From Big Bend to Carlsbad

Number Seventeen:
The W. L. Moody, Jr.,
Natural History Series

From Big Bend to Carlsbad

A Traveler's Guide

by JAMES GLENDINNING

TEXAS A&M UNIVERSITY PRESS
College Station

Frontispiece photo by Blair Pittman

The paper used in this book meets the minimum requirements
of the American National Standard for Permanence
of Paper for Printed Library Materials, Z39.48-1984.
Binding materials have been chosen for durability.

Library of Congress Cataloging-in-Publication Data

Glendinning, James, 1937–
    From Big Bend to Carlsbad : a traveler's guide / James
Glendinning. — 1st ed.
        p.   cm. — (W. L. Moody, Jr., natural history series ; no. 17)
    ISBN 0-89096-652-4
    1. Big Bend Region (Tex.)—Guidebooks. 2. Big Bend National Park
(Tex.)—Guidebooks. 3. Carlsbad Caverns National Park (N.M.)—
Guidebooks. 4. Carlsbad Caverns (N.M.)—Guidebooks. 5. Guadalupe
Mountains National Park (Tex.)—Guidebooks. 6. Guadalupe Mountains
Region (N.M. and Tex.)—Guidebooks. I. Title. II. Series.
F392.B54G58 1995
917.64'93—dc20   95-6059
                                                          CIP

Contents

Illustrations

Acknowledgments

Many people were helpful in giving me information about the Big Bend area and Carlsbad, New Mexico, and I thank them all.

On a practical level, the Chamber of Commerce in Alpine gave me a space to do typing, and the Small Business Administration at Sul Ross State University let me use their office for printing.

Several people wrote short pieces which are incorporated into this book. These are: Jem Welsh, "Music in the Big Bend"; Adam Lowcock, "Big Bend Area Golf Courses"; and David Busey, "What is Cabrito?" Others, such as The Desert Candle and the Apache Trading Post, let me use pieces already written. Thanks to them also and to Barabara Kellim for editorial assistence and to Sue Lockey for proofreading.

Time passes, things change. There may be facts that are no longer correct in the book and perhaps some questionable judgments. Readers are invited to write to me to suggest corrections or additions to the copy. In this way more people can learn about this wonderful region.

From Big Bend to Carlsbad

Chapter 1

◆

Natural Highlights

Three national parks and five state parks/natural areas comprise this spectacular tourist attraction. Travelers should visit at least one of these points of interest during their stay in the area and take advantage of the special programs that can enhance their enjoyment and appreciation of these natural highlights.

Big Bend National Park

DESCRIPTION

"A heap of stones thrown down by the Great Spirits after they had finished creating the Earth." That was the explanation the Apache Indians gave for the formation of the soaring Chisos Mountains in Big Bend National Park. Geographers see a different picture. The southeasterly course of the Rio Grande is blocked by a mountain range, and it turns towards the northeast as it forces its way through, forming a deep canyon. At this point there is a big bend in the river.

For geologists the region is unique. It is where the two dominant mountain ranges of the United States, the Appalachians and the Rockies, come together. The Rockies (a spur, really) continue as the Sierra Madre Oriental southward into Mexico. And separate from these two ranges, standing on its own just to the north of the Rio Grande, is a huge pile of volcanic rock, the Chisos Mountains, the centerpiece of the Big Bend National Park.

For birders, there are more species (434) than in any other national park. For other naturalists, there are over 1,100 plant types and 76 species of mammals. Biologists find in the park a unique combination of desert, shrubland, woodland, and grassland. For ordinary visitors, there is just a chance they may see a black bear.

Here is a national park (the nation's fifth largest) of 1,100 square miles, a vast expanse of desert with a mountain massif one and a half miles high in the middle. Open to the public since 1944, it has comparatively few visitors and is on the way to nowhere. In 1992 this empty corner of Texas on the Mexican border was visited by fewer than three hundred thousand visitors—the number who visit Yosemite every four weeks. But those who do make the long drive from the east or northeast, or who make a rail or air connection at Alpine, find a majestic wonderland.

In and around the park, visitors may find relics of earlier lifestyles: Native American, homesteading or mining, and reminders of a completely different culture just across the Rio Grande, or as the Mexicans call it, the Wild River of the North. They may also find vestiges of the life of primitive hunters from tens of thousands of years ago, or of much earlier animal life, such as dinosaurs and flying pterosaurs.

This is the Big Bend National Park, vast in size, varied in topography, and remote.

WHEN TO VISIT

Most visitors come during the winter and spring months when the temperatures are more manageable, especially when traveling at lower altitudes. Spring is the best time to visit, when the wildflowers provide a riot of color, starting in late February. Spring break is the peak time; if you arrive late, even the primitive campsites will be full, and you will only have "zone" camping (out of sight of the highway, in the desert area only, with no facilities). Thanksgiving and Christmas also create maximum demand for motel accommodations in and near the park.

May, June, and July are the hottest months, when the average maximum temperature on the desert floor can be over 100° F and can reach 115° F in the river canyons. During the winter, the average minimum temperature in the higher campsites falls below freezing. Average temperatures range from a minimum of 35° degrees in January, to 68° in July, and a maximum of 61° in January to a maximum of 94° in June. Add five to ten degrees to these temperatures along the Rio Grande, and take off five to ten degrees in the higher mountains. Annual rainfall averages fifteen to sixteen inches, with August being the rainiest month. These amounts vary from four inches in Castolon, to twenty-five inches in the High Chisos. For month by month temperatures, ask for the National Park Service free pamphlet, *Big Bend General Information.*

PARK HISTORY

When the State of Texas deeded 707,894 acres to the park service in 1944, it marked the end of many years of planning and action by scores of people. Principal among these planners was Everett Ewing Townsend, the "father" of the national park. Townsend, a cowboy, later a Texas Ranger, sheriff of Brewster County, and subsequently a lawmaker, was probably the first to think of the region as a park.

Another vital figure was Amon Carter, publisher of the *Fort Worth Star-Telegram* and an early influential advocate of the national park idea. He became chairman of the Texas Big Bend Park Association, an organization of prominent citizens across the state, whose goal was to raise money to buy the land for the park.

But the man who was on the spot at the critical time of the acquisition was Ross A. Maxwell, a geologist and later the first superintendent of the park. He was also a diplomat. Previously, over three thousand people owned land in the Big Bend, although only fifty-five actually lived there. It was Maxwell, who lived in the region alongside the ranchers and who decided to devote extra time to this project. During a difficult period of drought, he convinced them to move their stock off the park land. His name is rightly remembered for his work during the transition period from private to public land and is commemorated in Maxwell Scenic Drive. Even today, pockets of private land still remain within the park boundaries, toward the northern limit.

STATISTICS

A recent survey by the park service showed that typical visitors were families (62 percent) and 44 percent were between fifty-six and seventy years old. Seventy-three percent of them stayed more than one day, and 80 percent visited the Chisos Basin, but only 53 percent day hiked. Forty percent camped without hookups.

The National Park Service would like for visitors to stay longer so they can get to know more of the park, to get out of their cars so they can smell and listen to their surroundings, to avoid the overcrowded Chisos Basin, and to get to know the desert, one of the features that distinguishes this park from many others. Most people dismiss the desert as an empty

Dr. Ross Maxwell was the first park superintendent of what is now Big Bend National Park. A surface geologist, Dr. Maxwell has written the definitive book on the geology of the region. Photo by Blair Pittman.

wasteland; however, a guided walk with a ranger or an evening slide show at one of the campgrounds will show how full of life the desert is.

Advance preparation: reading some of the National Park Service pamphlets during the long drive to the park will help you to make the most of your time in the park.

PLANNING

Write to the National Park Service, Panther Junction, Big Bend, TX 79834. Their telephone number is (915) 477-2251. They publish two free general information pamphlets. The first, *Big Bend*, is a comprehensive color foldout, with a map and a wealth of information on the animal and plant life of the three zones in the park—river, desert, and mountain. The second, a black-and-white folder called *General Information*, gives all the necessary practical information, including temperatures, do's and don'ts, what to do with your pets (don't bring them), camping fees, and so forth. In addition, they print ten free specialized pamphlets: *Archeology; Hiking and Backpacking; Castolon Valley; Geology; Encounters!; Reptiles; Biological Diversity; Glenn Springs; Border Towns—Santa Elena and Boquillas; Dinosaurs, Pterosaurs, and Crocodiles.*

RECOMMENDED READING

The following books and a collection of more than three hundred other publications, plus maps, videos, posters, and cassettes, can be bought at the main entry point, where you pay admission at Panther Junction. You may also buy these in advance at any good bookstore (except for the National Park Service *Handbook*).

In the *National Park Service Handbook*, part one briefly introduces the park's history. Part two concentrates on the area's natural history. Part three is a travel guide with reference materials. The price is $5.95 from U.S. Government Books, P.O. Box 371954, Pittsburgh, PA 15250. Or order by phone by calling (202) 783-3238.

Also read *Naturalist's Big Bend* by R. H. Wauer ($11.95); *Chronicles of the Big Bend* by W. D. Smithers ($18.95); *Texas Big Bend Country* by George Wuerther ($15.95); *Big Bend Country* by Ross Maxwell ($9.95); and *A Homesteader's Story* by J. D. Langford ($8.95).

The most practical and popular books bought upon arrival are: *Hiker's Guide to Trails of the Big Bend National Park* ($1.25), describing thirty-six trails; *Road Guide to Paved and Improved Dirt Roads* ($1.25); *Road Guide to Backcountry Dirt Roads* ($1.25), describing more than 250 miles of these.

Buy each guide individually or all three for $3.00. The *Chisos Mountain Trails* pamphlet (50¢) lists the trails within the Chisos Basin, gives a brief description, and marks all the backcountry campsites. There is a topographical map, waterproof and tear proof, of the entire park for $6.95. The map is vital if you are planning to go off the trails, but not so necessary for those doing Chisos or other trails since the guidebooks have adequate maps.

Useful magazine articles about the Big Bend are: "Big Bend," *Travel & Leisure*, September, 1991; "Around the Bend," *Condé-Nast Traveler*, February, 1992; "Big Bend National Park," *Travel Holiday*, May, 1992; "Riding the Tex-Mex Trail," *Travel & Leisure*, February, 1993; "Big Bend," *Texas Monthly*, March, 1993.

HOW TO GET THERE

Personal car. From Marathon, Texas, it is 40 miles to the north entrance on U.S. 385. From Alpine, Texas, it is 80 miles to the west entrance on Texas 118. From Presidio, Texas, to Study Butte on Ranch Road 170 (see "Big Bend Ranch State Natural Area and the River Road" for a description of this beautiful drive), take Texas 118 to the west entrance, for a total of 65 miles.

Airline. The nearest commercial airport serving the large carriers is Midland-Odessa, which is 225 miles from the north entrance. By comparison, El Paso is 301 miles to the west, and San Antonio, by way of Del Rio, is 368 miles to the east. To save time you may fly into Alpine, only 80 miles from the west entrance, and rent a car, even camping gear. Dallas Express Airlines flies five times weekly from Dallas (Love Field). Lowest round-trip fare is $189. 1-800-529-0925.

Car rental. In Alpine rental cars are available from Big Bend Areo, whose fleet of vehicles include vans, compacts, 4-wheel drives, and limousines. Rates run from $20 daily and $140–$180 weekly, plus 10¢ a mile. (915) 837-3009 or 837-2744. Arrivals on the late train from the west can arrange for the car to be ready for them at Alpine's Amtrak station. A week's car rental at the Midland-Odessa airport will set you back $139–$159 per week for a small- to medium-sized car with unlimited mileage. For information at Midland/Odessa Airport, call (915) 560-2200.

Bus and Train. Greyhound passes through once a day in each direction from El Paso and San Antonio. All-American Bus Lines have north- and southbound daily services from Midland via Alpine to Presidio. For details call (915) 837-5302 from 7:30 to noon, 1:00 to 5:00 P.M. Monday–

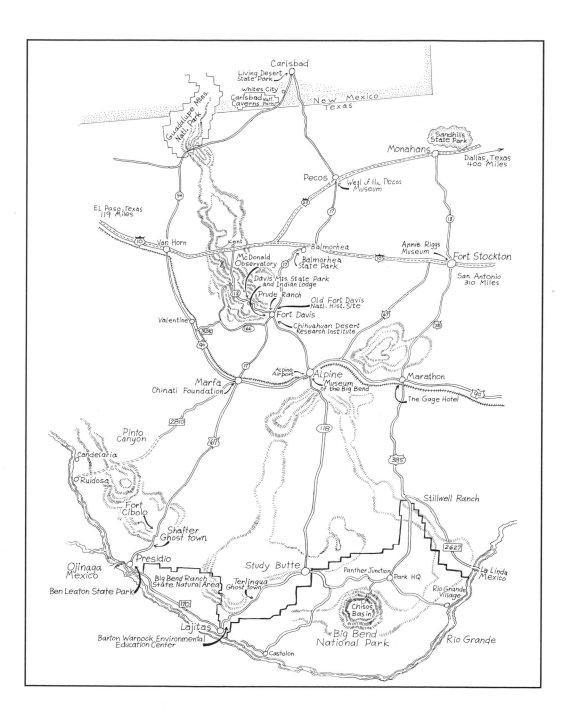

Friday and 7:30 to noon Saturday. Amtrak's Sunset Limited train stops three times weekly east- and westbound between Los Angeles and Miami. Call 1-800-USA-RAIL.

Shuttle. From Alpine airport or Amtrak Station Big Bend Shuttle Service a shuttle may help you get to the park, but you will still have transportation needs within the park unless you confine yourself to just one area. In Alpine, Far Journeys provides shuttle services to the Park (sample rate, $85 one way two persons). 1-800-753-5491 or (915) 837-3291. Big Bend Shuttle Service in Study Butte provides van service (sample fare $65 round trip per person, Alpine to Chisos Basin, minimum of 4) from Alpine to the Park. 1-800-729-2860 or (915) 371-2523. In Marathon Scott Shuttle can pick people up from anywhere and take them to the river from about $1 per mile, for a group of 4. 1-800-613-5041 or (915) 386-4574.

Camping equipment rental in Alpine. The Corner House Bed & Breakfast offers camping gear to rent. For rates, call (915) 837-7161.

INFORMATION

You will have to stop at the **Panther Junction Visitor Center** to purchase an entrance permit ($5 per vehicle). Golden Age Passports (for those sixty-two or older) are free, as are Golden Access Passports for the handicapped or disabled. A Big Bend Park Pass ($15) permits the holder to unlimited free entry from January 1 to December 31 of the purchase year.

Take a few minutes inside the Visitor Center to look at the large relief map of the whole park to gain an overall idea of the ups and downs of the topography. There are several dioramas about the park's past; there are also updates of the weather, river, and road situation, and information on registration for primitive campsites. Get your permits for these here.

Take a few minutes outside and follow the short nature trail to see for yourself the plants which you may have read about already and which you will surely see more of if you spend any time at all in the park. A quarter-mile away there is a gas station and small convenience store.

Before you leave Panther Junction, check the weekly list of interpretive activities: talks, guided walks, and slide programs. Depending on the season, there can be up to three of these programs daily, each lasting from one to two hours, at different locations in the park. The talks and slide shows are held at one or more of the four ranger stations in the park: Panther Junction, Rio Grande Village, Castolon, and Chisos Basin.

Interpretive ranger trainees lead walks into Santa Elena Canyon, and their bubbling enthusiasm for the towering 1,500-foot limestone walls is catching. A guide will present the group with some thought-provoking ideas on the value of the natural world and how everything in it is connected, and what happens when we try to change the natural balance by, for example, introducing a new species of tree (tamarisk). In this instance, the new species crowds out the native riverbank plants. You may listen to a more serious admonition during a slide show about the animals of the park and of what happens when you feed human food to animals. They like it but it makes them ill. Their fur or feathers lose their shine, and they get out of condition since the chemicals and preservatives in human food do not agree with their digestive system.

You may go on a guided walk with the senior interpretive guide, Gus Sánchez, and hear a man so obviously in tune and at ease with the environment that he seems made for this job. Take one of the walks, listen to one of the talks, or attend one of the slide shows, and your understanding of the area will increase—and with it, your enjoyment.

WHERE TO STAY

Motels

Chisos Mountains Lodge. (915) 477-2291. With seventy-two rooms, the lodge operates as a concession and provides the only motel accommodations within the park. The setting, within the Chisos Basin, is magnificent, and the view from the dining room is particularly impressive. Advance reservations are definitely recommended and, for peak periods such as spring break, Thanksgiving, and Christmas, vital—even one year in advance. Mid-February through mid-May is the busiest stretch. Write to Chisos Mountains Lodge, Big Bend National Park, TX 79834-9999, or call (915) 477-2291 for reservations.

There are no televisions in the rooms, although there is one in the lobby, nor any telephones. But there are pay phones outside each building. There is no pool and only one restaurant. The lodge is open all year round.

Rooms (prices quoted are for two persons) range from $58–$62, with $10 for each additional person, plus tax. If you have a choice, specify the newer motor lodge units at the slightly higher rate since these rooms have a balcony which faces the wooded mountainside. Try to avoid the older motel rooms which look onto the parking lot. For many people, a cottage is a better deal. Although not air-conditioned, they are tucked away higher up the mountainside and provide three double beds each. The rate (for three persons) is $66, with $10 per extra person, plus tax. Ask for

Number 103 with a view from the back porch of the Window, one of the prime sights in the park.

You may not have a great deal of choice in reservations unless you book particularly early. The supply and demand situation of this monopoly concession weighs against the "Texas Friendly" reception found elsewhere in the region. A lobby which looks like a T-shirt store and a staff who is mainly imported from elsewhere should not put you off enjoying the superb setting.

There are other motel accommodations outside the park and, in the case of visitors to the west part of the park, they are just as convenient as the Chisos Mountains Lodge, although they do not enjoy the same incomparable setting.

Big Bend Motor Inn and **Mission Lodge.** Study Butte, 3 miles from the west entrance to the park, 1-800-848-BEND, (915) 371-2218, or (915) 371-2555. The inn (45 rooms) and the lodge (36 rooms) both charge $63.55 and $52.95 (tax included) for a double. See Chapter 3, Study Butte, for description.

Easter Egg Motel. (915) 371-2430. Has 24 rooms and charges $45 for a double. See Chapter 3, Study Butte, for description.

Badlands Motel. Lajitas, 17 miles from the west entrance to the park, 1-800-527-4078, or (915) 424-3471. Has eighty-one rooms in four different locations, as well as condominiums, cabins, and a bunkhouse. All these are bookable through the same telephone number (listed above). Room rates for a double are $65, plus tax. Weekly rates and summer discounts are available. See Chapter 3, Lajitas, for description.

On Texas 118, **Wildhorse Station,** 7 miles from the west entrance to the park, has mountain cabins only, fully furnished, with kitchen, from $35 for two persons. Call (915) 371-2526. See Chapter 4, Texas 118 South, for description.

Longhorn Ranch Motel. 15 miles from the west entrance to the park, (915) 371-2541. Has twenty-four rooms, one suite. A double is $49.95. See Chapter 4, Texas 118 South, for description.

Terlingua Ranch. 35 miles from the park, (915) 371-2416. Has thirty-four cabins for $33 per night. See Chapter 4, Texas 118 South, for description.

Gage Hotel. Marathon, 40 miles from the north entrance, (915) 386-4205, or 1-800-884-GAGE. Seventeen rooms in the main building, each from $42. Twenty additional rooms and suites in the new section, Los Portales, range from $80. See Chapter 2, Marathon, for description.

Marathon Motel. (915) 386-4241. Has eight rooms at $30 per night. See Chapter 2, Marathon, for description.

Campgrounds

All campgrounds function on a first-come, first-served basis, with no advance bookings except for groups.

Rio Grande Village RV Park. (915) 477-2293. The only campground with hookups inside the park, for $12.50. Register at the Rio Grande Village Store. There are also gas, beer, and a self-service laundry available, and it is the only place within the park where there are coin-operated showers (75¢ for five minutes).

NPS Campgrounds

All National Park Service campgrounds are self-register and pay upon arrival.

Rio Grande Village. Has one hundred sites, toilets, a dump station, and water for $5 per night. A second overflow campground charges $3 per night for more limited facilities.

Chisos Basin. With sixty-three sites, charges $5 per night for all facilities, except showers.

Cottonwood Campground. With thirty-five sites, charges $3 per night. It has pit toilets and no dump station.

Note: in spring and fall, all lodging and campgrounds may be full. Before leaving the last town nearest the park, call (915) 477-2251 and ask for the dispatcher for information on availability. In addition, at busy periods signs are posted at the entrances to the park advising visitors of the availability of spaces.

Outside the park, there are plenty of RV campgrounds at Study Butte, Lajitas, Stillwell Ranch, and on Texas 118 from Alpine.

Primitive Campgrounds

There are fifty designated backcountry sites, available on a first-come, first-served basis. Permits must be obtained for all of them but there is no charge. You have to take your own water, remove your trash, and take care of your own toilet requirements (i.e., dig a hole), which you will be briefed about by the ranger who issues your permit. Most sites can be reached by vehicles with normal clearance and without four-wheel drive. The rangers will advise you which campgrounds are accessible for your vehicle when you make your reservation at Panther Junction or, in the case of the Chisos Mountains sites, at the Chisos Basin Ranger Station.

Backcountry Camping

For the more adventurous or for those who, if they are properly equipped, arrive during spring break to find all the lodging and all the campgrounds full, there is still the possibility, or the preference, of camping almost anywhere outside of the Chisos Mountains—provided you are a specified distance from any road, trail, or spring, and out of sight. If you are alone, the NPS will take your footprint, probably to persuade you to treat the desert seriously when going off the road or trail, but also so that you can be traced if you disappear. As part of this exercise, you will need to leave a sticker inside your car window and drop off one part of your permit at a ranger station upon returning from your overnight camping.

WHERE TO EAT

Chisos Mountains Lodge. (915) 477-2291. Has the only restaurant and fountain service inside the park. The view is magnificent and the service is cheerful. Breakfasts (7:00–9:00 A.M.) are standard. Lunch (noon–2:00 P.M.) includes a healthy-looking chef's salad ($4.60), a practical traveler's box lunch ($4.60) for take-out, and a border burger ($3.60). During non-meal hours, the soda fountain takes over for light snacks. Their specialty is cherry milk shakes. Dinner comes as a disappointment for those who might wish to round off a memorable experience with something more inspired than fried chicken. There are, of course, other dishes (rib eye steak, deep-fried jumbo shrimp) and their version of a dinner special (lasagna). The prices are honest, the service is competent, but there is simply no imagination or expertise to offer some special dishes to go with a special experience. This is coffee shop fare when the setting merits a dining room.

Within the park, the only other foods available are groceries, which you may buy at Castolon, Panther Junction, and Rio Grande Village.

Outside of the park, Study Butte and Terlingua have seen an increase and improvement in the cafe-deli-restaurant situation.

WHAT TO SEE AND DO

The park's most outstanding feature is its variety. It offers mountains, desert, and the river. It also offers fossil bones, mining remains, homesteader and ranching history, varied and abundant flora and fauna, amazing geological formations, and above all, spectacular views.

To see all of this, visitors can use the 160 miles of paved roads and the 256 miles of unpaved roads within the park. They can also (and slightly more than half the visitors do) get out of their vehicles and take hikes, using any of the thirty-six developed and primitive trails.

SCENIC DRIVES

For people driving their cars, and particularly for short-term visitors (a quarter of the visitors stay less than one day), the most popular route is from Basin Junction, 3 miles west of the Panther Junction Visitor Center, to Chisos Basin. This road (6.25 miles) goes into the heart of the Chisos Mountains. Because of the steep grades and switchbacks, trailers longer than twenty feet are not allowed. As the road climbs through Green Gulch, the rounded, intrusive igneous rocks of Pulliam Ridge are to the right, and the blocky extrusive igneous rocks of Panther and Lost Mine Peaks are to the left. Desert plants give way to woodland species such as oaks, piñon pines, and junipers as the terrain rises. The road

crests at 5,800 feet at Panther Pass, where there is a parking lot at the head of the self-guided Lost Mine Trail, the park's most popular.

Dropping down into the Basin, a depression about three miles in diameter almost two thousand feet below the surrounding peaks, one gets the feeling of driving into a crater. Actually, the Basin was formed by natural erosion taking place over millions of years. About one mile from the pass, a road leads off to the right, where the campground and an amphitheater are located. Just ahead is the Chisos Mountains Lodge, a store, and a ranger station.

To do better justice to this drive, and to the five other drives on good roads within the park, visitors would be well served by reading *A Road Guide to the Geology of the Big*

West Texas Bluebonnet, Lupinus havardii. *By Elva Stewart.*

Bend National Park ($6.95). This well-produced book is for people who want a detailed idea of the geological situation within the park. It offers an odometer guide, listing and explaining in detail what you will see. For example, at Stop Number Three, with the odometer showing 4.15 miles, you read: "Park on pullout at the Green Gulch interpretive exhibit. Pulliam Ridge on the right. The flat, box-shaped mountain directly ahead to the south is Casa Grande, literally translated from the Spanish as Big House. Home to peregrine falcons, Casa Grande is composed of volcanic rocks from both the Chisos and South Rim formations."

For those visitors with only one day to spend and who are intent on staying in their vehicles, there should be time to take the 32-mile **Ross Maxwell Scenic Drive,** on a well-surfaced road which winds up and down, affording some marvelous views with the option of twenty different stops.

At the start, from the Santa Elena Junction (13 miles from the west entrance, 13 miles from Panther Junction), the Chisos Mountains are to the left, and soon the Window comes into sight with the Casa Grande peak visible through it. Shortly after that, there is the chance to stop at a parking area and take a short trail to the adobe ruins of the Sam Nail Ranch House, also called Old Ranch, where a windmill still pumps water, which attracts birds and other wildlife. Just past Blue Creek Ranch, a short road goes to Sotol Vista, which is perhaps the finest view accessible by paved road in the whole park. A little farther on, as the road drops steeply back into the desert, you have the option of taking a side road which dead-ends after 3.5 miles at an arroyo which comes out of Burro Mesa. The main road now winds through one of the most magnificent geologic areas of the park, passing such volcanic features as Goat Mountain, Mule Ears Peak, Tuff Canyon, and Castolon Peak.

About one mile past Castolon Peak, the road drops farther down to the village of Castolon. Built and used as an army post, Castolon has been a frontier trading post since the early 1900s. A store and ranger station are here, and gasoline is available. The road now runs along the Rio Grande flood plain, where cotton and other crops were grown until 1959. The Cottonwood Campground is here as well as a dirt road which leads one mile later to the crossing to Santa Elena, Mexico.

Eight miles beyond Castolon is the Santa Elena Canyon overlook and a short distance further is a parking area. Now is the moment, time permitting, to get out of the car and take one of the most dramatic short trails in the park, a 1.7 mile round-trip that takes you across Terlingua Creek (if the water level is not up) and requires a short climb. Then it rewards you

Sotol Mesa view. Big Bend National Park, looking south toward Mexico. Photo by Blair Pittman.

with entrance to the majestic canyon itself—but only briefly, until the canyon walls close and there is no pathway left.

OTHER SCENIC DRIVES

Paved Roads

Maverick (west entrance) to Panther Junction, 22 miles long, passes through the painted desert, Big Bend's badlands. It skirts the northern end of Burro Mesa, a huge fault block, the geologists' term for a separate piece of mountain. It then passes the Ross Maxwell Scenic Drive turnoff (to the right) and three backcountry roads, leading to primitive campsites to the right.

Panther Junction to Rio Grande Village (20 miles) and to Boquillas Canyon (23 miles) is mostly downhill, from foothill grasslands through typical Chihuahuan Desert, to the banks of the Rio Grande. There are turnoffs to the abandoned village of Glenn Springs (8 miles on an unpaved road), to Dugout Wells, where a schoolhouse stood in the early 1900s (on a short, improved gravel road), and farther on, to Hot Springs (2 miles on an improved dirt road). In Rio Grande Village, there is a ranger station, campgrounds, a store, and gasoline. Boquillas Canyon Road turns off to the left and takes you in 4 miles to the canyon overlook and the trail parking area, passing a dirt road on the right, which goes down to the Boquillas crossing into Mexico.

Persimmon Gap to Panther Junction (26 miles), is the best approach to the park. Forty miles from Marathon, on U.S. 385, you approach the park entrance and a ranger station. Going due south with the backdrop of the Chisos Mountains slowly getting larger in front of you, the drive passes the turnoff to Dagger Flat, which has a concentration of giant dagger yuccas. After passing through Tornillo Flat, one of the barest areas in the park, a gentle climb begins towards Panther Junction, passing the Hannold Grave and pioneer homesite on your right.

Backcountry Roads

There are improved dirt roads and primitive roads. The problem is not so much the need for four-wheel drive as for high clearance. The rangers will advise you about this precaution, bearing in mind the weather conditions, the particular route you are interested in, and the make of your vehicle.

Improved Dirt Roads

Old Maverick Road (14 miles long) linking Santa Elena Canyon with Maverick is convenient since it avoids having to drive back along Ross Maxwell Scenic Drive and is manageable by any vehicle. It passes by the jacal (a low-ceilinged dugout house) of the legendary Gilberto Luna, who lived simply (and healthily) on his own crops, fathered more than fifty children, and died at the age of 108.

Croton Spring Road, 1 mile long, 3 miles east of Santa Elena Junction, shows evidence of Indian habitation.

Grapevine Hills Road, 8 miles long, is just west of Basin Junction. Its features include large trees, a spring, and a rock water tank.

Dagger Flat Road, 8 miles long, is located 10 miles south of Persimmon Gap. The small valley is filled with ten- to fifteen-foot-tall yuccas, seen to best advantage when in bloom in the spring.

Hot Springs Road is 2 miles long. It is 18 miles southeast of Panther Junction. It includes the store and other buildings of homesteader Langford's health resort and bathhouse on the banks of the Rio Grande.

Primitive Roads
For primitive roads, including the 51-mile River Road, which extends across the southern part of the park, see the NPS publication, *Road Guide to Backcountry Dirt Roads* ($1.25).

On Foot—the only way to get close to nature
The Big Bend National Park is remarkably well served by its road network, allowing drivers to get to many out-of-the-way corners of the park. But, having gotten there, the next step is to get out of your car. Let the senses take over and make the body do the work. Removed from the smell of leather seats or exhaust fumes, the nose can pick up the scent of a mountain pine tree. Away from highway traffic noise, the ear can pick up bird calls.

Self-Guiding Trails
There are eight of these trails within the park, all with leaflets available at the start or with signs en route.

Lost Mine Trail is the most popular (4.8 miles round-trip, medium difficulty), and **Santa Elena Canyon Trail** (1.7 miles round-trip, medium difficulty) is also extremely popular and sometimes has ranger-led walks. (See description at end of Ross Maxwell Scenic Drive section in this chapter.) All the others are easy, ranging in length from 50 yards to 2 miles. The Panther Path at the Visitor Center is a quick and easy way to get acquainted with the desert plants.

Rio Grande Village Nature Trail is unusual because of its variety and the message contained on the signs. It starts at site Number Eighteen in the campground and proceeds through dense vegetation, climbs into arid desert, then descends to the Rio Grande. On the way back, a promontory affords a fine view into Mexico and along the Rio Grande. Sunset is awe-inspiring as the rays of the sun strike the cliffs of Boquillas Canyon. The message on the signs invites contemplation of nature's marvels and our own place in this changing and varied wonderland.

Developed Trails
Window Trail is of medium difficulty, 5.2 miles round-trip. It is popular because of the impressive ending to the trail and its accessibility from the Chisos Campground and Basin parking lot. It is downhill going there, uphill coming back. From an open area of grasses, you move into the shaded Oak Creek Canyon. The canyon narrows, and trees eventually give way to polished rock. Finally, with a width of only twenty feet across,

you are at the base of the Window. The trail offers a wide variety of plants and a fair selection of birds. Coming back, the Casa Grande, framed by oaks and maples, provides a striking sight.

The **South Rim** is a strenuous day hike, a 13- to 14.5-mile round-trip. A long loop hike with many interesting highlights, it can easily be done in one day by those traveling light and in good physical shape. Another alternative, for those with the equipment, is to incorporate this hike into a High Chisos camping trip. In either event, allow time when you get to the rim to let the panoramic views work their full effect. The cliffs drop 2,500 feet from where you sit, and in front of you is spread a jumble of canyons, ridges, buttes, and peaks. In the background, beyond the Rio Grande (about 15 miles away) rise the blue-hazed mountain ranges of Mexico. Birds wheel effortlessly above you, a breeze blows up from below, your muscles are beginning to recover—it has been worth the climb.

There are fourteen other developed trails, from the easy 0.3-mile Window View Trail starting at the Basin Trailhead to others, over a 10-mile round-trip. **Emory Peak** is a must for many people, a 9-mile round-trip from the Basin Trailhead, using the same well-graded, gradual climb of 3.5 miles and 1,500 feet up the Pinnacles Trail to Pinnacles Pass, then taking a spur trail of one mile to the highest point in the national park (7,835 feet). The final fifteen feet require a scramble, but you will find adequate space on top among the radio antennas to enjoy the panorama.

PRIMITIVE ROUTES

The next step for those wanting to get to know more about the desert is to try a primitive trail, of which there are seventeen in the park. For any of these trails, the relevant topographical map, obtainable from the Panther Junction Ranger Station book shop, is necessary and also a compass and the knowledge of how to use the two. You don't need a backcountry permit for day use of these trails, but a ranger will suggest which trail to take. You will also be cautioned about the dangers and advised on what to wear and what to carry.

The routes are detailed in the *Hiker's Guide to Trails of Big Bend National Park* according to the NPS classification, which is cautious but prudent. The majority are rated as strenuous. Routes vary in length from 3 to 31 miles. Some have water, usually available at a spring, but most don't and, in any event, no hike should be attempted without adequate water to take you back to your vehicle. One gallon per person per day is the standard recommended quantity of water for desert use.

Chimneys Trail is considered of medium difficulty and of short length (4.8 miles round-trip). It is a good introduction to primitive routes (although there is no water), with the option of a little cross-country desert walking on the way back. The parking lot and trailhead are clearly marked with a sign on the Ross Maxwell Scenic Drive 1.2 miles south of the Burro Mesa Pouroff spur road. For those new to the desert, it is reassuring to be able to see where your vehicle is located at any point during this four-hour hike. From the paved road, follow an old roadway, marked with small piles of rocks, downhill for perhaps forty-five minutes to the "chimneys," which are clearly visible from all directions. You are walking almost due west, and Kit Mountain is on your left. The chimneys are the still-standing parts of an eroded dike. Indian petroglyphs can be found on the walls of the southernmost chimney, and nearby there are remains of shelters used by herders. You can easily climb to the top of one or other of the chimneys, take out your binoculars, and do some scanning of the desert. Or you can find shade behind and below one of the chimneys and have a snack.

If you were to continue on the trail, heading west for 5 miles, you would reach the Old Maverick Road and the old dugout house of Gilberto Luna. But this side trip would require arranging for a vehicle to pick you up at the other end.

A short cross-country diversion is possible at this point and will add variety to the hike. Almost due north from where you are sitting on one of the chimneys, and only 1 mile distant, is a huge cottonwood tree, clearly visible, which marks Red Ass Spring. You can head off towards this tree, using your common sense to find the route, and take another rest in the shade upon arrival. From there, you can head directly back cross-country, if you like, gradually ascending towards the outcropping of rock next to the highway behind which your car is parked. Allow four to five hours, including rest stops, for the whole trip. Unless it is in the dead of winter, start early to arrive back at your vehicle before the hottest time of day.

TRAIL RIDES

The Chisos Remuda in the Basin has closed down. The only available alternatives are the stables at Study Butte or Lajitas (see Chapter 3 under these headings).

RIVER FLOATS

This activity, reaching into the third area of Big Bend National Park's diversity, is not to be missed if time and budget permit. There are three canyons (Santa Elena, Mariscal, and Boquillas) along the 107 miles of river, which form the park's southern boundary, and four different outfitters will offer you a variety of escorted trips. You may also do float trips yourself, but you will have to arrange the shuttle to and from the river, pay the user's fee, and do the work yourself, but it is certainly possible. You may also choose to go by canoe, which brings you closer in touch with the river and requires some extra effort and different skills. Plan, if you can, to spend an overnight on the river or at least a full-day trip, since getting to and from the river can take some time. Consider the season (it can get powerfully hot inside the canyons in summer), and ask about the water level, which can vary dramatically season to season, and whether water upstream is being diverted.

For all the options, see Chapter 4 (River Trip Outfitters).

SPECIAL ATTRACTIONS

Hot Springs, the destination of early 1900s pioneer homesteader J. D. Langford, had long been used by Indians. They left rock paintings on the limestone cliffs on the banks of the Rio Grande and holes in the bedrock where they had ground their mesquite beans and seeds. Langford, seeking to regain his health, arrived here, sight unseen, in 1909 and proceeded to build a house for himself and his family with the help of a Mexican man who was already living at the site. Langford later had a stonemason build a bathhouse of limestone rocks over the hot springs. Alarmed by increased fighting along the border and by news of the oncoming Mexican Revolution, Langford and his family moved to El Paso for their safety in 1913. They did not return to Hot Springs until 1927 when he proceeded to build a tourist center, with a post office, store, and a motel.

To see Hot Springs today, visitors can drive along the 2-mile improved road from the Panther Junction–Rio Grande highway and then take a 2-mile round-trip on a self-guided trail. Or they can take the 3-mile Hot Springs Canyon primitive trail from Rio Grande Village.

Whichever route they take, they will find the remains of the post office, buildings, pictographs, middens along the self-guided trail, remains of the bathhouse, and an abundant supply of 105° F water. Visitors can take a midnight moonlit stroll or a daytime (better in winter and spring) walk. They can sit in the shallow water of the stone bathtub right at the edge of the Rio Grande, conversing with their fellow bathers or communing with nature. For relief from the hot water and a chance to splash around a bit, many visitors plunge into the muddy waters of the river.

CROSSING INTO MEXICO

Within the park, there are two easy crossings, each by rowboat and involving a small fee, to villages on the Mexican side. Santa Elena is reached from Castolon, and Boquillas from Rio Grande Village. In both Mexican villages, you may eat in restaurants, buy souvenirs, and stroll around.

Because of the large numbers of people crossing from Rio Grande Village, the Boquillas crossing has become more exploited and the village risks losing the appeal which makes these crossings so different from others along the border. For full details, see Chapter 4, "Crossing into Mexico."

FIESTA

International Good Neighbor Day takes place in October, and the park service goes to great lengths to celebrate with its Mexican neighbors the unique location they share. Included are music, dancing, food, and speeches.

LEARNING MORE

To be more aware of the surroundings and to get a better feel for the place, listen to the experts. In addition to the NPS interpretive activities, visitors should take advantage of other learning opportunities.

The **Big Bend Natural History Association** offers half-day, full-day, and longer seminars on a variety of topics, all conducted by experts. Prices may be as low as $40 for a one-day seminar on, say, Mountain Lion Behavior to $375 for a four-day Biodiversity Photography Workshop, including accommodations and some meals. For the catalog, write Big Bend Natural History Association, P.O. 68, Big Bend National Park, TX 79834 or call (915) 477-2236.

Alternatively, **area outfitters** (see "River Trip Outfitters," Chapter 4) provide informative guides and vehicles for in-park tours, even into Mexico.

For birders, **Jim Hines Big Bend Birding Expeditions** ([915] 371-2356) offers a variety of tours by raft or vehicle from $70 per person (with a two-person minimum). Based nearby at Terlingua Ranch, Hines also offers three-day birding workshops in July, August, September, and October for $350 per person.

For an individual guide, **Jim Bourbon,** a qualified, experienced interpreter and guide, takes small groups and individuals on excursions, by appointment only, for $150 per day. See Chapter 3 (Study Butte) for more information. (915) 371-2202.

Having a specialist interpret the park, its geology, and wildlife could well make all the difference between admiring remarkable scenery and gaining real insight into the vast and varied life in the desert and mountains, and understanding the earth's history in stone.

The Big Bend National Park is deservedly the number-one attraction. Visit it at all costs, but allow enough time for it to work its magic on you. Choose your season, and go prepared with suitable clothing, equipment, food, and water. Plan ahead, and consult the rangers when you arrive. If you are able, walk rather than drive; camp rather than stay in motels.

Big Bend Ranch State Natural Area and the River Road

BACKGROUND

This recent arrival to the Texas State Parks System is a mouthful to pronounce and a vast area to explore, although only a small part of it is open to visitors at this time. Acquired in 1988 from local ranchers, the Big Bend Ranch State Natural Area (part of the state park system but with a more protective philosophy regarding use by the public) covers some four hundred square miles. The park offers a unique rock formation (Solitario) caused by a gigantic explosion millions of years ago, a wealth of plant life, and a record of ten thousand years of human habitation. The Big Bend Ranch State Natural Area (BBRSNA) is equal in size to all the other state parks combined.

The parks department policy on opening up BBRSNA is a cautious one. They have undertaken an inventory of the area to see exactly what there is and are in the process of deciding which areas to develop—with the overall intent of introducing as little disturbance as possible in the way of paved roads, power lines, and other signs of civilization. The idea is to gradually open up the area, with emphasis on low impact facilities, like primitive campgrounds and trails for horses, as well as hikers. This exciting development will be underway as this guidebook appears.

As the book goes to press, the public can see part of the park by driving along the River Road (no fee, since this is Ranch Road 170) or taking an all-day bus tour, given twice monthly, into the interior of the ranch. The fee is $55, includes lunch, or $30 for Texas Conservation Passport holders (conservation passports cost $25). There are also three hiking trails, including the two- to three-hour Closed Canyon Trail, and the two- to three-day Rancherias Loop Trail. There are three primitive campgrounds and one picnic area along the River Road.

INFORMATION

First, obtain information, a map of the park, and permits where applicable at one of the two entrances, the Barton Warnock Environmental Educational Center in Lajitas or Fort Leaton in Presidio. For Texas Parks and Wildlife Information call 1-800-792-1112; for bookings call (512) 389-8900.

The Barton Warnock Environmental Education Center, just east of Lajitas on RR 170, presents a comprehensive archeological, historical, and natural history profile of the Big Bend region. There are separate rooms featuring archeology, geology (including a seismograph and a model of the Solitario uplift), history (camels, contraband, candelilla), western heritage, and wildlife. In the latter room, you will see stuffed lions, deer, roadrunners, javelinas, pronghorn, and other frequent inhabitants of the area.

Also in the wildlife room, and seen in greater numbers outside in the rambling Desert Garden are, among many other plants of the Chihuahuan Desert, the four plants which provided primitive man with food: prickly pear for syrup and jelly; mesquite seeds for flour and its wood for tools; persimmon juice for dye and its wood for tools; and sotol for food.

The center is open daily from 8:30 to 4:30. The entrance fee is $2.50 for adults, free to conservation passport holders, and $1.50 for children from six to twelve. (915) 424-3327.

Prickly pear, Opuntia engelmanii. *By Elva Stewart.*

At the other end of the River Road, 44 miles west along RR 170, almost in Presidio, is **Fort Leaton,** open daily from 8:00 to 4:00; the entrance fee is $2 for adults, free to Conservation Passport holders, and $1 for children six to twelve. (915) 229-3613.

This imposing adobe fortress, built on a low bluff overlooking the Rio Grande floodplain, dates from 1848,

Fort Leaton. Photo by Blair Pittman.

when Benjamin Leaton crossed the Rio Grande from Mexico, where he had been employed as an Indian scalp hunter by the Mexican government, and built a fort.

Today the fort is a museum commemorating life on the border and the trading and agriculture which still form the economic base of this community. Although it still bears Leaton's name, local residents call it El Fortín, unwilling to recognize the evil man who collected scalps for bounty. There are many rooms, mostly empty, but the fascinating part is the exhibition, with commentary, of the lives of the early agricultural Indians and the Spanish colonizers. The north-south trade route established in those days is still in active and increasing use today, with a new bridge facilitating busy, two-way trade.

THE RIVER ROAD — EL CAMINO DEL RÍO

The fifty miles **between Lajitas and Presidio** ranks as one of the most scenic in North America, according to *National Geographic.* More particularly, it is the stretch within the Big Bend Ranch State National Area, south from Redford, where the road twists and undulates, revealing new views at every corner, which is the most exciting. On one side lies the desert grassland, and beyond it the mountains of the park; across the Río Grande, now a more substantial river and brown in color with occasional rapids, due to the additional flow from the Río Conchos, are the higher mountains in Mexico. Immediately to the side of the road is the floodplain of the Rio Grande with its green riverside vegetation and cultivated land.

The road is a narrow but well surfaced two lanes. The curves are sharp and some of the hills are steep. Coming from Lajitas, the steepest gradient is 15.9 percent; don't stop once you are embarked on this ascent. Also, watch out for stray grazing animals. This is free-range territory, and if you hit an animal, the driver is held responsible.

You won't hit the mules at **Fresno Ranch,** 6 miles from Lajitas, since they do not stray onto the road. Here, an interesting experiment is taking place. The Sleepers, a family of mule raisers, have set out to reverse the mule's stubborn stereotypical image and historic role as beasts of burden. "Folks often don't understand a mule's intelligence," the Sleepers say, "and many mules get ruined. There are ways to raise and breed mules (including telepathy) that can produce a superior partner and companion, more like the smartest dog you ever met than a horse." They train and sell mules, and their slogan is "Mules looking for a good human to take care of." Call (915) 424-3318 if you are a prospective mule buyer.

Primitive campsites ($2 per night, permit required and obtainable at Fort Leaton or Warnock Center) are available at Grassy Banks, Madera (Monilla) Canyon, and Colorado Canyon. Boats can also be put in at these points. The campsites provide toilets and trash bins, but there is no water.

At **Madera Canyon** (13 miles from Lajitas), there is a picnic site with tepees and tables.

Ten miles farther towards Presidio is the **Closed Canyon Trail.** This short (1.4 mile round-trip) canyon is narrow and shaded, ideal for a scramble on the smooth rocks and good for a family picnic in the shade. As you hike farther into the canyon, the walls get closer and the pour-off drops steeper. Make sure not to go too far if you are on your own; the limestone rock is smooth and the hand and footholds get scarcer. Some people have taken ladders with them to get back up the steeper drops, but most people turn back before the descent gets too scary. The trail ends at a series of impassable pour-offs. You cannot reach the river. A permit is required for this trail.

King of the road. Highway 170 from Lajitas, Texas, to Presidio is considered the most beautiful view in Texas. Since there is a shortage of fences, watch for wandering livestock. Photo by Blair Pittman.

Rancherias Canyon Trail is longer and more demanding, but can also be an easy day trip of 9.6 miles round-trip, requiring six to eight hours. It starts half a mile from Closed Canyon, from the West Rancherias Trailhead. A permit is also required here. Be sure to get a *Trail Guide* and ask for precise details on getting on to the trail from the trailhead parking area because the markers sometimes get shifted. Once in the drainage of the canyon, it is a relatively easy walk all the way to the seventy-foot-high Rancherias Falls. There you can sit in the cool water which comes from the Rancherias Spring.

RANCHERIAS TRAIL

This 19-mile hike, usually done in two to three days, requires reasonable effort and some attention to route finding but affords the delight of discovering remote springs and enjoying high country solitude.

Most trekkers start from the East Rancherias Trailhead, since this route provides a more gradual ascent. This means that upon completion you find yourself at the West Rancherias Trailhead and need to hike or hitch 2.5 miles to find your car.

The *Guide to Trails of the Big Bend Ranch State National Area,* and the *Backcountry and River Map* are both important on this route to keep you on the trail, to advise you where you should not tread because of the fragile ecological condition of the terrain, and to make you aware of the geological and historical features of the landscape. The nineteen-page trail guide is a gem, packed with illustrations and information. Briefly, you ascend 1,515 feet on the first section, descend into a canyon to find an adobe homestead, where there is water, then climb again, passing a cave shelter until you reach a jeep road. You now turn due west and follow this jeep road for about 4 miles to Rancherias Spring, a sizable area with large cottonwood trees. Later, turning south, you join a wagon road that takes you steeply downhill to the trailhead.

You'll meet few if any people at all on this road. But you'll surprise flocks of quail, hear the wind rustling the leaves of the cottonwood trees, and smell the flowers of the catclaw bushes. You'll probably get hot (carry one gallon of water for security) and a little tired, but it will seem a small price to pay for the experience.

BUS TOUR INTO THE RANCH

There are two departures each month. One leaves from Fort Leaton (Presidio) on the first Saturday of each month on a 74-mile round-trip.

The second departure is from the Warnock Center in Lajitas and leaves on the third Saturday of each month on a 136-mile round-trip. Each tour lasts eight to nine hours and costs $30 to conservation passport holders. An excellent chuck wagon lunch is provided, and there are free cold drinks. The refurbished military bus is air-conditioned and has a restroom. These tours are very popular and often sell out early, depending on the season. Bookings are accepted ninety days in advance. Call (915) 424-3327 or (915) 229-3613 for more information, or to make a reservation call (512) 389-8900.

SEMINARS AND WORK-STUDY PROJECTS

There are other means of getting inside the BBRSNA and of participating in the exciting discoveries which are to be made there. Throughout the year, the **Big Bend Natural History Association** offers programs ranging from a half-day ($20) to six days ($275), covering natural photography, mountain biking, wildlife, geology, and plant life. These seminars are conducted by some of the best-known and qualified people in their respective fields. Most involve some walking, and some require extensive hiking.

A new addition to the list of courses is the **Desert Survival Workshop,** a three-day introduction. The course gives training in such things as locating water sources, making fire by rubbing sticks together, recognizing medicinal plants, and creating shelter, and is proving very popular with all sorts of people. For the catalog *Big Bend Seminars*, write to Big Bend Natural History Association, P.O. Box 68, Big Bend National Park, TX 79834. The program applies to the Big Bend Ranch State National Area, Big Bend National Park, and Amistad National Recreation Area.

A second organization, **Texas Adventures,** part of the Texas Parks and Wildlife Department, offers seven-day programs relating to research and study at the BBRSNA, living and working in the park, and enjoying a hands-on experience. The cost is $875. Write to Texas Adventures, 4200 Smith School Road, Austin, TX 78744-9989.

These are early days for the state's largest park with all its diverse resources and primitive character. But without doubt, a lot more of the park will be made accessible, including access by the personal vehicle to the center of the park. Equestrian, mountain bike, and camping and hiking possibilities will also become available.

Carlsbad Caverns National Park

DESCRIPTION

Carlsbad Caverns is part of the same geological formation as El Capitan, the distinctive sheer-sided mountain, 30 miles to the southeast. But whereas the mountain stands 3,000 feet above the salt flats of West Texas, the caverns reach 800 feet and more underground. Both are part of the same Capitan Reef, a layer of marine limestone 1,600 feet thick that was formed two hundred million years ago on the floor of the Permian Sea, which covered much of this area at that time.

Many millions of years later, roughly sixty-five million years ago, the continent buckled. The Rocky Mountains appeared, and the Capitan Reef was also thrust upwards into the daylight. In one section of the mountain range, cracks occurred on the surface during the upheaval; water, slightly acidic, flowed through these cracks and, over the years, dissolved the limestone and carved out caverns and tunnels. Later, when the water table dropped, air replaced the water, and caves and corridors were waiting to be discovered.

There is evidence from pictographs on the entrance wall, from mescal-roasting pits nearby, as well as discarded items, that native Americans lived around the caverns. How far they ventured inside the cave is just conjecture. It was Jim White, a cowboy turned guano miner, whose curiosity lead him into the depths of the caves. He is credited as the discoverer of the caverns.

Bats were the clue to the cave. Every evening a whirlwind of these strange mammal bats flew out of the cave in search of insects to feed on. In the morning, they returned. The dung, known as guano, which they left in the cave in huge quantities, dried out over the centuries and was discovered to be one of the richest natural fertilizers. The guano was lifted out of the caverns by buckets and sent to fertilize the citrus orchards in California.

What made Carlsbad Caverns different was the immense variety of rock formations under the surface. Even before the demand for guano was fading due to transportation costs, Jim White had begun to explore the inner recesses of the cave during his off hours. Using smoky kerosene lamps, whose marks are still visible on some walls today, he crawled and climbed his way through the caverns and was the first man to see and name the enormous variety of structures and shapes underground. For twenty years, White explored, built trails, and escorted the first tourists

Temple of the Sun, Big Room, Carlsbad Caverns National Park. Courtesy National Park Service.

underground, using the guano bucket to transport the visitors. What the tourists saw then and what visitors see today is a wonderland of sculptures—some gigantic, some delicate, waterfalls, curtains, organ pipes, and columns—which turn the caverns and chambers into cathedrals and forests. Seeping drop by drop into the cave system, water absorbed mineral calcite en route and later dropped the tiny mineral load as a crystal. These crystals are what form the underground sculptures.

Although not the only underground caves administered by the park service and not the largest cave system in North America, nevertheless Carlsbad Caverns, designated a national monument in 1923, has sufficient appeal to attract over three-quarters of a million visitors annually. Such is the excellence of the underground engineering and construction, that even with six thousand visitors a day, the system can cope. And the possibilities for expansion are exciting. There are many more corridors and caverns waiting to be found, and already some of the lesser-known routes are being opened up to the public. In addition to the standard self-guided tour of the Main Corridor and the Big Room, there are now ranger-guided tours of Slaughter Canyon (23 miles away) and a number of special guided programs (with helmet and lights) to other parts of Carlsbad Caverns.

WHEN TO VISIT

Since the temperature underground remains almost constant, the main concern is with crowding. All the holiday weekends are very busy, especially Easter when a lot of tourists from Mexico visit.

The summer months are generally more crowded since it is a popular vacation time; fall is when tour groups are more numerous. By contrast, mid-week in January and February the caverns are so quiet that guided tours are offered. If you want to hear the Bat Flight Program, it takes place (no extra charge) every evening from Memorial Day weekend through the end of September. Since the starting time coincides with sunset, you need to call (505) 785-2232 for exact times. In late October or early November, the bats migrate to Mexico for the winter and return to Carlsbad in May.

PLANNING

Write or call the National Park Service for any of the following information sheets: *Carlsbad Caverns Official Map and Guide* (color); *Area Information, Where to Stay in Whites City and Carlsbad; Cavern Information*—hours of operation, what to wear, possibilities for photographs; *Blue and Red Tour* with descriptions of each; *The Bat Flight; Slaughter Canyon Cave* (New Cave); *Cave Swallows at Carlsbad Caverns*. Write to National Park Service, 3225 National Parks Highway, Carlsbad, NM 88220 or call (505) 785-2232. For twenty-four-hour recorded information, call (505) 785-2107. If you are already in Carlsbad, drop in at the NPS office; it is directly on U.S. 62/180 to Whites City.

U.S. NATIONAL PARK SERVICE

The National Park Service feels strongly about preserving Carlsbad Caverns for future generations. They would much rather interpret the underground and aboveground wonders of the park than act as policemen. Yet, with more than eight hundred thefts of rock formations each year, the caverns are slowly being stripped, and very little of the rock is still growing. So, the request, backed by law, is don't touch and don't go outside the marked pathways (movement detectors are having to be installed). Instead do ask about all the special programs accompanied by the rangers, including the surface programs available from May through October, and join in.

The NPS urges everyone to attend the Bat Flight Program. Learn about these intriguing animals, how they live, how they navigate, and what their usefulness is in the environment. Particularly for children, understanding bats will remove their ignorance of them and help counteract their negative reputation. According to the NPS, bats are good guys.

HOW TO GET THERE

Personal car. The Caverns can be reached from the east by U.S. 62/180 from Carlsbad, New Mexico, to Whites City (20 miles), or from the south and west from Van Horn by Texas 54 and U.S. 62/180 (99 miles), El Paso on U.S. 62/180 (144 miles), or Guadalupe Mountains National Park (35 miles). The Visitor Center, the start of the Caverns tour, is 7 miles from Whites City.

Bus. If coming by bus, see "Whites City" in chapter 3 for details of bus service to Whites City. From Whites City there are two morning buses to the park headquarters.

FROM THE PARK ENTRANCE

The two-lane road offers three exhibits which are worth stopping for, time permitting: the fossil reef; Indian Rock Shelter, which includes a short walk identifying eleven plant and tree species; and Walnut Canyon vista. There is also a 9.5-mile Desert Drive, a loop trail, which can be taken after visiting the caverns and which finishes up near the entrance gate. There is a pamphlet (50¢) available at the Visitor Center describing the eighteen points of interest on this drive.

A **restaurant aboveground** (table service), open daily from 8:30–5:00, offers burgers ($2.75), a BLT sandwich ($3.10), and a taco plate ($4.75). The **underground lunchroom** (self-service) offers a fried chicken box lunch ($4.25), a ham and cheese sandwich box lunch ($3.95), a burrito ($2.95), apple pie ($1.65), coffee, and soft drinks.

A **gift shop** offers a wide variety of standard items, including batteries (important for the special tour participants) and books, such as *Silent Chambers—Timeless Beauty* ($3) and *The Bats of Carlsbad Caverns* ($4.95).

In the auditorium there is a seven-minute film about bats, running more or less all day long. A well-stocked book shop near the ticket desk also rents earphones for the tour (50¢).

BLUE TOUR—RED TOUR

The **Blue Tour** (Main Corridor, Scenic, Big Room) is the complete walk-through trip (3 miles). It begins at the Visitor Center, travels about 300 yards over a surface trail, and then enters the cave through its natural entrance (where the bats come out). It takes about three hours and, although not strenuous, may be a problem for people with health or walking limitations. For those desiring an easier walk, take the shorter Red Tour. There is, on average, one visitor carried out each day whose knees, feet, or stamina have given out. The Blue Tour goes downhill for 830 feet and then goes up 80 feet, just before the lunch room. This is 1.75 miles. The route then joins that of the Red Tour and the surface is fairly level for the 1.25-mile circle trip of the Big Room. You return to the surface by elevator. Start at any time you want, and go at your own pace; rangers are present throughout the cave to give information or assistance.

The shorter **Red Tour** takes the visitor down by elevator. About one and a half hours are usually needed to complete the Big Room (1.25 miles). There are places to sit down. You may want to talk with a ranger or let a group pass; there is no reason to hurry, and your radio receiver will keep playing the relevant information about what you are looking at.

Some highlights include the following: on the Blue Tour—Bat Cave, Green Lake Room, King's Palace, Queen's Chambers, Papoose Room, and Boneyard; on the Red Tour—Giant Dome, Twin Domes, Temple of the Sun, Lily Pads, Mirror Lake, Bottomless Pit, and Top of the Cross.

Natural entrance, Carlsbad Caverns National Park. Courtesy National Park Service.

HOURS

Visitor Center opens at 8:00 A.M. year-round and closes 7:00 P.M. in the summer and 5:30 P.M. in the winter.

The first Blue Tour and first Red Tour each start at 8:30 A.M. The last entry of the Blue Tour is at 3:30 P.M. in the summer and at 2:00 P.M. in the winter. The last entry of the Red Tour is at 5:00 P.M. in the summer, 3:30 P.M. in the winter.

The last elevator is at 6:30 P.M. in the summer and at 5:00 P.M. in the winter.

FEES

Adults, $5. Children six to fifteen, $3. Under six free. Golden Age Pass holders, $2.50. Golden Access Pass holders, $2.50. Golden Eagle Passes are not applicable.

SPECIAL TOURS

At the Information Desk inquire about the special tours available. To join these conducted tours, with names like Lower Cave, Spider Cave, and Left Hand Tunnel, which are on a first-come, first-served basis, you need to be at the Visitor Center around 8:00 to 8:30 A.M. The tours are arranged on a day-to-day basis and have a maximum number on each program (612 usually). But, in addition to the Red or Blue Tours, and to the bat program, these additional aboveground or underground tours offer a new range of learning and experience with the thrill of exploration.

The **Slaughter Canyon Tour** (New Cave) ($6) is different in that you need to make reservations. It starts from the Slaughter Canyon Cave parking area, which is 23 miles from the Visitor Center. First, it involves a stiff hike (forty-five minutes) to the entrance of the cave. Bring your own flashlight and water, and wear shoes or boots suitable for the steep, slippery slopes inside the cave. Two rangers escort the group, which is limited to twenty-five people. This primitive tour has been available since 1974 and offers a somewhat more demanding visit to one of the more scenic caves in the park. The tour takes place on weekends only in winter, at 10:00 A.M. and 1:00 P.M., and on a daily basis during the summer, at 9:00 A.M. and 12:30 P.M. You must book and pay in advance and be at the cave entrance by the appointed time. Temperatures can be very hot in summer and very cold in winter. You may bring cameras but not tripods or videos.

SPECIAL PROGRAMS

Several different special programs are offered in addition to the Bat Flight Program and the Bat Flight Breakfast, which operate on a regular basis. Which one happens to be scheduled on the day you arrive depends on which rangers have been assigned that day. Each ranger has a special area of expertise.

Lower Canyon Trip covers an area that has long been explored but only recently opened as a special program. On a recent trip our ranger told us we needed two hours, had to wear a helmet and provide batteries for the headlamp, and sign a release saying we did not hold NPS responsible for any accident. We were also advised that the trip would be demanding but equally rewarding, and we were cautioned not to carry any unnecessary hand luggage.

Duly helmeted and having signed the release paper, five of us and two rangers took the elevator 750 feet down along with the other visitors. We immediately parted from the larger group and went down four different ladders into the darkness. We said, "On ladder" or "Off ladder" to let the next person know his turn to move. What we found at the bottom was a sizable cavern with our route marked with red reflecting tape.

At our first stop we heard a brief history of the discovery of the cave. Later we saw Jim White's signature scratched on a rock ("Jim Nov 1906"), and the nail beside it that he used to make his marks. Sometimes we saw black smudges where a kerosene lantern had scorched the rock. At another point, we saw the remains of an earlier ladder dangling down.

We needed our helmets as we crouched down to pass through a narrow low entrance. We were now in the bat dormitory. We found out that bats hang upside down when sleeping and that their muscles are tense when they are relaxed, directly opposite of humans.

We used stepping stones to cross over some deeper water and stopped to hear the basic talk on stalactites and stalagmites, on how the sculptures were formed by water, producing calcite. We saw how delicate some of the tracery is and learned about the secondary growth called popcorn. We also saw cave pearls, like oyster pearls, which used to be given to the early visitors as souvenirs, and we understood how brittle and breakable some of the formations are, an easy temptation for thoughtless visitors.

After easing our way through a keyhole opening and turning off our headlamps, we listened in complete darkness to the deafening sound of silence. The ranger illustrated the reflective property of calcite by using a camera flash, and the glow remained for some time. We crawled for a short stretch, and the rangers had some fun with us, pretending that they had lost their way.

But, of course, they hadn't, and we shortly recognized our previous route when we regained one of the larger chambers and prepared to go back up the ladders. We saw the lights from the visitors on the Red Tour shining above us, and we were glad we had just the slightest taste of how it feels to be exploring without the level pathways, the positioned lighting, and the crowds of tourists.

An even more difficult tour than this one involves a substantial amount of crawling, but this one should be able to be handled by anyone who is not overweight, who is in good health, and who doesn't mind getting his feet wet or his hands or clothing dirty.

During the **Bat Flight** program, you learn that more than 95 percent of the half-million bats that roost in Carlsbad Caverns' bat cave are Mexican free-tails. They arrive from the south in May to give birth in June and raise their young. The best bat flights normally occur in August and September when the baby bats join the flight.

The bat flight talks are usually scheduled from Memorial Day through the end of September, but the scheduled time changes and gets later with each passing day. Call (505) 785-2232 for exact times. From early May through October, the bats start to leave the caverns at sunset. For about one hour, a vast dark, moving mass, whirling counterclockwise, spills from the hole in the ground and flys off to scavenge for insects, using a sonar-like navigation system to locate their prey. They spend the night ranging the area and around dawn return to the cave's entrance, executing a dramatic dive from hundreds of feet above, without collision or injury, to reenter the cave. Early risers can watch the reentry, with bats approaching from all directions, some at twenty-five miles per hour, using their navigation system and completing a safe and speedy return to the cave.

The **Bat Flight Breakfast** is held one day each year, usually on the second Thursday in August, 5:00 A.M.–7:00 A.M. The park service sponsors the breakfast (small fee) and a special program. Call for topics and times.

There has been a dramatic decline in the bat population over the past few years, but nonetheless the sheer drama of the still massive formation reentering the mouth of the cave as if they were orchestrated by some divine hand is a truly amazing experience.

Guadalupe Mountains National Park

DESCRIPTION

Driving across the desert from El Paso in the west or Van Horn in the south, the visitor will notice in the distance, rising like a sentinel, the sharp outline of El Capitan. To the Spanish explorers the bold outline of the cliff face resembled a captain leading his men, so they called it "The Captain." To pioneers, the landmark was like a lighthouse rising above the desert sea.

The reference to the sea is appropriate since millions of years ago this mountain chain, stretching south and east from New Mexico, was under water. At that time, this whole area, now known as the Permian Sea, was a vast shallow ocean. Below the water, an offshore reef was being formed, caused by a buildup of the sand and silt being washed out from the shore. Only when the sea evaporated some million more years later, and when a later buckling of the earth's surface thrust this section upwards, was this limestone reef revealed, and then only part of it. Imagine roughly an upside-down horseshoe shape extending north from Van Horn, turning east around Carlsbad, and descending to near Alpine. This is the Capitan Reef and only three stretches—the Apache Mountains near Van Horn, the Glass Mountains near Alpine, and the Guadalupe Mountains, by far the longest, stretching forty miles to Carlsbad—are visible today. The rest remain buried.

This wedge of mountains cutting into the northern border of the 900-mile-long Chihuahuan Desert offers a remarkable diversity of plants and trees. At this southern latitude, cacti and other desert plants thrive. In contrast, only half a mile away but two thousand feet higher, northern trees like maple, fir, and even aspen flourish as well the beautiful and rare Texas madrone, which grows only in West Texas and on the Edwards Plateau. This Rocky Mountain ecosystem spills into the Chihuahuan Desert, and it all happens within a small area of only ten miles square, where deep canyons cut into the mountainside and lead up to a forested bowl on the mountain top.

The abrupt intrusion of the mountain onto the desert floor also has a profound effect on the westerly winds, funneling them and increasing their intensity, particularly during the spring months. Readings of over seventy miles per hour at the ranger station at the park entrance are not unusual.

WHEN TO VISIT

The weather can be tricky at any season ("potentially extreme" is the park service's cautious description), but April (when you hope the winds will relent), October, and November, for the astonishing fall colors (maple leaves in particular) in McKittrick Canyon, seem like good choices. In summer,

Giant dagger, Yucca. *By Elva Stewart.*

you have the satisfaction of climbing above the desert heat to the wooded shade of The Bowl.

RAINFALL AND TEMPERATURES

July, August, and September have rainfall of three to five inches per month. The other months register around one inch only. Temperatures at the campsites range from an average low of thirty degrees in January, to highs in the upper eighties in June, July, and August.

HISTORY

The Guadalupe Mountains National Park is one of the newer additions to the National Park Service's areas of responsibility. In 1957 the Pratt family made a gift to the U.S. government of 5,632 acres, comprising the most famous part of the park, the McKittrick Canyon. Seventy thousand acres were subsequently purchased from J. C. Hunter. Hunter, a banker and politician from San Antonio, had an ambitious plan to establish sheep and goats in the higher elevations of the ranch. He installed substantial numbers of water tanks there, which are still visible, with water pumped from two thousand feet below, to sustain the herds. However, the Department of the Interior purchased this acreage, and the park was opened to the public in 1972.

Although nearly 800,000 visitors a year go to Carlsbad Caverns, only 35 miles away, it is surprising, at first sight, that less than one-quarter of that number visit the Guadalupe Mountains National Park. One reason may be that this is a hiking park; there are almost no driving roads (except for one eighteen-mile round-trip stretch to Williams Ranch, of limited interest, requiring a vehicle with high clearance). The park service, by limiting facilities within the park and by designating over half the total area as a wilderness, seems to be planning to keep it that way. There are no easy circle trips for those who want to stay in their vehicles.

PLANNING

Visiting the park requires some advance planning. It is relatively isolated and some distance from motels and food supplies; also the camping facilities within the park are limited in number. There are twenty tent sites and twenty RV sites at Pine Springs Campground, on a first-come, first-served basis (toilets but no showers and no dump service). When the sites are full, you may park in a nearby picnic area on U.S. 62/180 or travel 35 miles to an RV site at Whites City.

There is no food for sale in the park, not even vending machines. It is 5 miles to the nearest cup of coffee or hamburger. Therefore, the best advice is to arrive early (checkout time is 12:00 noon).

At peak times of the year (spring break, holiday weekends, and sometimes during the summer), you will need to be around the campsite early in the day to occupy the site of a departing camper. At any time of the year, if you are approaching from Carlsbad, you can check with the Park Information Office there—3225 National Parks Highway, Carlsbad, NM 88220, (505) 785-2107—during the day, so they can call ahead to check availability at the campground. They also have a twenty-four hour recorded information message at this number. The Visitor Center number is (915) 828-3251.

Be prepared. Fill up with gas before you leave your last point of departure. It is 30 miles westbound from the park to the first gas station (Dell City junction with U.S. 62/180), and 35 miles eastbound at Whites City. Food supplies should be bought in Carlsbad, Van Horn, or El Paso. Grocery supplies at Whites City are expensive.

This park is not for everyone. Anyone who wants to learn about the special nature of Guadalupe Mountains National Park and who intends to do more than a short day hike must come prepared to expend some energy on the trails. You will need to protect yourself against thirst and bad weather. There is no water in the backcountry, so every drop must be carried uphill. One pint weighs one pound. The rangers recommend one gallon per person per day in the summer. Even on the flat and undemanding McKittrick Trail, you must carry your own water. And everyone going up Guadalupe Peak, or on one of the longer trails, should carry rain gear, bring high protein snacks, and have suitable footwear. Sprained ankles and twisted knees are the most common injuries the rangers have to cope with (there is a horse for carrying out the disabled). Tents and cooking stoves are also necessary for overnights.

HOW TO GET THERE

Air and car rental. See details under Carlsbad (Chapter 3), or fly into El Paso or Odessa and rent a car.

Personal car. Driving from Carlsbad, New Mexico, the park is 55 miles south on U.S. 62/180. From El Paso, it is 115 miles east on U.S. 62/180. From Van Horn (I-10), it is 63 miles north on Texas 54, and Midland-Odessa is 170 miles away.

Bus. Three buses pass daily by the park entrance on the El Paso–Lubbock route. The northbound stops at 5:00 A.M., 3:50 P.M., and 10:00

P.M. The southbound stops at 12:25 A.M., 6:00 A.M., and noon. This is a flag stop. When buying a ticket and boarding the bus on your way to the park, you must notify the driver of your intended stop at Pine Springs at the park entrance, since this is not a regularly scheduled stop. And you must flag down the bus when waiting to board at Pine Springs. Buses leave El Paso at 3:00 A.M., 1:45 P.M., and 7:25 P.M.; and Carlsbad at 4:40 A.M., 10:50 A.M., and 11:15 P.M. Call the bus company at (806) 765-6641.

WHERE TO STAY

RV Parks and Camps

Pine Springs Campground. At elevation 5,840 feet, this camp contains twenty well-placed tent sites, twenty-nine RV sites, "dry dock" only, no hook up, no dump station. Two group tent sites are available, but must be reserved in advance. All other sites are on a first-come, first-served, self-pay basis ($6 per site per night). Campground hosts are usually on duty during the summer months. Toilets, dishwashing facilities, and trash containers, but no showers, are provided. During busy periods (spring break, holiday weekends) all sites are likely to be taken quickly. Plan to arrive during the morning since checkout time is twelve noon. Otherwise, "full" signs will be posted, and you will have to ask at the Visitor Center or see the campground hosts for alternative overnight sites. Some possibilities are roadside picnic spots on U.S. 62/180; the RV site at Whites City, 35 miles north; and the Bureau of Land Management property over the state line 20 miles north.

Campground at Dog Canyon. This site is at the second entrance to the park, situated at 6,300 feet elevation on the northern side, a two-hour drive from Carlsbad, New Mexico. There are nine walk-in tent sites and five RV sites. Water and restrooms are provided, but no showers or dump station. There is a ranger station here which can issue back country permits.

Motels

The nearest substantial motel accommodation is at Whites City (see "Whites City"), with considerably more in Carlsbad, 20 miles farther on. At Van Horn, 63 miles south, there are seventeen motels.

INFORMATION

The Pine Springs Visitor Center, a stylish building completed only in 1990, is visible from the highway and is staffed from 8:30 A.M. to 4:00 P.M.

daily. There is no entrance fee to the park. The twelve-minute slide show in the auditorium provides a visual treat on the park's varied moods. There is also a static display of the park's animal life, and a push-button video recreation of the geological history of the reef. In addition to the usual well-stocked bookshelves with items for sale, free pamphlets, *Guadalupe Mountains* and *Official Map and Guide* (in color), are available. Printed in black-and-white are four pamphlets—*Guadalupe Mountains, Information and Map; Pine Springs Campground, Dog Canyon,* and *Suggested Day Hikes.* All these items can be obtained in advance by writing or calling Guadalupe Mountains National Park at HC 60, Box 400, Salt Flat, TX 79847-9400, (915) 828-3251.

Retail items which might be of interest include: *Natural History Note Series* (15¢) on specific subjects (e.g., the Texas madrone tree); *Canyon Notes for McKittrick Canyon* (50¢) also available at McKittrick Canyon Visitor Center from a machine; and *The Guadalupes,* a thirty-four-page description of the geological and natural history of the park with information on the early pioneers. There is also an evocative piece called *On the Trail* and some first-rate full-page color photographs for only $3.00. If you buy *Trails of the Guadalupes* (a hiker's guide) for $3.50, you will probably not need the topographical map ($7.95) unless you are planning to go cross-country (which is permitted).

WHERE TO EAT

State Line Bar and Cafe. 19 miles east. Despite the "Where Friends Meet Friends" slogan on the outside wall, there is more action inside around the pool table, at the Texas lottery machine, and at the bar than in the cafe, which sells snacks only. Forty miles west at Cornudos, if you are traveling to El Paso, the rangers say there is a good hamburger. Such is the sparse situation regarding eating places in the immediate vicinity. The nearest real restaurant is in Whites City (see "Whites City").

WHAT TO DO

If you are staying overnight, attend one of the **ranger slide programs** on the nature of the park (geology, reptiles, mammals, etc.). They are held every night from Memorial Day to Labor Day at around 8:00 P.M. for an hour or so. Or inquire at the Visitor Center if there are any guided walks along McKittrick Canyon or elsewhere.

Drive or walk to **Frijole Ranch** (1.5 miles away). At the ranch, now a cultural museum, you can read how the Smith family grew vegetables here and transported them overnight for 60 jolting, dusty miles to sell them in Van Horn. It must have been a fast journey. Inside the house, you can get an idea of the hard struggle of the daily lives of the early pioneers. The best spot is probably outside in the garden, shaded by trees and close to the flowing spring water. This is a lovely place to picnic.

From the ranch, there is a 2.3 mile round-trip hike to two springs, **Smith** and **Manzanita,** to give you an introductory idea of some of the plant and animal life in the park. This is an easy trail which goes slowly uphill through desert scrub brush. Entering a canyon, it suddenly comes across a spring, green and fresh with small pools. On the way back, the path passes by Manzanita Spring, where you may possibly see elk. This trail is the best introduction to the terrain of the park for the visitor with limited time. It might end with a picnic at Frijole Ranch, whose highlights include two delightful springs.

SAMPLE TRAILS

McKittrick Canyon is the single best-known and most-traveled trail. The limited length (4.6 miles round-trip to the Pratt Cabin, with 1.1 miles more to the Grotto picnic area) and the level surface make it possible for the less energetic to achieve the satisfaction of crossing and recrossing the spring-fed stream and enjoying the fragile beauty of the canyon. In the fall, the colors are a delight, and a further climb up the ridge beyond the Grotto permits a wider look along the canyon itself and of the surrounding ridges. *Canyon Notes,* which you may be carrying with you, gives some insights into the previous inhabitants of the canyon and surrounding areas. For twelve thousand years there has been human life there, according to archeological evidence. More recently, around six hundred years ago, the Mescalero Apaches hunted and gathered in the canyon, using all their ingenuity with the various plants to make food, clothing, medicine, or household articles. If you are lucky, you may hear a ranger talk and give a demonstration on how versatile and imaginative the Mescalero Apaches were in using every single growing substance for their daily life. This is also a hike to take if the weather is windy. The McKittrick Canyon Visitor Center has a visual display, offers a detailed and invaluable guide and map for sale (50¢), and has a video with commentary by Mr. Pratt himself. There is drinking water, restrooms, and a ranger on duty during the summer. Note that the gate to the highway is locked at 6:00 P.M. every night, and all hikers, except those doing backcountry trails, are expected to be gone by then.

The **Nature Trail Loop** (just under 1 mile), leading off from the Visitor Center, has all the desert plants clearly marked and their characteristics and uses noted. Here you can start to distinguish between the agave, or century plant, the yucca, and the sotol. The Mescalero Apaches got their own name from the heart of the agave plant, mescal; it was a most important source of food. All sorts of other plants are identified, like the prolific creosote bush, the lechuguilla ("lettuce," in Spanish, but bearing no resemblance to that harmless vegetable), and the best known of all, the prickly pear. The desert will soon start to appear to be full of variety and full of life.

Guadalupe Peak Trail starts at Pine Springs Campground and ends at Guadalupe Peak. It is a 9-mile round-trip, taking three to eight hours, and involves a 3,000-foot ascent. It leads to the highest point in Texas, with stunning views on clear days for 360° around. This can be a strenuous hike with an elevation gain of just under three thousand feet. Although the trail itself is easy and for the most part gradual, it takes a long time to get there. Depending on one's condition and determination, the hike to the top may take from one to four hours. And then there is the descent, by no means easier. Take water, food, sun protection, and foul-weather gear. At the top, the effort seems worth it, as the landscape lies before you: the salt flats, the continuation of the reef, and the other lower peaks. Be sure to sign the summit book. Previous entries make for interesting reading—pain, joy, humor, and spiritual reflections are all spontaneously recorded. Read comments like "Well—step aerobics paid off," and "Many thanks to the makers of Black Rock boots!" and "Thank you, Lord, for giving us these places to come to and the strength to do it." There are also plenty of "awesomes" and "gorgeous." For most, this trip can be a one-day hike. But you can also

Lechuguilla. By Elva Stewart.

camp out for the night at the Guadalupe Peak campsite, after having obtained a permit from the rangers, and enjoy the sunrise.

To really appreciate what makes up the appeal of the Guadalupe Mountains National Park, you need to spend one night up top in the **Mountain Zone,** perhaps in **The Bowl,** or stay at the Mescalero Campsite. The Bowl is a large depression in the high country filled with fir and pine and is the heart of the park. The **Mescalero Campsite** is one of ten backcountry campsites. There, tent locations have been cleared like terraces, facing east for the sunrise; look for the secluded site Number One. To get there, you have to go up one of the two trails to The Bowl, en route seeing what the 1990 fire did to the vegetation as you pass through the burned area. Note the remains of water pipes and appreciate the hardships the ranchers endured to ensure that their livestock would survive. Later you can walk through tall pines and enjoy the forest silence. As you cook your supper, mule deer may approach cautiously, and turkey vultures will drop down to inspect you.

Note that there are specified horse trails, even a shared trail up to Guadalupe Peak, but you have to bring your own horse since there are none for hire. Mountain bike riding is permitted on only a few roads, such as the Williams Ranch Road. Dogs are not permitted on the trails.

Some Other Trails

From Pine Springs Campground to Williams Ranch, **El Capitan Trail** is almost 10 miles one way; it skirts the base of El Capitan and has gentle gradients.

Devil's Hall Trail is 5 miles round-trip from Pine Springs Campground, taking four hours. It features a rock experience, both clambering around them and studying the stratification from below. There is little elevation gain. This trail is popular because it's different.

From Pine Springs to Dog Canyon Campground, **Tejas Trail** is a through hike of 11.7 miles, requiring eight to twelve hours. It involves a 2,000-foot ascent, fairly gradual, and has a good view of The Bowl and also of all the Guadalupe peaks. It connects with other trails (see map).

Bear Canyon Trail gives an alternate route to the high country, but it is a stiff climb. It takes three to four hours and is 3.4 miles long. From time to time, you see the pipeline laid to bring water to The Bowl. At the top you connect with The Bowl Trails, one with a spur to Hunter Peak.

Bush Mountain Trail is 11.4 miles, requiring eight to ten hours, from

Tejas Trail to Dog Canyon Campground. It passes Bush Mountain and an earthen dam, Cox Tank, and offers good views.

Permian Reef Geology Trail starts from McKittrick Canyon Visitor Center and is a long and steep 2,000-foot ascent; it leads to Wilderness Ridge campsite (4.1 miles away) in a beautiful wooded area. Once the ridge has been gained, there are good views to the north of the park; it is 4.7 miles one way to the park boundary.

Pleasantly devoid of overcrowding and offering the variety of vegetation which comes with significant altitude gain, the Guadalupe is a hiker's and camper's delight. Beware of those fierce spring winds, and in the fall head for McKittrick Canyon. Even the most jaded spirits should be lifted at the sight of the profusion of autumn colors.

Chapter 2

◆

Other Principal Sights

Big Bend and its surrounding area offer tourists an unusual combination of smaller state parks, historical sites, and popular tourist attractions.

Balmorhea and Balmorhea State Park

The two miles which separate Balmorhea, situated midway between Fort Stockton and Van Horn on Interstate 10, have made all the difference to the life of this town of 757 people. Named after three early settlers (Balcom, Morrow, and Rhea), the town presents a sleepy image to those passing through. Peace and quiet reign here. The tree-lined main street (Texas 17) features, on one side, a swiftly flowing stream, which comes from the nearby San Solomon Spring. Artifacts indicate that Indians used this productive spring before settlers came to the area. Today, the spring is responsible for Balmorhea's main attraction, Balmorhea State Park, as well as for the irrigation of the surrounding farmland.

Those who turn off I-10 at this point are probably heading south towards Fort Davis, the Davis Mountains, or the McDonald Observatory. Some may be visiting the Balmorhea State Park to camp, swim, or scuba dive; a smaller number may be headed for Lake Balmorhea one mile southeast of the town for some fishing or birding. Those who pause in town will find a quiet community that offers the visitor two motels and five cafes. There is a rural, old-fashioned charm about the place: a reed-encrusted water wheel rests in the stream and a sign outside the Methodist church reads, "Does it mean nothing to you, all you who pass by?"

Balmorhea State Park, 4 miles south of Balmorhea in Toyahvale on Texas 17, claims the title "Oasis of West Texas" and provides forty-three acres of lawns and trees as well as the largest spring-fed swimming pool in the world. Not only is this the largest (1.75 acres and 3.5 million gallons) pool, but it is also the deepest (30 feet), with a constant temperature between 72 and 76 degrees. The spring is home to eight species of fish, including catfish, crayfish, and perch. A slight nibbling sensation on your toes reminds you that the pool may be constructed by humans, but it also belongs to the fishes.

The Civilian Conservation Corps built the pool and the canals in the campground and later added the Spanish-style cottages between 1935 and 1941. Thirty-four campsites are available for RV and tent campers, and San Solomon Springs Court offers eighteen units, some with a kitchen. Two rare and endangered fish (pupfish and mosquito fish) are found in the canals (no swimming allowed). Outside the park entrance, to the left, is **Branding Iron Barbecue,** open weekends from Memorial Day to Labor Day for sandwiches and barbecue plates.

Opposite the Branding Iron is **Desert Diving,** a full-service dive center. A complete scuba diving set rents for $25 per day. Inner tubes are also available for rent for $4 per day, and camping and diving gear is for sale. In addition, Desert Diving offers a mobile home for rent (up to 6 persons) for $45 a night, plus tax. (915) 375-2572.

The entrance fee to the park is $5 per vehicle. Campsites are $7 with water, $10 with water and electricity.

ACCOMMODATIONS IN THE PARK

Rates for the San Solomon Springs Court units are $35 for one person, $5 for each additional person, and $5 for kitchenettes (no utensils provided). A TV, clothesline, and central heat and air are included. At peak periods (spring break, July 4) advance bookings are strongly suggested, and some hundreds of swimmers can make this a noisy, crowded place.

Normally, this is a small and quiet campground, although the occasional car or truck can quickly drown out the numerous bird calls. The setting, amidst fertile agricultural land with the craggy outline of the Davis Mountains in the background, is soothing, and with an elevation of 2,500 feet, the temperature is usually agreeable. There may not be more agreeable overnight stops, after hours of charging along I-10, than the comfortable, red-roofed cottages in the park, with the canal flowing past the door, in the shade of large cottonwood trees. Reserve in advance for the cottages and for camping, through the central reservation number (512) 389-8900, 8:00 A.M. to 6:00 P.M., Monday–Friday. The park office is open from 8:00 A.M. to 5:00 P.M. daily. (915) 375-2370.

There is now year-round swimming, from 8:00 A.M. until a half-hour before sunset. Lifeguards are on duty from late May to Labor Day, when the entire pool may be used. At other times, once you have signed a liability release, you may swim in the side sections. Children aged twelve and under must be accompanied by an adult; swimmers aged thirteen through seventeen must have written permission from their parents. Complete bathhouse facilities are available, and a food and refreshment concession operates during the summer months.

Lake Balmorhea, one mile southeast of town, presents a different, un-tended image. The lake is well known to bird-watchers as a stopover for migratory birds. Get hold of *Birds of Balmorhea State Park and Vicinity, A Check List*, if you want to get serious about identification; it is free from Texas Parks and Wildlife Department, 4200 Smith School Road, Austin, TX 78744. A sign by the lake suggests one should obtain permits for fishing and camping at the store. There is no cafe here, public toilets are of the primitive variety, and the area has an unkempt look to it. But, for the serious bird-watcher or fishing enthusiast who does not need a well-tended RV site, this is a good alternative to Balmorhea State Park. The six-hundred-acre lake is stocked with perch, catfish, bass, and crappie. There is an annual tournament each May. A fishing permit costs $2 for those with Texas state licenses ($13), primitive camping is $2, RV hookups, $8. These fees are paid at the store, where bait and beer can also be bought.

WHERE TO STAY

Motels

Country Inn. P.O. Box 295, Balmorhea, TX 79718, (915) 375-2477. Located right on the main street, this two-story building, built ten years ago, offers fifteen rooms of adequate quality at $30 per room for one person, $35 for two, and suites from $45 to $100 (sleeps six). Ask for a room at the back which looks out over the small canal. This motel sometimes gets filled up with scuba divers on weekends and with hunters in the fall, so book in advance. Meals can be eaten across the street at the **Fillin' Station Cafe.**

Valley Motel. On Main Street, (915) 375-2263. With eleven rooms, it has looked run-down for a number of years but is now in the process of being improved. Ask for one of the new rooms with color TV, new bathroom fixtures, and new carpet. Close to Dutchover's Cafe and the Bear's Den Cafe. Rates are $20 for one bed, and $25–$30 for two beds.

RV Park

Prices at **Balmorhea State Park** are listed earlier in this chapter. Desert Diving near the park entrance offers "dry" sites.

At **Balmorhea Lake,** the fee is $8 for a hookup, and next to the Fillin' Station Cafe, the fee is $10 for a hookup.

In town, **Blue Quail RV Park,** near the Fillin' Station Cafe, offers a few sites.

WHERE TO EAT

Dutchover's Cafe. On Main Street. Pink is the color here for walls, tablecloths, and even the inside of the coffee mugs. It is very clean, offering a good breakfast choice and a mostly Mexican-food menu. It is open from 7:00 A.M. to 2:00 P.M. (915) 375-2338.

Fillin' Station Cafe. On Main Street. Formerly a steak restaurant, it now serves Mexican food and burgers. Open seven days a week. (915) 375-2233.

Bear Den. Near the Valley Motel, originally catered to local students, but is now expanding in size and in the breadth of its menu. Lots of enchilada and taco plates are offered, along with fajitas and chicken-fried steak. Try the Bear Plate at $4.25.

Balmorhea Drugstore. On Main Street (established in 1916). Delightful, cool in the summertime, and old-fashioned. There is a soda fountain, ceiling fans, and a collection of hats and ballpoint pens.

Circle Bar and Steak House. In contrast to the drugstore's nostalgic atmosphere, this functional new structure has opened next to the Chevron gas station, three miles east of town at I-10 and Texas 17, featuring steaks. The restaurant is open Thursday–Sunday; the bar opens daily at 5:00 P.M. A rib eye steak (eight ounces) is $8.95; a sixteen ounce T-Bone is $14.95; chef's salad, $4.95; and a burger, $2.75.

Greasewood Cafe on Main Street. Watch for this new restaurant, which is about to open as this book goes to press. Initially, the restaurant will serve dinner 5:00 to 10:00 P.M. (closed Wednesday), from a menu reflecting several cooking traditions: American, Cajun, and French. There will be vegetarian dishes and the bread will be home-baked. The Greasewood Cafe has a wine and beer licence, and will be open late (until midnight) on weekends for dancing. The menu and the ambience are designed "to provide a peaceful, esthetically pleasing atmosphere integrating the natural qualities found in the region," says owner Kate Vigneron. (915) 375-2658.

Chihuahuan Desert Visitor Center

Founded in 1978 and linked to Sul Ross University through its administration and staffing, the center is not actually in the desert but in prime rangeland 4 miles south of Fort Davis and is always looking for funds for its continued development. The Chihuahuan Desert is the largest desert in North America, with 80 percent of it lying in Mexico. The center itself,

Century plant, Agave americana. *By Elva Stewart.*

located in an area with an average rainfall of fourteen inches annually, falls just outside the precise desert boundary, but this in no way limits it usefulness to scholars or its enjoyment for the public.

Picked for its easy access to Alpine (22 miles south) and Sul Ross State University, where the center has its office, the unfinished project comes as a pleasant, unheralded delight. The visitor's first sight, at the end of a mile of dirt road, is of an outdoor classroom and temporary gift shop.

After a short walk through a rock outcropping, visitors find themselves entering the Arboretum, a living collection of plants native to the Chihuahuan Desert region. The plants in this forty-acre arboretum have been grouped according to families, are well displayed, and offer a great variety. There are also one hundred species of trees and shrubs.

The incomplete nature of the enterprise actually adds to the impression that this is a working laboratory, where both staff and plants are in the process of growth. The institute (Chihuahuan Desert Research Institute), which owns the center, aims to be not only a desert museum, but also a functional source for research, says its director, Dennie Miller. The vast majority of plants have been grown from seed in the institute's greenhouse, and one gets the feeling that this really is an outdoor classroom. The greenhouse contains the largest collection of cacti in the Southwest, with more than two hundred species. The sixteen hundred-square-foot Visitor Center building, modeled after early military architecture of the desert Southwest, is still under construction and will be completed as soon as funds permit.

For exercise, visitors may follow the short Modesta Canyon Trail, (a half-hour round-trip), which visits some springs hidden in the canyon. Those who are more energetic can follow the self-guided, interpretive trail to the peak (allow two hours total), the highest point on the site.

The center is a wonderful place to spend an afternoon; it's casual and unfinished but offers plenty to see as well as the chance to take a stroll. There are crayfish in the springs, hawthorn and cherry trees nearby, piñon pine trees on the slopes above, and from the overlook looking southwest into a stone quarry, you may see some exotic aoudad sheep, imported by ranchers into the region for hunting purposes. If you come across any Indian artifacts, make sure to give them to the CDRI staff for identification and placement in the Museum of the Big Bend, located on the campus of Sul Ross State University.

When the gate on the highway (Texas 118, 4 miles south of Fort Davis, and 18 miles north of Alpine) is open, drive on through. No admission is charged, but donations are particularly welcome for this good cause. It is open from April 1 through Labor Day. The hours are 1:00 P.M. to 5:00 P.M. on weekdays and 9:00 A.M. to 6:00 P.M. on weekends. The one advantage this site has over a lower desert setting is that the summer temperatures at this altitude of around 4,700 feet are tolerable, even pleasant. Call (915) 837-8370 for more information, 9:00 A.M. to 5:00 P.M., weekdays.

EVENTS

In April, there is a Native Plant Sale, and in August a Picnic and Barbecue for members only.

Davis Mountains State Park and Indian Lodge

The modest introduction in the leaflet *Davis Mountains State Park* states that "its 2,150 acres encompass an unusually scenic portion of Texas." This statement does not do justice to the beauty of this small and wonderful park.

DESCRIPTION

The park is located 3 miles north of Fort Davis, on Texas 118, in the rolling foothills of the Davis Mountains. This mountain range, largest in Texas, measures 40 by 60 miles. But at the lower altitude of the park, the rounded, well-vegetated hills display a softer image. The flora and the fauna of the park represent a mixture of grassland and woodland species and offer excellent cover for birds, as well as deer and javelinas.

The park itself is small, only 3,300 acres altogether, including the recently added 1,400 acres of the Primitive Area, or about 5 square miles. But in this compact space, there is not only the imposing Indian Lodge, hiking trails to Fort Davis, and the Primitive Area, but also, most unusual for the Texas Parks and Wildlife Department, a superintendent who is a trained and dedicated bird specialist.

WHEN TO GO

The elevation in the park (4,900–5,500 feet) provides for cool summers, and spring and fall can produce energizing morning temperatures when it might be the time to take one of the trails. A 4-mile trail leads out of the park to historic Fort Davis, and there is a second trail in the Primitive Area on the other side of Texas 118. June is the hottest month of the year, and from July 4 through late August the park keeps busy while summer rains can keep the hillsides green. Spring Break and Thanksgiving are also busy periods. The average annual temperature is 63 degrees, with an average rainfall of 19 inches.

INFORMATION

First you must pass through the park headquarters. Unless you are proceeding to Indian Lodge only, you will need to pay the daily entrance fee of $4 per vehicle. Texas Conservation Passport holders ($25 annual fee) and Parklands Pass holders (free to those over 65 and disabled Vets) enter free. Camping rates are $8 for a water-only campsite and $11 for a site with electricity; also $13 for a full hookup site. There are also weekly rates. The park office number is (915) 426-3337. For State Parks information, call 1-800-792-1112. For reservations at Davis Mountains State Park, call (512) 389-8900.

WHAT TO DO

Go **birding.** The Davis Mountains are bird territory, and this area of West Texas contains an astonishing variety of birds, thanks to its location on the north-south migratory route. The park is equally fortunate in having as its superintendent Kelly Bryan, a bird enthusiast and a trained ornithologist who has banded over forty-five thousand birds.

Even if you are not a bird enthusiast, the three times weekly bird banding exercises (in spring and fall only) are too good, and too close, to miss. The nets are set in strategic locations in one part of the primitive area of the park. The birds fly into them, and are trapped (without injury). Along comes Kelly Bryan or volunteer park visitors who will help him to increase the bandings to a daily operation (in season); they identify the bird, note its condition, give it a cleanup, maybe a pat on the back, then release it. The report, as with others from around the continent, goes to the U.S. Fish and Wildlife headquarters.

Even before attending one of the banding exercises, if the season permits, everyone should take the time to recognize one or two of the most popular birds in the park. A free booklet, *A Checklist of Texas Birds*, obtainable from the park staff or volunteers, may help in this activity. First to visit your campsite will probably be the curious canyon towhee. This bird is useful for picking bugs off the radiator of your car. Uninvited, it will also venture inside your car or tent. The towhee is not harmful, cute but plain, except for a rust-colored crown.

The second most likely bird for you to spot will probably be the first one you hear. The plaintive and repetitive "Who cooks for you" sound comes from the white-winged dove. With its white wing patch and its larger size, you should be able to spot this vocal neighbor, whose call is often mistaken for the owl's.

A third bird, easily spotted around the park campground, is the acorn woodpecker, usually seen close to its nest on a telephone pole. Its red cap and the yellow patch on its throat give its face the appearance of a clown. In addition, Davis Mountains is the only state park which harbors the Montezuma quail, once abundant but now protected; park staff or volunteers can point you to a likely viewing spot.

Take a **back country trail.** The newly opened Primitive Area, on the other side of Texas 118, has added an additional 1,400 acres to the park's boundaries. At present this is a day-use only area, requiring the visitor to have a Texas Conservation Passport ($25, but with many cost savings) and to sign in and out for the day. A short (three- to four-hour round-trip) trail with a six-hundred-foot elevation gain is currently provided. You need to sign in at the Visitor Center and collect a map and instructions before leaving.

The trail starts from the parking lot on the other side of Texas 118, where the bird banding takes place. Follow an easy, level trail upstream towards Prude Ranch, and be prepared after a few minutes to branch off to the right when faded, orange tape markers appear. These have been tied to trees and bushes, and most of them are still there.

This trail takes you across the stream bed to the other bank, then continues, gaining altitude and bearing to the right. You will cross a fence, then join a jeep road where cairns indicate that you're on the right track. On the ridge, since you may now look out over the whole Prude Ranch central area, you have the choice of continuing in the same direction of the jeep road, which will take you along Sheep Pen Canyon to the farther limit of the park, or to bear sharply to the right and backwards, and then following this trail, crossing one more fence, to the Overlook. You will now be directly above the point you started from and have fine views all around to Mount Livermore, to McDonald Observatory, to Indian Lodge, and across the hill to Fort Davis.

There are plans to establish a six-tent primitive camping site here in the near future, and this site would certainly be a place suitable for a star watching and a camping party. But, in the meantime, you will need to get back to the Visitor Center to sign in.

If your time does not permit a hike, or the opportunity for bird watching or attendance at a program in the Interpretative Center, you should, at the very least, allow time for the skyline drive and overlook and for a visit to Indian Lodge.

March is the busiest month in the park, and December and January the quietest. Reservations for busy periods (e.g. Spring Break, July 4) are vital. For campsite reservations (these may be made ninety days in advance), call (512) 389-8900, from 8:00 A.M. to 5:00 P.M.

Visit **Indian Lodge.** Current estimates of park visitation indicate that an estimated 396,000 visitors annually pass through the entrance gate to the Davis Mountains State Park, and many of those are on their way to visit Indian Lodge. This pueblo-style hotel, built over fifty years ago by the Civilian Conservation Corps, is a highlight of the park.

The hotel resembles a multilevel Indian pueblo village with some of the original walls measuring eighteen inches thick. In the original fifteen rooms, which are much preferred, latilla cane ceilings, kiva fireplaces, and handmade cedar furniture, complemented by softly woven Indian furnishings, present a handsome appearance.

Built high in the Limpia Creek Valley, the building blends naturally with its surroundings. From its windows, the visitor can look across the hillside, perhaps fresh and green after a summer rain shower, to the skyline outside the park. In 1967 twenty-four additional rooms were built, together with a swimming pool and restaurant.

In this splendid setting is a tastefully furnished lodge with creative new management; the prices, determined by the Texas Parks and Wildlife Department in Austin, remain eminently reasonable.

Daily room rates (for one or two persons) are (old section) double bed $66.00, king-size $77.00 and (new section) two double beds $60.50. These prices include tax and a breakfast buffet. A child over 12 years is $10.00. Children under 12 years are free. Cribs, rollaways, and room service are not available. This is, not surprisingly, a very popular place. The rooms are priced below market value. It is essential to book and secure your reservation by sending a deposit (one night's accommodation); credit cards are not accepted over the phone, although they may be used as payment when checking out. (915) 426-3254.

The Lodge's **Black Bear Restaurant** provides a full menu, but recently the lackluster service and the strictly average quality of the cooking have not done justice to the fine setting. The exception is Sunday lunch, noon to 2:30 P.M., which at $7.75 per person for a good help-yourself buffet, is as popular as ever with local people. Now, however, with a rewritten menu and a tighter control in the kitchen, things are looking more promising. The breakfast provided to the guests is also available for walk-ins: $3.00 for Continental breakfast and $5.00 for a cooked breakfast. And theme evenings at Indian Lodge, with an appropriate buffet, have proven very popular—Oktoberfest, a Mardi Gras evening with Creole and Cajun cooking and Dixieland jazz ($12.95), and a St. Patrick's Day celebration (Irish singalong in the lobby, with a choice of Irish stew, cider chicken, or corn beef and cabbage for $10.95) draw crowds. At Christmas, Open House features performances by area choirs and musicians. The Lodge is very much a feature in the lives of local people as well as visitors to the area.

Historic Fort Davis

Today, Fort Davis National Historic Site is open to visitors from 8:00 A.M. to 5:00 P.M., between early September and late May, and from 8:00 A.M. to 6:00 P.M. for the rest of the year. The site is closed on December 25. The cost is $4 per car, or $2 per person. Educational groups, individuals

Fort Davis, enlisted men's barracks and stables, 1886. Courtesy National Park Service.

under sixteen, and holders of Golden Eagle, Golden Age, or Golden Access Passports enter free of charge.

What greets the visitor is a large parade ground, a tall flagpole with the Stars and Stripes snapping in the wind (at least in the springtime), and six carefully reconstructed buildings with their original contents: the enlisted men's barracks, the commanding officer's quarters, a lieutenant's quarters, the commissary, an officer's kitchen, and an exhibit of twelve-pound mountain howitzers, Gatling guns, and mule escort wagons. As one tours these remains, which are the most extensive of any nineteenth-century post on the southwestern frontier, the loudspeaker system periodically breaks into martial music or bugle calls, which were the daily accompaniment to the soldiers' lives.

In the squad room, the neat rows of beds, blankets folded, hats and helmets placed on top, would satisfy any sergeant. In the commissary, the provisioning order forms list "baked beans, 3 lb can. Sauce, Worcestershire, 1 pint bottle." Beef was seven cents per pound, and codfish balls were also available. This post was a major installation; the second fort took two hundred men to build, and at its peak, twelve companies were stationed here. The careful reconstruction, the military music, and the display of small details of daily life combine to create a vivid impression of life on the frontier.

A twelve-minute slide show in the auditorium outlines the history of the fort and the region, and there are also audio programs. The bookstore at the Visitor Center is well stocked, and there is a static display of maps, artifacts, and pictures in the museum.

Old faces stare out from the pictures in the museum, including that of Vitorio, the Warm Springs Apache chief who was "the greatest commander, white or red, who ever roamed these plains" (this characterization is from W. W. Mills, a prominent Anglo businessman and politician from El Paso in the late 1800s). Significant attention is paid to the buffalo soldiers, the black troops given their nickname by the Indians because of their close-cropped hair. The military view is clearly stated: "forcing the Indians from the region and keeping them out of it" (Major General Ord 1879). And, finally, another caption on the wall: "With the Indians conquered, the Davis Mountains became a cattleman's empire. Mail protection was no longer needed."

Allow one to two hours for the feel of this vivid re-creation to get through to you. Or spend a little longer and try one of the hiking trails. There are three loop trails (1–2 miles each) and a longer trail, which takes you to the Lookout Tower in the Davis Mountains State Park (2 miles) or to Indian Lodge on the other side of the park (4 miles).

McDonald Observatory

Sitting high on top of Mount Locke at an elevation of 6,800 feet and enjoying amazingly clear viewing conditions (which was why, of course, the site was chosen) is the University of Texas McDonald Observatory, which, despite its primary research objectives, has an active program of public tours and information.

The first stopping point is the W. L. Moody Visitors' Information Center, where you can easily spend an hour looking at the astronomy exhibits, viewing films, or buying at the gift shop (astronauts' ice cream, $1.45). The Visitors' Center is open daily from 9:00 A.M. to 5:00 P.M. except Thanksgiving, Christmas, and New Year's Day.

At 2:30 P.M. (check-in 30 minutes before) there is a daily tour of the observatory, which houses the 107-inch telescope (there are three other smaller telescopes housed nearby). You can get inside the white housing dome, probably see the doors open, look at the outside of the telescope, and learn about how it works. The tour lasts about an hour. Those with large RVs or trailers can leave them at the Visitors' Center and travel up to the telescope by van. This option is useful and fascinating to some but not "hands-on."

Twice daily, at 11:00 A.M. and 3:30 P.M. weather permitting, there is a solar viewing program from outside the Visitors' Center. As with the observatory tour and the star parties, there is no charge, and it is here that the infectious enthusiasm and good humor of the guides comes into play. The solar viewing uses telescopes specially equipped with filters to provide a safe view. Clouds permitting, you may see solar features such as sun spots and flares, and because of the filter, the sun appears a lovely orange color. You learn that the sun is only a star ninety-three million miles away; the guide compares it to a gas-filled, layered onion. It contains most of the mass of the solar system and provides us on earth with life-giving warmth.

Up on the hill is the 107" telescope, the observatory's largest. Once a month there is an evening program open to the public, and reservations are required six months in advance. Admission is $5.00 for adults, $4.00 for students and senior citizens, and $2.50 for children under twelve.

In this program a professional astronomer shows how a large telescope is used in research. The astronomer discusses the research at hand and, if clouds allow, you might look at a planet through the scope. However, you'll learn that the telescope was not designed to be "looked through." Instead, the scientists attach gadgets to the telescope that gather certain data about the universe. This is the largest telescope at the observatory and therefore attracts interest but, if you want beautiful views of our universe, read on.

During the daytime, the 107" is not available for public use. Still, you should take the self-guided tour and read about how the telescope is used for research every clear night of the year.

The most fun activity, certainly the most popular, is the **Star Party,** which takes place every Tuesday, Friday, and Saturday starting at 6:30 P.M. or 9:00 P.M., depending on the month and, of course, on the state of the sky. It is here that you may use telescopes that are built to provide, in striking detail, some wonderful views of objects in space. You'll stand under a canopy of stars with your star-guide and learn constellations. You can enjoy an astronomy video, and hot beverages may be purchased. No reservations are necessary—just show up, dress warmly, and be prepared to be patient in the event that there are any school buses or tour groups.

Astronomy is the study of light and is a non-tactile science. The various films shown in the Visitor Center touch on the mystery of the sky, the enormous distances involved, and the potential we all have to learn about the vast universe we are a tangible part of. The guides liken astronomy to scuba diving, another life experience. The sky is one of the things which has not changed much in our world, and you don't need a degree in science to appreciate its beauty or to learn in a natural setting about the layout of the night sky.

A new telescope at McDonald Observatory is due for completion in late 1997, and, with ninety-one hexagonal mirrors in a mosaic which has a diameter of 430 inches, it will be the largest of its kind in the world. But the main source of satisfaction—information gained, beauty experienced, and spirituality awakened—will continue to come from the Star Parties and their lively guides and interpreters, who also love kids.

The night sky is beautiful and dark, the guides are entertaining as well as knowledgeable, and with luck you can get to see through both the fourteen-inch and the twenty-four-inch telescopes outside of the center. The guides have already explained which way is north, the names of the constellations, and the location of the various planets. In these clear conditions, with this expert yet low-key explanation, one's own eyes or a pair of binoculars are sufficient for a major part of the enjoyment, even before a look through the telescope.

Once a month there is Public Night on the 107-inch telescope. Admission is $5 for adults, $4 for students and senior citizens, and $2.50 for children under twelve. You don't actually get to look through the telescope, as it is not of the reflector type. But you do get to understand how it operates and gain an appreciation of the work being done at the observatory on a daily basis. Reservations are required and must be made approximately six months in advance. A schedule of Public Nights can be obtained from the Visitor Center.

For details of Public Nights and for the changing times of the evening Star Parties, call (915) 426-3640, or write to Visitors' Information Center, Box 1337, Fort Davis, TX 79734.

Prude Ranch

John Robert Prude had a problem in 1985. The year before, he had borrowed about one million dollars and spent it renovating and adding to the family ranch, which had been taking in guests for sixty years. The trouble now was that in the year since he had borrowed and spent the one million dollars, oil prices had plummeted and with them the likelihood of much repeat business from existing guests, oil people from the Permian Basin.

The Prude Ranch had already been in what they called the "people business" since 1921, in addition to the original cattle business of the five-thousand-acre property, which had kept the family busy for four generations. And since 1951 they had been taking in summer camp groups for whom the mountain setting, the cool summer temperatures, and the outdoor activities were ideal. But the immediate loss of the bulk of his steady customers, added to the burden of paying back the loan, meant that John Robert had to make a sudden switch in strategy to attract a new clientele to fill the enlarged bunkhouses, family rooms, and guest lodges.

The switch involved attracting new group business, such as the Elderhostel program; offering new programs, such as environmental education courses, in addition to board and accommodation; and marketing within the travel trade and in the media in order to attract family and individual visitors. To promote the ranch, the owners have visited international travel trade fairs overseas and even produced videos with Japanese commentary.

What the visitor now sees is a sizable and varied operation, with a staff of twenty-five, offering different types of accommodations to youth groups, tour buses, RV travelers, tent campers, or tourists in cars who are looking for a bed, some food, and something more than a traditional vacation. The something more can be a horse ride or the chance to take a walk through a working ranch in beautiful high country scenery.

For groups, there are more options, including hayrides and chuck wagon feasts, square-dancing instruction, slide shows about the Chihuahuan Desert, or Star Parties with staff from nearby McDonald Observatory.

John Robert stresses that the Prude Ranch should not be confused with other dude ranches, for high rollers and hard drinkers. The Prude Ranch's goal is to provide simple satisfaction by doing simple things. There are tennis courts, a swimming pool, and exercise machines, but the setting of the ranch and the chance to ride one of the eighty horses on the open range (escorted) or to hike through canyons or over mountains makes just being there the main enjoyment. Staff are considered family, and they are involved in the running of the ranch.

ACCOMMODATIONS AND RATES

Individual guest lodges are on the mountainside and separate from the accommodations for groups. There is a rustic feel to the cabins, with vaulted ceilings and Southwestern décor. Although there is no TV, there is a chance to sit out on the porch and enjoy the view across to the hillside. In each room, there are either two double beds or one double and two single beds, sometimes bunked. The rate for one person is $65; double occupancy is $75. Each additional person per night is $5.

Family bunk rooms include one double bed and twin-sized bunk beds (up to six). The rate for one person is $40; double occupancy is $49. Each additional person per night is $5.

The ranch bunkhouse accommodations can house from eight to twenty persons per room. All beds are bunked beds. Guests must provide their own bed and bath linens. Rates are according to the size of the groups and whether meals are included.

RV hookups are $12.50. Tent sites with water and electricity are $8.50. Tent sites with no services are $6.00.

MEALS

Prices quoted include all-you-can-eat meals. Menus, meal times, and meal prices are posted daily in the ranch office. Breakfast is provided every day, but other meals are included only when visiting groups warrant it. Check the board; if the group menu does not appeal, Indian Lodge is just next door, and Fort Davis is only 6 miles away. Breakfast is from $5.50; lunch is from $6.00; dinner is from $7.95.

There is no charge for using the tennis or swimming facilities or the exercise machines. Individual fees for horseback riding are $8.50 per hour.

Chapter 3

Towns and Communities

Several picturesque towns mark the route between Big Bend and Carlsbad, and each one offers a unique contribution to your vacation memories.

Alpine

Approaching Alpine from the east or west, so gradual is the ascent that one is scarcely aware of the increase in altitude. After miles and miles of dry, flat desert scenery, suddenly and dramatically a tree-lined oasis appears, ringed on three sides by mountains, at an elevation of 4,400 feet.

Set in this pleasant location, providing a small university, a hospital, golf course, and a movie theater, Alpine pursues its own life as the county seat of Brewster County (Texas' largest) and as a service center to the region. It is a town where the sense of community is still strong.

A community of people exists here, including an increasing number of retirees who are attracted to the climate, the quiet, and the absence of crime, and who find the unchanged nature of Alpine agreeable. Alpine (population 5,600) is also the transportation hub of the region, providing visitors and residents with five-times-weekly air service to Dallas, thrice-weekly rail service east- and westbound on the Southern Pacific Line and bus links north and south, east and west.

Like other towns in the region, Alpine's economic development dates mainly from the coming of the railroad to West Texas in the late 1880s. At that time, the town's name was Murphyville, named after Dan Murphy, who had leased his nearby spring to the railroad company. Cattle were shipped on the railroad, and later, various metals from the mines in the south of Brewster County.

Another impetus to the economic development of Alpine was the founding of Sul Ross College, now a university, in 1920. In the 1940s, the establishment of Big Bend National Park helped to bring more tourists into the area. With the resumption of air service in 1993, Alpine's role as the gateway to the region was further enhanced.

There is a wonderful diversity about Alpine: working cowboys wearing spurs buy their groceries at the supermarket, artists exhibit their work in seven galleries, and students from all over the state attend the flourishing Sul Ross State University. The Museum of the Big Bend is being enlarged, and there are two new bed and breakfast homes and a brand new 75-bed motel in town. But to see what influences the lives of the people of Alpine, take a look at the mural in the post office, step inside the town library, and hang around to observe one of the local parades or join the crowds at the Cowboy Poetry Gathering.

HOW TO GET THERE

Personal car. By car, U.S. 90 brings you from Marathon, 30 miles to the east, or Marfa, 26 miles to the west. The majority, arriving on I-10 from the east or northeast will angle down from Fort Stockton (67 miles) on U.S. 67. Easily the most scenic approach to Alpine and the region can be appreciated by getting off I-10 at Balmorhea (47 miles west of Fort Stockton) and taking Texas 17 over Wild Rose Pass to Fort Davis (32 miles) and then going a farther 26 miles to Alpine.

Car rental. Big Bend Aero at Alpine Airport has an expanding fleet of cars and vans for rent. These are late eighties and early nineties models, including four-wheel drives, compacts, and wagons. Flying in or arriving by train, then renting a vehicle for your local travel, can save time and avoid that feeling towards the end of your Big Bend stay that you still have hundreds of miles of driving left before you get home. Rates run from $20 to $50 per day, plus 10¢ a mile. Call (915) 837-3009 or 837-2744.

Airline. Dallas Express Airlines provide service from Dallas (Love Field) via Abilene five times weekly. Rates are from $189 round-trip. Call 1-800-529-0925.

A charter flight connection from Midland-Odessa can be made with George Merriman's Skies of Texas; one- and two-engine planes provide easy connections into the region. Sample fare: from Midland-Odessa, $84–$112.50 per person; from El Paso, $110 or $150 per person (for a party of four or two, respectively, including baggage). Call (915) 837-2290 for reservations.

Rail. Amtrak offers service east- and westbound three times a week on the Southern Pacific Line from Los Angeles to Miami. The train from the east arrives at 11:10 A.M. on Tuesday, Thursday, and Sunday; the train from the west arrives at 9:59 P.M. on Monday, Wednesday, and Saturday. Contact Amtrak for fares at 1-800-USA-RAIL; from Houston, for example, the round-trip fare can be under $100, depending on availability, and this is a convenient overnight run of about thirteen hours. Expect the train to be two hours late on average. In Alpine, Alpine Travel acts as the agent for Amtrak. Their telephone number is (915) 837-3356.

Bus. The bus going north to Fort Stockton and Midland leaves daily at 11:00 A.M.. It stops at Midland-Odessa Airport. Going south, the bus to Marfa and Presidio leaves daily at 10:15 P.M.

Going west, buses to Van Horn and El Paso leave daily at 3:50 A.M. and 8:35 P.M. Going east, buses to San Antonio leave at 1:15 A.M. and 7:30 A.M. Journey times: to El Paso, five hours; to Midland-Odessa Airport, four and one-half hours; to San Antonio, eight hours.

WHEN TO VISIT

As its name suggests, Alpine has a mountain climate. In summer, daytime temperatures may sometimes go above 100° F, particularly in June. But in the evenings, the temperature drops considerably to the mid or low 60s; in fact, visitors to the outdoor summer theater in Kokernot Park are advised to bring a sweater. Sunshine is abundant, and the infrequent periods of cloudy weather occur mostly during the winter months. The average annual rainfall is around sixteen inches. In winter, Alpine is partly protected from the cold air masses which move south across the plains. Most of these fronts turn east before reaching Alpine. Snow falls occasionally, but most often it is light and remains on the ground only a short time. Equally, cold spells rarely last for more than two to three days. Relative humidity is low, averaging about 50 percent annually. The Davis Mountains to the north block the northerly winds so that the prevailing direction is westerly from November through May. A southeasterly flow prevails throughout the summer and early fall months.

INFORMATION

Visit the Chamber of Commerce at Third Street and Avenue E., or call (915) 837-2326. They are open Monday through Saturday from 9:00 A.M.

to 5:00 P.M. There you can pick up a map of the town, the current *Big Bend Area Travel Guide*, numerous pamphlets, a copy of the local newspaper, the *Avalanche*, and also of the free bimonthly regional newspaper, *The Desert Candle*. The staff who answer the phone and deal with walk-in visitors have a helpful manner and are well informed.

WHERE TO STAY

Hotels and Motels

Seven motels, with one new arrival, provide 330 rooms of mainly standard quality. All except the Antelope Lodge and the brand-new Ramada are on the east side of town. In addition, one historic inn provides 10 comfortable and tastefully decorated bed-and-breakfast rooms. There are two bed-and-breakfast homes, with a total of 12 rooms. There are 2 RV parks with a total of 55 sites. The following prices quoted exclude tax. All motels will pick up and drop off for rail or bus.

Antelope Lodge. On west U.S. 90, (915) 837-2451. This cozy motel has thirteen compact cottages that circle a shady park. Kitchens are in all units, and there is a laundromat, but you need to specify if you want a phone. Ask for one of the newly decorated rooms. Or, for a splurge, if your muscles are aching after too much horseback riding or hiking, request the hot tub cottage. Rooms have low rates, simple decor and furnishings. A single is $26; a double, $29; the hot tub cottage, $44.

Ramada Limited, 2800 W. Highway 90 (1-800-272-6232), is a welcome arrival in Alpine. Located on the west side of town, with fine views towards Twin Peaks, this motel provides rooms from $55 (including continental breakfast) up to $125 for the two-bedroom Twin Peaks suites. There is no restaurant on the premises, but the Ramada offers TV, shuttle service, and clean, new rooms with no railroad noise.

Siesta Country Inn. Just as you leave the one-way system going east, directly opposite the Sul Ross campus, 1-800-972-2203, (915) 837-2503. This family-run, home-style inn includes lots of personal home touches in the fifteen rooms, all of which are a little different; some are nonsmoking, some with kitchenettes. A laundromat and compact swimming pool are included. TVs have remote controls. A single room is $24, a double, $32; add $2 for nonsmoking, and $4 for a kitchenette.

Bien Venido Motel. 809 East Holland, (915) 837-3454. Within walking distance of the railroad station, this two-tier structure is a bare-walls operation, offering the lowest rates in town. Rates are from $22 single, $25 double, laundromat available, some kitchenettes, and a restaurant (same name, different ownership) next door for breakfast. Discounts are available for seniors and for long-stay residents.

Sunday House Motor Inn. Further east on U.S. 90, 1-800-247-0862 or (915) 837-3363. Visible with its size and blue-painted doors, Alpine's largest motel has eighty rooms. The restaurant claims the most complete menu in West Texas, and there is also a supper club, where you can buy alcoholic drinks. The barracks-like building has appropriately large rooms. There is a laundromat and a small pool. Prices are $34 for a single, $38 for a double (add tax of 13 percent here).

Days Inn. On U.S. 90 East, (915) 837-3417. Opposite the Sunday House is the one-story Days Inn. You'll find a friendly reception, compact rooms, and a minute pool. The popular Ponderosa Restaurant is right in the center of the motel (try huevos rancheros for breakfast). A single room is $25.56 (including tax) and doubles are from $31.95. You need to ask for a TV remote control at the reception desk.

Highland Inn. On U.S. 90 East, (915) 837-5811. This motel is owner managed. An effort has been made to maintain this sizable property with friendly front-office staff and by doing the necessary repairs when something goes wrong. It has forty-four rooms and ten suites and is located opposite the Sul Ross campus. A twenty-four-hour convenience store is next door. They have a pool and restaurant (open for breakfast and lunch only) and a supper club. Doubles are $34, plus tax.

Holland Hotel. 207 West Holland, 1-800-535-8040 or (915) 837-3455. This historic hotel was converted into a bed-and-breakfast operation a few years ago. The results are ten very tastefully furnished rooms of character, each one different, all spotless. Check-in is at the bar downstairs. Continental breakfast is included in the price. Rates run from $40 to $65 (tax included) for the room. All rooms have coffee makers, TVs, and baths; most of the rooms have a wet bar, refrigerator, and microwave. You can hear Amtrak's Sunset Limited pass just in front of the hotel, an occurrence that doesn't please everyone. The stylish Cinnabar Restaurant is downstairs.

Corner House Bed and Breakfast. Corner of U.S. 90 and Texas 118, (915) 837-7161. Five rooms are provided for bed-and-breakfast guests in this brick-built 1930s house. There is a colorful garden outside (the herbs are used in the cooking), and inside is an international collection of artifacts in addition to works by local artists. There are four bedrooms, two with a private bath, the others sharing a bathroom. One has an open fireplace. The four breakfast choices include egg-in-the-hole, home-baked bread, granola, and pancakes. Breakfast can be served on the porch. Prices range from $50 to $60 per room for two, and from $38 to $45 for one person.

The White House Inn, 2003 Fort Davis Hwy. (915) 837-9247. Set back from the highway on spacious, landscaped grounds, this two-story bed-and-breakfast property with imposing columns offers seven bedrooms, each with private bath and phone. One bedroom is handicap accessible. The breakfast is buffet-style, with special dietary requirements met upon request. Price from $60, plus tax. There are facilities for small parties and events, including private dining for lunch and dinner parties.

RV Parks

Pecan Grove. 1902 U.S. 90 East, (915) 837-7175. Located on the west side of town, it has thirty-one shaded spaces with raked gravel driveways. Well organized and welcoming, it has full hookups, cable TV, showers, and a laundry; the rate is $13 (no tax), based on two persons. Tent camping, $8 for two, is also available. Book in advance.

Danny Boy. On U.S. 90 East, (915) 837-7135. Opposite Pizza Hut, it has twenty-four sites with full services and is close to several restaurants. Family owned, it is close to open land, with views over Alpine and freely roaming wildlife. The rate is $11 (no tax), based on two persons.

La Vista RV Park. 6.5 miles south on Texas 118, (915) 364-2293. Located in a high mountain basin. You will enjoy clear, starry nights here; it is new, spacious, and picturesque. Somewhat bare of trees or services, it nevertheless has great views. Full hookups are included. The rate is $12, based on two persons.

Woodward Agate Ranch. Further south on Texas 118, (915) 364-2271. The ranch is reached by a 1.7-mile dirt road, 15 miles from Alpine. Ample facilities are found here for $10 a night. Also primitive camping is available, two miles farther along a gravel road, down by a creek. There is rock-hunting fun here, or you can buy the samples already collected.

WHERE TO EAT

There are the usual number of fast food places, with McDonalds having the prime site and the largest sign; Sonic, Dairy Queen, Pizza Hut, and Subway are all visible on the main highway through town.

Little Mexico. 204 Murphy Street, (915) 837-2855. Located on the other side of the tracks, this restaurant has a good following and is popular with visitors. Clean, colorful, and friendly with a variety of dishes, it is run by the well-known Valenzuela family. There are vegetarian dishes and a Kiddie Korner menu. You have a choice of cheddar or mozzarella cheese, and salsa and chips come free. There are plenty of starters (try mozzarella sticks). The Mexico Plate for $5.95 is popular with visitors; burgers, chicken fajitas, or salads are also available. And, if you're feeling guilty about overeating, read the message on your placemat. Open from 11:00 to 9:00 daily, except Sunday.

La Casita. 1104 East Avenue H, (915) 837-2842. This is the sort of place favored by those with a keen interest in Mexican food. It's a little hard to find, but the trip is worthwhile. Low prices, with everything prepared when you order it, the place looks like the front room of someone's house, which it is. It closes around 8:00 P.M. daily and is closed on Sunday.

Alpine Bakery. 302 East Holland, (915) 837-7279. Pink curtains, blue carpet, magazines to read, and sometimes Mozart to listen to make this a pleasant change for coffee or a snack. The bakery section is somewhat limited in choice, but lunch has a wider variety with soups and sandwiches. Breakfast is more promising with three-egg omelettes and ultra light pancakes, reflecting the hobby of the owner-chef. It is open from 7:00 A.M. to 5:30 P.M., Monday through Friday, 7:00 to 3:00 on Saturday, and closed on Sunday. Now open evenings Thursday–Saturday, 6:00–9:00.

Longhorn Cattle Company. 801 North Fifth, (915) 837-3692. Located half a mile from downtown on the left side of Texas 118 North, this is a popular restaurant with a predictable and consistent menu. It has a bright and clean atmosphere, without any discernible character; brisk and friendly service; some seating in booths. An excellent salad bar ($3.95), substantial hamburgers, including salad ($5.95), barbecue, and plenty of steaks round out the menu. It is solid and reliable.

Corner House Cafe. (915) 837-7161. Part of the bed-and-breakfast of the same name. The emphasis here is on natural foods, including herbs from the garden, plus some more sturdy meat dishes. Some typical lunch plates are quiche (with soup, salad, and bread), roast beef and Yorkshire pudding—reflecting the owner's country of origin—Waldorf salad, shepherd's pie, and baked chicken in a honey herb sauce. Soups, chilled and hot, are a specialty, and all the bread is baked on the premises. Seating is available inside, on the porch, or in the tree-shaded garden, complete with fountain and hammock. Open Tuesday through Saturday from 11:30 to 2:00 P.M. and Thursday through Saturday 6:00–9:00.

Alicia's. On the other side of the tracks, (915) 837-2802. At the other end of the dining scale is this hamburger and burrito joint—full of character, tasty, inexpensive, and with limited counter and table seating. Excellent French fries. You will spot the place after crossing the tracks on Texas 118 going south, before you turn to the left; it is ahead and slightly to the right, just beyond a stop sign. Food here is functional and filling; buy here before driving south to Big Bend. This is not to be missed.

Golden China. 104 North Phelps at Avenue E, (915) 837-3878. Tony Cheng, owner and chef, recently moved to Alpine from Fort Stockton and seems to have found the right spot. Open daily, 11:30 to 9:30; the lunch specials at $3.45 with soup, choice of two items, rice, and sweet biscuit are filling and unexceptional. More interesting are the items such as chef's special shrimp or Kung Pao beef. Specify if you want the dish hot, and it will be done. The decor is colorful, the service variable.

Ponderosa Inn Restaurant. On U.S. 90 heading east (on the outskirts of town), (915) 837-3321. Lewis Gordon, chef and owner, actually enjoys cooking, and his customers follow him faithfully—in this instance to his own restaurant. It is open daily 6:00 A.M. to 10:00 P.M.; some more interesting items include chicken and dumplings, and liver with onions. It is popular at breakfast for huevos rancheros.

Cinnabar. In the Holland Hotel, (915) 837-3455. This is the classiest place in town, from the Southwestern-style decor to the full-scale bar. It has a varied and imaginative menu to match the site and the decor, and is open for lunch and dinner, except for Sunday. The dinner menu offers plates like desert-blackened salmon with cilantro sauce ($13.95), blue corn chicken enchiladas with green chili sauce ($8.95), and charcoal shrimp and linguini pasta tossed with cilantro pesto ($8.95), in addition to steaks.

Sunday House Restaurant. East Hwy 90 (915) 837-2817. Next to the Sunday House Motor Inn. Open seven days a week 6:00 A.M. to 10:00 P.M. with a full menu. Popular because of its supper club license, the special evenings buffets—for example, fajitas ($5.95) on Wednesdays, and Chinese food ($5.95) on Fridays—and the noon buffets.

Sul Ross State University Dining Hall. (915) 837-8237. This place is worth mentioning for its special interest and good value. It is open when the university is in session, seven days a week, for the benefit of Mountainside Residence Hall occupants. (Enter the dining hall through this residence hall; take Gate Four.) Pay on entering and you can eat all you want. Breakfast is $3.75, lunch is $4.25, and dinner is $4.75. It is aptly and imaginatively run, with a substantial choice of meat dishes, hamburgers and spaghetti, a deli, salad bar, and a dessert cart with a minimum of four choices. Call regarding the hours of opening.

Sunshine House. 205 East Sul Ross (downtown), (915) 837-5402. If you are over fifty-five, this friendly and welcoming center offers a lunch menu for $2, Monday through Friday at 11:30 A.M. There is also a gift shop. If there are more than three in your party, you should call in advance to let them know you plan to come.

Martinez Bakery. 202 West Avenue G. (915) 837-2940. A good destination for a stroll across the tracks. Very clean, with a varied selection of baked goods, including breakfast burritos ($1.65), pumpkin empanadas (45¢), and banana bread (45¢). On Friday and Saturday, there are barbecue and roast beef sandwiches. Open 7:00–5:00; closed Sundays.

Casa Blanca Cafe. Hwy 188 south, next to Jackson Field. (915) 837-5552. Open for lunch and dinner, Monday through Saturday. A practical burger and sandwich place, with the addition of some Italian dishes served with garlic bread. Cold sandwiches (BLT, $3.50) come with potato salad. The Western Burger is packed with bacon, ham, two cheeses, and mushrooms and comes with fries or onion rings ($5.25). Italian dishes are spaghetti, meat lasagna, and manicotti cheese ($6.25–$7.50). There are seniors' and kids' dishes.

The Outback Bar and Grill. East Avenue G. (915) 837-5924. Open seven days a week, 11:00 A.M. to midnight. An ambitious and welcome arrival in town, this promises to be a lively destination for those wanting a sports bar, DJ music, and dancing (on weekends) and a variety of grilled foods. To get there, cross the tracks on Hwy 118 going south, turn right at Alicia's Burrito Place, and you will find the Outback 100 yards along on your right.

Reata Restaurant, 203 N. 5th Street. (915) 837-9232. Open six days a week (closed Sunday). In the old Downtown Brown's restaurant, opposite the bank, this new and classy place has ambitions to be a cut above your standard West Texas steakhouse. A lot of attention has been paid to the decor, with all sorts of cowboy trappings hanging on the walls. The steaks are from nearby Clear Fork Ranch. Chef Grady Spears, formerly at the Gage in Marathon, has planned a substantial and attractive menu, with plates like smoked cabrito enchiladas with a chipotle sour cream sauce, mesquite grilled quail with plum baste, some pasta dishes, and a sixteen-ounce cowboy steak with pico de gallo. Prices for the entrees range from $6.95 to $16.95. There will also be direct access to the garden area in the rear for weekend music; this will please the people who used to frequent the popular outdoor live music evenings at Downtown Brown's.

Gallego's Mexican Restaurant. 1102 East Holland. (915) 837-2416. Lunch buffet $5.75 Monday–Saturday.

Señor Sisi's Cafe. 903 West Avenue E. (915) 837-7391. This cafe, on the west side of town, is open for breakfast and lunch.

Stetson Restaurant, next to Highland Inn, 1401 E. Hwy 90 (915) 837-5811. Breakfast and buffet lunch.

WHAT TO DO

Climb the **hill behind Sul Ross State University,** perhaps at sunset. It's not always easy in Texas, where 93 percent of the land is privately owned and fenced off, to find an accessible place for a short hike. This land is state property. There is animal life and a great view over the town, whatever the time of day.

Try the large, indoor **pool at Sul Ross State University** ($1 admission); call (915) 837-8226 for hours of opening. Or swim in the open-air pool in City Park (June–August, 50¢ admission), where there is also a half-mile walking and jogging trail and a nine-hole golf course. (See "Big Bend Area Golf Courses"). There are also tennis courts on the university campus, free to the public if they are not being used.

Wander around town. Look at the markers outside the courthouse. Look at the old photographs in the entrance lobby. Watch the trains go by (Amtrak stops three times a week in each direction). Visit the cozy library, where you can sit on the floor and browse through old books about the area or catch up with the daily newspapers. Visit the post office and look at the mural. Admire the workmanship that went into building Kokernot Field in 1947, paid for by a rich local rancher who was an avid baseball fan. Stroll over the tracks and look at the variety of architecture in the barrio.

Visit the **Museum of the Big Bend.** On the campus of Sul Ross State University, a former bowling alley is now a fascinating museum, due to move soon into larger premises in Lawrence Hall. There is one permanent exhibit showing the life and history of the Big Bend. The other half of the space features changing exhibits by local and regional artists. Enter through the gazebo gift shop on the upper level. The museum is staffed by volunteers, and entrance is free; donations are accepted and well spent. This museum is well worth a visit. Open Tuesday–Saturday 9:00–5:00, Sunday 1:00–5:00; closed Monday. (915) 837-8143.

Attend **Theater in the Park.** Get a schedule of the summer theater program from the Chamber of Commerce. A musical and a play are offered by the repertory company (university and town) each summer in July and August. Be sure to take a sweater or a blanket as protection from the cool evening air. Check with the Activities Office at Sul Ross (837-8061) for a listing of campus activities open to the public.

See a **movie.** Try the small-town movie theater (two screens) on Holland Avenue East, downtown. On Thursday night the entrance fee is reduced to $1.50. On the other nights it is $3.00. The movies are current, but the equipment and the comfort are definitely not big city.

ALPINE'S RECEPTION COMMITTEE

In 1986 Kaaren and Bob Florstedt moved to Alpine. Bob had retired after a career in the foreign service. Nine months later, hearing the train's whistle one day, Kaaren said, "The train's in; let's go look". They went, they looked, and found an architect from Houston who needed accommodations. And they helped him out.

Six years later, they are still meeting trains, six arrivals a week. They wear a "Welcome to Alpine" badge now and hand out free literature about Alpine, the Big Bend National Park, and other tourist attractions. Sometimes they have driven visitors to their destinations in Alpine; more often they can point to the phone in the waiting room (now refurbished and stocked, thanks to their urging) and help the visitor arrange for a hotel pickup. Bob has recently been formally appointed as station caretaker.

When the Florstedts are on vacation they have the Amtrak crews, who change shifts here, trained to take care of any stragglers. If the train is late, and especially in the middle of the night, many first-time visitors to Alpine, particularly those from abroad, have been very grateful for this unexpected, voluntary reception. Letters from across the country and around the world are sufficient thank you to the ever-active Florstedts.

SERVICES

Car rental. See Big Bend Aero—Chapter 1, How to Get There.

Flights. Last Frontier Ultralight Flites, is operated by Gene Cornelison, owner of Alpine Bakery and a passionate enthusiast of ultralight flying. His fifty-horsepower engine can take a passenger up to four hundred feet for ideal viewing, then skim over the grasslands at a mere four feet. The cost is $25 for a half-hour flight. See him at the bakery, or call (915) 837-7279.

Skies of Texas charter flights has one- and two-engine planes available for charter, both for sightseeing by the hour or point-to-point. Contact

George Merriman at (915) 837-2290. See "Flying Down to Mexico for Breakfast" (Chapter 4).

Alpine Travel, located at Ten Communications Square on Texas 118 North, is the only full-service, fully appointed travel agency in the neighborhood. They offer special tie-in fares with Lone Star Airlines, connecting in Dallas with the long-distance carriers. You may book rail tickets here (not at the station), and book or change any airline ticket. Call (915) 837-3356.

SHOPPING

Shops

Ocotillo Enterprises. 205 N. Fifth, 1-800-642-0427 or (915) 837-5353. A striking landscape on the side of a building greets you as you drive into Alpine from Fort Davis. This is Ocotillo Enterprises, a well-filled, fascinating downtown shop. Named after the ocotillo plant, it is open daily. Books are the strongest suit—a strong and varied selection relating to the region. Plus, they offer a rocks and beads collection, a variety of unusual items such as pan pipes, a Chinese accordion, native American flutes, and tapes, videos, and cards. Not the least attraction is the owner, Judith Brueske, a source of local information since she is also the editor of the free bimonthly newspaper, *The Desert Candle.*

Apache Trading Post. On U.S. 90 West, (915) 837-5149. Easily the best advertised store in the region, its signs greet you on every approach to Alpine. A wide variety of Mexican and native American items, Western memorabilia, cards, knickknacks, and a strong line of maps—raised relief maps, and maps of just across the Mexican border. Located four miles west of Alpine, it is open daily.

Books Plus. 608 East Avenue E (at the corner of Phelps), (915) 837-3360. Four rooms of mainly used paperbacks are worth a mention because of the wide selection of subject matter, should you need a book for evening reading. They are closed on Sunday.

Sprigg's Boots and Saddles. 608 East Holland (near Phelps), (915) 837-7392. For completeness of stock and the wonderful evocative aroma of leather, visit this fascinating store. They carry boots, chaps, spurs, and all the other paraphernalia of ranching apparel, with a nod to other interests (hiking boots) and other animals (pets). Also, boot repairs are done here, and some gift items are available.

Big Bend Saddlery. On U.S. 90 East, (915) 837-5551. Much larger than Sprigg's, it contains a huge workshop and a display room. A must-see place for visitors to the region if they are interested in seeing quality, handmade articles of the cowboy way of life. This is a cultural experience as well as a buying treat. The Big Bend Saddlery also puts out a lavish sixty-eight-page catalog, listing saddles ($2,500), spurs ($70–260), and more esoteric items like snaffle bits (around $40).

Johnson's Feed and Western Wear. 109 South Cockrell, (915) 837-5792. Johnson's is also in the field of supplying western wear but more directed to apparel, belts, ties, etc.

Arts and Crafts Mall of the Big Bend. On Holland Avenue at Fifth Street, (915) 837-7486. Over five thousand square feet of antiques, gifts, and western memorabilia are effectively presented and easily viewed in separate sections of this modest-sized mall. Look for the locally made brooms. Closed on Mondays.

Second Saturday Market. Across the railroad tracks, just opposite the station, is the warehouse where sheep's wool and mohair used to be stored. On the second Saturday of each month there is a general sale here— everything from household to agricultural items. On the street outside, vendors sell from the back of their pickups. It is worth a look, if only to observe some of the participants.

Galleries

A recent influx of artists into the region and the opening of several new galleries in Alpine have warranted the inclusion of Alpine in the guidebook *The 100 Best Small Art Towns in America*. The principal galleries are:

Mescalero Gallery, Hwy 118 South. (915) 837-5045. Open 10:00–5:00 daily, and by appointment. This gallery features beautiful pictures of regional flowers, as well as antiques and collectibles. Private lessons in watercolors and oils are also given by co-owner Carol Happ.

Kiowa Gallery, 105 E. Holland Avenue. (915) 837-3067. This gallery is not only geographically central in Alpine but is the leader in producing enterprising displays by regional artists. You can't miss Kiowa Gallery when you are downtown, since the whole of one long exterior wall is taken up by a vast mural of a night crossing of the Rio Grande by Milton Faver, a successful early pioneer. Regional artists are featured in regular exhibitions, in addition to the permanent display.

Blue Fox Gallery, 118 N. 5th Street. (915) 837-3298. Hours by appointment. More of a studio than a gallery. Its owner, Linda Chase, a transplant from Washington, D.C., creates sometimes large and always impressive canvasses. You are invited to see the process as well as the product of this imaginative artist.

Heather Ceramics, 106 N. 6th Street. (915) 837-5309. Open 1:00–5:00 Monday through Friday, or by appointment. Greenware, finished, or custom work; paint and supplies. Free lessons and firing. Beautiful array of finished goods.

The Alpine Studio, on West Murphy, across the tracks from the Amtrack station. Two students at Sul Ross, Antonio Guerrero and Kelly Dyal, have pooled their resources to display their work in this new studio. Open daily. The artists do all their work here, and the visitor sees a great variety from paper masks (actually molded from subjects' faces) to sculptures in metal and clay, and from literal impressions to contemporary fantasies.

Big Bend Weavers and Spinners, 105 N. 6th Street. (915) 837-2052. This creative group opens their door from 1:00 to 3:00 weekdays and often on Saturdays from 10:00 to 2:00, for visitors interested in watching a demonstration or taking a course.

Sixth Street Studio, 114 N. 6th Street.

Prickly Pear Studio, 901 W. Sul Ross Avenue.

J. Davis Studio, 901 W. Holland Avenue. (915) 837-3812.

Cinnabar Restaurant, 207 W. Holland Avenue. (915) 837-3455.

Quetzal Arts and Imports, 500 S. Lackey Street. (915) 837-2410.

P. B. Kime Gallery. 801 E. Holland Avenue. (915) 837-7063.

For work done by local artists, see Chapter 4 (Regional Artists).

Workshops and Studios
Mahala Sibley. 114 N. Sixth Street. (915) 837-5029. This place offers hand-painted tiles, featuring desert images, set into wrought iron tables.

Michael Stevens. He is nationally known for his fine, custom-made guitars. Call (915) 837-5989 for more information.

EXCURSIONS

Woodward Agate Ranch, sixteen miles south on Texas 118, is a working ranch, which mixes cattle raising with the tourist business. A 1.7-mile drive on a dirt road brings you to the ranch buildings. (You can camp here overnight in the simple RV park—hookups, but limited amenities). You can, with the enthusiastic directions of the host, either go off by yourself and pick rocks, for which you pay 50¢ a pound, or you can pay various prices for a wide variety of rocks already on view. See Chapter 4 (Highway 118 South).

Chihuahuan Desert Research Center, sixteen miles north on Texas 118, is open from April 1 through Labor Day or by special arrangement for groups. This easily visited five-hundred-acre site, with a visitor center, is an invaluable way of understanding life in North America's largest and highest desert. This living desert museum shows the visitor over four hundred species of plants and also offers the Modesta Canyon Trail, a half-hour hike that provides the opportunity to view bird life and wildflowers in a peaceful setting. See Chapter 4 (Some Itineraries from Alpine).

EVENTS

Contact the Alpine Chamber of Commerce for exact dates and details of these annual events:

March	Cowboy Poetry Gathering
April	Gem and Mineral Show
May	Cinco de Mayo festivities
July	Fourth of July celebration
July–August	Summer Theater of Big Bend
October	National Intercollegiate Rodeo
December	Mountain Country Christmas

Carlsbad and the Living Desert Zoo and Botanical Garden State Park

Named after Karlsbad in Czechoslovakia, because of the similarity of the spring mineral water in each town, Carlsbad, New Mexico (population 30,000), is only 22 miles from the entrance to Carlsbad Caverns. It offers a variety of restaurants, over one thousand motel rooms, and three camp-grounds. There is an excellent, unique zoological and botanical state park, 5 miles northwest of town on a hilltop; and in town are a riverfront park, beach, and amusement playground. Air connections with Albuquer-que, bus service to El Paso and Lubbock, and car rentals are available.

HOW TO GET THERE

Personal car. Roswell, New Mexico, is 76 miles to the northwest on U.S. 285. From Pecos, Texas, 85 miles to the southeast on U.S. 285. From Hobbs, New Mexico, 69 miles northeast on U.S. 62/180; from Whites City, and the entrance to Carlsbad Caverns National Park, 20 miles southwest on U.S. 62/180.

Car rental. Hertz is available at the airport; sample prices: $47.99 per day with one hundred free miles, plus 30¢ per mile, for a medium-sized car; and $193 per week for the same size car with 600 free miles, then 30¢ per mile for additional mileage. Call 1-800-654-3131 or (505) 887-1500.

Airline. From Albuquerque, New Mexico, there are three flights daily (Monday through Friday) and two flights on Saturday. The lowest round-trip fare with twenty-one day advance purchase is $101. Call Mesa Airlines at 1-800-637-2247.

Bus. There are three buses daily going west to El Paso, and north and east to Lubbock. Departures from El Paso are at 3:00 A.M., 1:45 P.M., and 7:25 P.M.; from Lubbock, 1:40 A.M., 7:45 A.M., and 7:00 P.M. Departures to El Paso are at 4:40 A.M., 10:50 A.M., and 11:15 P.M.; to Lubbock, at 6:10 A.M., 5:00 P.M., 11:15 P.M. Journey time to El Paso is three and one-quarter hours, to Lubbock, five to six hours. Call TNM & O Coaches at (505) 887-1108 for more information.

Shuttle. Shuttle service from El Paso Airport, is available twice daily for $33 each way. It leaves El Paso Airport at 10:30 A.M. and 5:30 P.M. The shuttle leaves Carlsbad at 7:00 A.M. and 2:00 P.M. Journey time is two and one-half to three hours. The telephone number is 1-800-522-0162.

INFORMATION

About the Area
The **Visitor Center** at the Chamber of Commerce, Canal (U.S. 62/180) and Greene Streets, puts out a *Carlsbad Visitor Information* pamphlet, a comprehensive but undiscerning listing of lodging, city attractions, and area attractions. The Discover Carlsbad Scenic Drive is described, and you can use this folder as you follow the trailblazers which mark the route. The Center also has a detailed map of the city, a glossy color brochure, entitled *All Roads Lead to Carlsbad*, and a color pamphlet with pictures. It is open Monday through Friday from 8:00 A.M. to 5:00 P.M. Their telephone number is (505) 887-6516. When they are closed, a dispenser by the front door has these publications. For twenty-four-hour phone service, a recorded message gives details of local current events. Call (505) 885-CAVE.

About National Parks
At 3225 National Parks Highway, there is a NPS Information Office, which gives advice on the Carlsbad Caverns and on Guadalupe Mountains National Park. This information is especially useful before making the 55-mile drive to Guadalupe Mountains National Park to find out what camping accommodations exist. It is also useful before driving to Carls-

bad Caverns National Park for evening bat watching to find out what time they exit the cave (it changes throughout the year). This office is open from 8:30 A.M. to 4:00 P.M. daily. (505) 785-2107.

WHERE TO STAY

Almost all the motels are located along U.S. 62/180, which turns into Canal Street as it approaches the city center. Familiar chain names (Travelodge, Motel 6, etc.) are easily seen, with their rates posted. Towards downtown, the less expensive motels appear with rates (for two) in the high teens and lower twenties.

Quality Inn. 3706 National Parks Highway, 1-800-321-2861 or (505) 887-2861. The inn is a few miles south of downtown on U.S. 62/180 and offers a restaurant, lounge, pool, free shuttle to the airport, and free all-you-can-eat breakfast. For two persons the price is $51, plus tax. Discounts are available for AAA and AARP (for two persons) for $46, plus tax.

Best Western Motel Stevens. 1829 South Canal Street, 1-800-528-1234 or (505) 887-2851. It is a large (200 rooms) and busy motel with restaurant, lounge, pool, and free shuttle. For two, the price is $55, plus tax. For AAA and AARP the cost is $49.50, plus tax.

Rodeway Inn. 3804 National Parks Highway, (505) 887-5535. With 104 rooms, it also claims the best buffet in the West for $9.95, and kids eat free. In the busy seasons, there is also a breakfast buffet for $6.95. The rate for two persons is $52.95, plus tax. There is a 10 percent discount for AAA and AARP.

RV Parks

Carlsbad RV Park & Kampground. 4301 National Park Highway, (505) 885-6333. "The park with the pecan trees" is south of town. There are 80 sites, an indoor pool, showers, a small store, a laundry, and a recreation room. For RV hookup, the cost is $11.59, including tax. For a tent site, the price is $8.57 including tax.

Lake Carlsbad Campground. North on Muscatel off U.S. 62/180 east, (505) 885-4435. Conveniently located almost downtown, but since it has lake frontage and a golf course to the back, it is not noisy at night. It has showers and toilets only, and is clean but not new. It is well supervised, and the price is $4 per night for RV or tent.

WHERE TO EAT

Furr's Cafeteria. 809 W. Pierce (505) 885-0430. It offers all-you-can-eat lunch and dinner with substantial choices and the best prices in town.

Lunch price on Monday through Friday is $4.95. Dinner is $5.49, except for Sunday, when it is $5.99.

The Palm Court. On South Canyon, it offers Greek food, including spanakopita (spinach pie) for $3.25, stuffed grape leaves for $2.50, and a combination plate for $4.25. It is closed on Sunday.

Golden China. 509 South Canal Street, this place features an all-you-can-eat lunch for $4.95, and dinner for $5.95.

Cowboy's Lounge. 222 West Fox Street. (505) 887-0934. Try this restaurant for elegant dining. Fettucine with chicken is $9.95, rainbow trout with orange teriyaki is $8.25, and prime rib is eight ounces for $10.95, and twelve ounces for $14.95.

Lucy's Ltd. 701 South Canal Street (505) 887-7711. Lucy's has been a landmark for Mexican food for years and remains a good choice.

SERVICES

The excellent **Carlsbad Laundry** is for those who may have been camping for some time. It is located at 610 West Church Street at Guadalupe. (505) 885-6225.

World Wide Travel Service at 513 South Canal Street offers very helpful advice. (505) 887-2808.

WHAT TO DO

The Museum and Art Center on Fox Street, one block west of Canal Street downtown, is worth a visit for its prehistoric and pioneer items, bird carvings, and a display of Taos artists' work. It is open Monday through Saturday from 10:00 A.M. to 6:00 P.M. Admission is free. (505) 887-0276.

Riverfront Park, Lake Carlsbad Water Recreation Area, and **George Washington Paddlewheel Boat** are all attractions that have resulted from building a dam on the Pecos River that flows through town. They provide a variety of recreational activities and an attractive center to the town. In the Riverfront Park is a steam locomotive that was the first one to haul potash when mining started in the 1930s. This mining activity and the proximity to the Carlsbad Caverns provide the economic life of Carlsbad.

Living Desert Zoo and Botanical Garden State Park, just off U.S. 285 as you exit Carlsbad going northwest (505) 887-5516. This is an excellently sited and imaginatively constructed introduction to the desert.

Unlike many other parks in the region which feature desert trails illustrating plant life and pictures of animals, this one has live animals.

The park is situated on top of the Ocotillo Hills overlooking Carlsbad. If you want to take a picnic, this would be a good place to have it. Refreshments are available here, but they are minimal. Allow at least one and a half hours to walk around.

Desert plants are identified, and just before the exit there is a greenhouse featuring succulents of the world, some of the largest, most amazing tropical plants, oversized and extravagant cacti from Peru, Argentina, and Ecuador, rich hibiscus and bougainvillea blooms, and even a pine tree from Norfolk Island in the South Pacific.

But it is the animals which make all the difference, plus the ingenious and easy layout of this hilltop park. First, the aviary reveals ravens, hawks, and eagles, and a great horned owl sits placidly on a branch looking as wise as Solomon. Then there is a walk-through cage with double doors so that the smaller birds can't escape.

You can feed some animals (water fowl, prairie dogs, and deer); the inquisitive, energetic prairie dogs provide a particular attraction. Nocturnal animals and snakes are in their own confined areas.

The larger animals, including deer, elk, and bison have more space to wander. The Mexican wolf, elegant and gray, catches the eye; *Ursus Americanus*, the black bear, actually a rich shade of brown, is standing on hind legs intent on catching a darting lizard; but the lizard is too quick and escapes higher up the wall of the cage.

Park hours: open daily except Christmas. In winter the hours are from 9:00 A.M. to 5:00 P.M.; in summer, from May 15 to Labor Day, it is open from 8:00 A.M. to 8:00 P.M.. Admission is $3 per person, and children age six and under are free.

Fort Davis

A sign at Fort Davis greets you: "Welcome. From Fort Davis the rest of Texas is downhill." Fort Davis is indeed the highest town in the state. It is a mountain town in a desert setting, and the combination of altitude and dry heat results in reasonable temperatures most of the year.

Fort Davis (population 1,262) is a tidy, pleasant place with an above-average selection of accommodations, a good variety of restaurants, a library in the old jailhouse, and a nice cultural choice of galleries, a museum, and of course, the fort itself.

Forty years ago, before air-conditioning, Texans used to visit Fort Davis (elevation 4,800 feet) in the summer for its cool temperatures. More recently, the whole area has become better known for its varied attractions, and Fort Davis has benefited, without losing its small-town appeal. Within easy distance are: Balmorhea, with its large swimming pool, McDonald Observatory, Prude Ranch, Davis Mountains State Park and Indian Lodge, and Marfa and its Mystery Lights.

But the town still keeps its character despite the increase in tourism. A female resident who is a banker by day also plays guitar in the local band. Charley Bergman, the local Mr. Fix-It, is willing to take time from repairing a leak in a restaurant, or doing some electrical wiring, or driving the ambulance, to repair the camping stove of a tourist who has run into difficulties.

Here is a town where you might actually prefer to walk along the street instead of driving, or might feel inclined to take a blanket and sit on the lawn under the trees outside the county courthouse and watch Fort Davis going about its business.

By nine every evening, the sidewalks are rolled up, figuratively speaking, and Fort Davis settles down to another quiet night.

INFORMATION

The Chamber of Commerce works out of the Hotel Limpia and produces a comprehensive newspaper, the *Fort Davis Visitors Guide*. For this sheet, write to Fort Davis Chamber of Commerce, P.O. Box 378, Fort Davis, TX 79734 or call (915) 426-3941.

WHERE TO STAY

Hotels and Motels

Hotel Limpia. On the town square, 1-800-662-5517 or (915) 426-3237. Built in 1912, this hotel has been painstakingly restored by its owners, a local family, Joe and Lanna Duncan. The attention to detail in this imposing building can be seen in the effort to present history (rocking chairs on the porch) and gracious living (period oak furniture). There are smaller touches, too—matching leather bags in the entrance hall, a piece of local stone holding down the page of the Visitor's Book. Nothing has been spared to achieve comfort in the public rooms and the bedrooms, an indication of an alert and caring management. You are right in the center of town, and you feel part of its life. There are thirty-four rooms, including eight across the main street in Limpia West. Prices run from $65 for a regular room to $75 for a two-bed, two-bath suite, plus tax. In addition, Mountain Cottage, owned by the hotel and located half a mile away under the cliffs, rents for $112 a night and can accommodate six in self-contained comfort.

If you want to feel part of Fort Davis try the first floor corner suite, which looks directly out onto Main Street. Meals can be taken at the Limpia Restaurant, next door. Call for reservations.

Old Texas Inn. On Main Street (above the 1950s-style drugstore), 1-800-DAVIS MT or (915) 426-3118. This inn has six comfortable rooms, each furnished with a different motif (e.g., Judge Roy Bean). Each room costs $40 for one person, with $5 added for each extra person. This family-oriented accommodation (air mattresses are permitted on the floor), together with the drugstore and soda fountain downstairs, make the inn an entertainment in itself.

Stone Village Motel. On Main Street (near the Fontainebleau RV Park), (915) 426-3941. This unpretentious thirteen-room motel offers clean and simple rooms (some with kitchenettes) at a bargain price. It is owned and managed by one of the town's characters, Malcolm Tweedy, a star of local regular stage melodramas. He is always ready to talk with visitors. Prices are $40 per room for two persons, with $4 for each extra person. Kitchenettes are $5 extra. Prices do not include tax.

Fort Davis Motor Inn. On Texas 17 North (just outside of town), 1-800-80-DAVIS or (915) 426-2112. This new, no-frills motel provides thirty-six rooms, including nonsmoking accommodations. The southwestern decor of the rooms compensates, in part, for the plain exterior appearance. Rooms have cable TV. Coffee is available in the lobby from 7:00 A.M., and the Poco Mexico Restaurant is just next door for those who want breakfast. The lobby closes at 10:00 P.M. Summer rates are $64.95 per room, plus 10 percent tax. There is a 10 percent discount for AAA, AARP, and government travelers. Winter rates are 10 percent lower.

Wayside Inn Bed and Breakfast. Situated halfway between the fort and the town center, 1-800-426-3300 or (915) 426-3535. The inn sits on slightly higher ground and offers a good view from the dining porch over the town. There are a total of seven rooms with king- and queen-sized beds, most with private bath. Two suites sleep six persons in each. Prices range from $60 per room, plus tax to $110 per suite, including tax. The inn is carpeted throughout with lots of family items displayed on the walls, including a wedding dress. There is a strong sense of family here and an old-fashioned atmosphere. Add to this a hearty self-service breakfast with scrumptious biscuits, pancakes, waffles, and scrambled eggs, and you can see why the Wards are popular hosts.

The Veranda. 210 Court Avenue, (915) 426-2233. This new bed-and-breakfast is a substantial historic building with high ceilings and long corridors; it previously functioned as a hotel. With its many antiques (some of which are for sale), the Veranda offers the feel of a different age. There are eight bedrooms, each with a sitting room adjacent and a private bath, although not all bathrooms are connected. Breakfast, an impressive affair, may be taken in your room, in the dining area outside the kitchen, or on one of the many verandas which overlook the sizable and productive garden. Close to the courthouse, its rooms rent for $65, plus tax.

Neill Doll House Museum and Bed and Breakfast. Half a mile from the courthouse, (915) 426-3838, 426-3969, or 426-3348. Set back in trees and among boulders, this large house offers the visitor a collection of three hundred dolls throughout five rooms stuffed with antiques and furniture from the late 1800s. Entrance to the museum is $2. The bed-and-breakfast (a hearty meal) is $65 for two persons. There are two rooms.

Boynton House Guest Lodge. 1-800-358-5929 or (915) 426-3123. Enter from Texas 118, half a mile south of town, and proceed uphill on a good dirt road. The lodge provides bed-and-breakfast and outstanding views overlooking Fort Davis from its position on top of Dolores Mountain. There are seven rooms, some elaborately furnished, with bath, TV and many extras. The spacious living room has features like musical instruments and games for guests. Air mattresses for children are permitted in the rooms. No smoking is allowed. Mrs. Boynton has a special interest in taking care of guests with infirmities. A complete breakfast is served. Prices from $60.00 a room.

Butterfield's. On Main Street, (915) 426-3252. These four brightly painted cottages are just behind the gift shop. There are Jacuzzi tubs, open fireplaces (wood supplied), and cable TV. The color scheme of the furnishings is restful. Sleeping bags on the floor are permitted for children. Breakfast may be taken next door at the Drug Store. The gift shop sells delicious homemade chocolates ($8.50 a pound) and handmade porcelain dolls. Rates are $60 per cottage.

RV Parks

Fontainebleau RV Park. Two blocks from the Stone Village Motel on Main Street, (915) 426-3094. This is a compact site with full hookup for

$12. Cable TV, toilets, and a laundromat are available. Tent campsites cost $5 per person.

Crow's Nest Park. Eighteen miles from Fort Davis on Hwy 117/160. Superb views alone make this RV park worth the trip. RV hookups and laundry facilities are available, and there are some primitive campsites. Horse trails are being established. Call ahead, (915) 426-3343, for rates and specific directions to reach the park.

There is also an RV park four miles north of town in the Davis Mountains State Park.

WHERE TO EAT

Hotel Limpia Dining Room. It has floral carpet, white-painted chairs and tables, dried flowers hanging from the ceiling, and rocking chairs on the porch outside—it shares a decor similar to the hotel itself. The menu is equally tasteful, two fish dishes, three types of chicken plates, a vegetable dish, two pasta dishes, as well as roast beef and steaks. The service is family style, and the dishes are brought to the table and left for you to help yourself. The host may appear bringing hot rolls directly from the oven. There are also children's plates and lighter dinners. Prices range from $5.95 to $12.95. Above the restaurant is the Suttler's Club, the only establishment serving cocktails in Fort Davis. Temporary memberships are available for $3, except for guests of the Hotel Limpia and the Stone Village Motel, for whom it is free. The only problem with this restaurant is that it is not open long enough. It is open every day except Monday from 5:30 P.M. to 9:30 P.M., but is open for breakfast and lunch only on weekends. (915) 426-3241.

The Drug Store. (915) 426-3118. Its 1950s decor is enhanced by a soda fountain and period music. The youthful staff offers a good selection of burgers, BLTs, chicken breasts, and fajita burritos, together with malts and shakes. "Be joyful always," the menu urges, and after a substantial burger, one well might be. Open daily, including for breakfast, but closes at 5:00 P.M.

Highway 118 Cafe. On Texas 118 (going south from town), (915) 426-3934. This is a highly visible and bright cafe that is popular with the locals. It is open from 6:30 A.M. to 2:30 P.M., then again from 5:30 P.M. to 8:30 P.M., but it is closed on Monday. Breakfasts are well featured, and burgers ($2), a taco plate, or fried chicken ($4.50) are other choices. There is a noon buffet four days a week.

Raul's. On Texas 118 going north (at the junction of Texas 17, (915)

426-3908. Here is the "tenderest, juiciest, and tastiest barbecue" in all of Texas, said someone who claimed to know about barbecue. In business for eighteen years, it is open daily from 10:30 A.M. until 7:00 P.M. but is closed on Tuesday. The hours may vary. The dining room seems to be part of the family home, but that only adds to the appeal of the place. There is little argument about the popularity of the brisket. Sandwiches sell from $3.15 to $4.50 for The Texan. Brisket by the pound costs $7.15–$8.00.

Cueva de Leon. On Main Street, (915) 426-3918. It offers Mexican food served in a nicely decorated dining room. Selections include a salad bar and chicken fajitas with guacamole and sour cream; or a salad for $3.50 was a tasty, light lunch. The service is reliable and friendly. A noon buffet (all you can eat) is $4.00. The fajita buffet for $5.95 is served on Saturday at 5:00 P.M. and Sunday at 11:30 A.M. They are open between 11:30 A.M. and 2:30 P.M., and again between 5:00 and 9:30 P.M., Tuesday through Sunday.

Poco Mexico. On Texas 17 North (next to the Fort Davis Motor Inn), (915) 426-3939. Breakfast is served 7:00 to 10:00 A.M., lunch 11:00 to 2 P.M. This is not a sophisticated place but is highly rated by those who know Mexican food. The interior is simple and clean, and the food, served on disposable plates, is mainly Mexican. The combination plate ($4.50) is popular, as are the green enchiladas. There are a few non-Mexican dishes, including a ten-ounce sirloin steak at the low price of $6.50.

T J's. On Main Street (near the entrance to the fort), (915) 426-3195. T J's offers burgers and fries, coffee, and cokes; also baskets of chicken strips, catfish, or shrimp. There is also outside seating and drive-through service. They are open every day from 11:00 A.M. to 9:30 P.M.

WHAT TO DO

General Sights
Follow the **Historic Intown Tour and Overland Trail,** with up to twenty-eight sites marked on the map and described in the text of the *Visitor's Guide.* In particular, visit the Methodist Church, the oldest Protestant Church between San Antonio and El Paso. The red-carpeted interior gives it a fresh look and, interestingly, attendance numbers and contributions from the previous week are posted. Nearby is the library, formerly the jail. In 1983, when the 1910 jailhouse was converted into a library, the newspapers had a lot of fun describing the event: "Old Jeffer-

son County Jail now booking readers," and the like. The four-cell jail has been left almost as it was, with the addition of a coat of gray aluminum paint, and the library now houses twelve thousand volumes.

The **courthouse,** easily the largest building in town, has memorial stones outside and photographs inside. Visit the courtroom, use the rest rooms, or study the posters on the walls to see what's officially going on. One poster (from the Texas Parks and Wildlife Department) analyzes the number of mountain lion sightings and mortalities over the last few years. In the Trans-Pecos region in 1992, there were 73 and 74, respectively. In all of Texas, for the same year, there were 266 sightings, and 136 deaths.

The **Pioneer Cemetery** is located on Texas 118 going south, opposite the Highway 118 Cafe; there is a parking area with a metal gate leading to a narrow fenced path. This brings you to the overgrown cemetery, which was in use from 1870 to 1914. Among those buried here in the scattered graves are the Frier brothers, shot as horse thieves by a ranger posse, and Mr. and Mrs. Diedrick Dutchover, whose pictures and story are told in the Overland Trail Museum.

Museums

The **Overland Trail Museum** is located as you head towards the fort, and signs to the museum are posted on Main Street.

In a ramshackle building, dating from 1880 and sorely in need of modernization, is this fascinating collection of all sorts of bits and pieces from the past. One room contains everything from arrowheads, to saddles, powder horns, a barbed-wire display, rawhide hobbles, and a pair of zippered boots.

There are old photographs everywhere, including one of Mr. and Mrs. Dutchover, whose descendants are widespread throughout the area today. In the mid-1800s, escaping from Belgium where he had been witness to a murder, Mr. Diederick arrived in Galveston. When asked for his name by the immigration officer, Diederick, not knowing English, was unable to reply. "He looks Dutch all over to me," said another immigration officer nearby, and this was how he came by his new name. Later, the newly named Dutchover was recruited into the army for a brief time and came to Fort Davis to help build the fort. There he met a Spanish woman, whom he married, and the Dutchover family began.

In the back of the museum stands the room where the previous owner, Jim Mersfelder, lived. A barber as well as justice of the peace, Mersfelder was a man of many skills. A photograph, posted on the door and taken by himself using a self-timer, shows him seated at ease in a chair.

For a general history of the area, in the home or on the ranch, this museum is fascinating. The haphazard display and the homemade signs actually add to the sense of history. As is often the case, the volunteers who run the museum are part of the history themselves. The museum is open Thursday through Saturday only (except for groups). The entrance fee is $1 for adults and 50¢ for children under twelve. The telephone number is (915) 426-3904.

The **Neill Museum** is situated half a mile from the courthouse; It was originally the historic Trueheart House, built in 1898, but purchased by the Neills in 1949 and restored. What the visitor sees today is a fine summer home, set in a garden of two acres which contains several large boulders. This house doubles as a bed-and-breakfast (see previous section, "Where to Stay").

Entering by a stone stairway, you will find inside a collection of three hundred dolls, dating from 1830, and also quilts, bottles, and toys. Of particular note are a dollhouse from 1730 and baby buggies. The Neill Museum is open from June 1 through Labor Day, or by appointment. (915) 426-3838. Hours are 10:00 A.M. to 5:00 P.M., Tuesday through Saturday, and 1:30 to 5:00 P.M. on Sunday.

Galleries

The **Chappell Gallery,** on Main Street just down from the Hotel Limpia Restaurant, is owned and operated by nationally known artist Bill Chappell. The display of Western art, encompassing oil paintings, many bronzes, and works in leather and silver, reflects thirty years of work by someone who was once a cowboy and whose art reveals that experience. Other artists are also represented. If the door is closed and the Chappells are in Colorado, where they spend six months each year, a phone call to the number posted on the door will bring someone to open up. Look in particular at the small bronzes, such as *Good Ole Boy*, or at a composite painting entitled *All in a Day's Work*, which depicts the daily cycle of the cowboy's life. Call the gallery at (915) 426-3815.

The **Adobe Hacienda Gallery,** located on Cemetery Road, the only named street in Fort Davis, is a gallery built four years ago by Bill Leftwich, Western artist and shade-tree historian. Some of his oil paintings are also in the Chappell Gallery, but in his own gallery you will get to see a larger collection. The telephone number is (915) 426-3815.

The **Fisher-Hill Gallery,** opposite Chappell Gallery, is pleasant and informal, and displays a variety of craft items by local residents. Toi Fisher crafts gourd creations, her mother weaves; local artists, such as former park superintendent Kelly Bryan, have pen and ink drawings on display. There are dried pansy pictures and Navajo jewelry. While you look around, you can taste one of the specialty coffees on sale by the cup. Their telephone number is (915) 426-3246.

The **Blacksmith and Cowboy Art Gallery** is an ambitious new project on Court Avenue, four blocks west of the courthouse. The aim is to show the many sides of everyday working life in the mid-1800s. Features include a blacksmith's shop and a windmill with an ocotillo fence. The walls are hung around with spurs, chaps, and branding irons. There is handmade country furniture and handthrown pots. There will be seasonal demonstrations of applepressing and cheesemaking. No admission charge. Open daily. 1-800-887-9187. (915) 426-3556.

Shopping

Brass Boot. Located in the Hotel Limpia, this substantial gift shop is in the same building as the restaurant. There are four or five rooms displaying a good selection of Texas books and plenty of gift items, like candles and potpourris. A good practical buy, for only $7.50, is an imported doormat.

High Country Nursery. On Texas 118 North, it offers local honey (three pounds for $4.99), a pueblo candle holder ($3.99), and cactus arrangements ($14.99), as well as all sorts of plants and shrubs.

The Book Keeper. In the center of town, next to the Drug Store, it offers an expanding selection of used books.

The Sleeping Lion. Next to the Fisher-Hill Gallery, it sells geodes, fossils, and electroformed jewelry.

Limpia Creek Hat Company. Sell western wear and specializes in cowboy hats. You can pay from $25 to $400 for one of their hats, and they make the better-quality ones in their own workshop.

S. S. Savage. Opposite the Hotel Limpia, it has a small, selective showing of fine objects of West Texas and the Southwest. There are textiles, fine folk art, books and music, Zuni jewelry, and Taxco silver. Local artists like Abby Levine from Fort Davis and Bob Hext from Alpine have their work on display here also. They are open 9:00 A.M. to 7:00 P.M., six days a week, and Sunday from noon. Their telephone number is (915) 426-3311.

Davis Mountains Horseback Tours offer guided trips of from one hour to a full day. A one-hour in-town tour ($10.00 per hour) gives you most of the sights of Fort Davis following a circle route. The two-hour ride costs $18 and goes to the top of Scobee Mountain; a sunrise or sunset ride costs $25. More lengthy trips take you out into high ranch land. The half-day trip, approximately six hours, costs $40; the full-day costs $90, with lunch included. A minimum of three riders is required for half-day and all-day trips. The horses look well groomed and maintained, and members of the staff are extremely attentive. Call (915) 426-3016 for reservations.

Bicycle rentals are by the hour, half-day, or full-day. Maps and tours are available from Fontainebleau RV Park, located on Main Street. Call (915) 426-3916 or 426-3461 (evening) for reservations.

The **Scenic Loop Tour** is a pleasant half-day car trip of seventy-four miles. It will take you into the Davis Mountains, passing all the notable points of interest (or stopping at these points if you want to make a full-day tour), such as Prude Ranch and the McDonald Observatory, and bring you out into the rangelands to the west. All the points of interest are described in the *Fort Davis Visitors' Guide*, with a plea for watching out for animals on the road. Also check to see if it has rained recently, since flash floods can occur in the numerous low dips in the road.

You can go clockwise or counterclockwise around the loop. If you plan to picnic, and are heading in a clockwise direction, the **L. E. Wood Picnic Area** will come up about halfway and provides picnic tables under tall trees. Going in the other direction, counterclockwise, the **Point of Rocks Picnic Area** comes after the fifteen-minute drive from Fort Davis and gives fine views over the grasslands. A plaque on the rock tells of the spring and watering hole for wagon trains. In either direction, you might prepare for your picnic by buying some brisket from Raul, and perhaps some beer, soft drinks, or a Texas wine from the Stone Village Grocery in the center of Fort Davis.

EVENTS

Fort Davis has a variety of events throughout the year and the town takes pride in the amount of local effort and participation in these events. See the last page of the *Visitors' Guide* for a listing of events during the current year. Also check with your hotel, or look for signs or in the local paper for any additional events.

There are regular events nearby at Prude Ranch, at the Davis Mountains State Park (bird banding), and at the McDonald Observatory (Star Parties). Some typical local events are:

April	Square Dance at Prude Ranch
	Easter Sunrise Service at Fort Davis National Historic Site
May	Hammerfest Bicycle Race
June	Black Powder Shoot
July	Old-Fashioned Fourth of July Celebration, street dance and accompanying melodrama acted by townsfolk
September	Apple picking at local orchards
	Restoration Festival at the fort
	Harvest Moon and Tunes Fall Festival
October	Halloween Party at Indian Lodge
November	Arts and Crafts Fair
December	Christmas at the Fort
	La Posada Pageant at Indian Lodge

Fort Stockton

In the past, it was the existence of springs that caused an interest in what is now Fort Stockton, originally called St. Gall when it was founded in 1840. Three centuries before, Spanish explorers, pushing northwards in their search for gold, doubtless felt relief when they came across the abundant water bubbling from the ground. The presence of water was also known to the Comanches as they traveled the area, and they in turn were the reason why, by the mid-1800s, the army arrived and established a fort to protect the increasing number of westbound settlers and the Butterfield Stagecoach service.

Today the water supply is less abundant; in fact, the springs themselves have dried up, but they still provide the theme for Fort Stockton's most popular annual event, the Water Carnival, which takes place in July. In this century, oil took over in importance (there is an oil field just north of town), but that too has declined in relative importance to the local economy. Its location halfway between San Antonio and El Paso on I-10 and its position as the first turnoff to the Big Bend for those driving from the east or northeast has been Fort Stockton's fortunate geographical chance.

But, besides benefiting from its geographical location on the interstate highway system, Fort Stockton has done a lot on its own to cater to visitors. Not far from the charmless main strip (Dickinson Boulevard), some farsighted planners of the local historical society and the city council have uncovered a surprising potpourri of sights on the Historic Tour, including the fort itself and the Annie Riggs Museum. In this way, Fort Stockton (population 8,520), the largest town in the region, has avoided becoming simply a pit stop on I-10. It has developd a character and a certain appeal of its own.

The history of the town can best be understood by taking the short, but varied, Historic Tour, which includes such novelties as a Sears mail order house and the eleven-foot-tall Paisano Pete statue, the world's largest roadrunner, as well as two museums and the fort itself. On a more practical note, 13 motels provide 798 rooms, 8 campgrounds offer 447 sites, and there are 22 restaurants.

INFORMATION

The Visitor Information Caboose at Exit 257 on I-10, is stockpiled with pamphlets and maps for the whole region (open daily 10:00 to 8:00 and Sundays 12:00 to 8:00) and is located next to McDonalds; or visit the Chamber of Commerce at 222 West Dickinson. The phone number is 1-800-336-2166 or (915) 336-8052 for the caboose, or (915) 336-2264 for the Chamber of Commerce.

Most of the motels and many of the restaurants stretch along Dickinson Boulevard, which is also U.S. 290. If exiting from I-10 at Exit 261, shortly after passing Paisano Pete (on the left), you will come across the Chamber of Commerce (on the right). One block further west along West Dickinson, on the left outside the Pecos County State Bank, a marquee lists the day's events.

Unlike many towns where the city center has become deserted, boarded up, and run down, Fort Stockton took the initiative to obtain outside funds to help develop its downtown center and earn the title of Main Street City, a revitalization program sponsored by the Texas State Historical Commission. You can see and hear for yourself what the city has done by taking their sixteen-point self-guided tour. Take a map and pay a $5 deposit for a cassette (refundable when returned). Or take the two-and-a-half-hour tour by bus, with a guide, which runs twice daily, at 1:30 P.M. and 5:10 P.M. (once each Saturday and Sunday at 1:40 P.M.), leaving from the caboose or the Chamber of Commerce, with free pickup at eight additional locations. Cost is $6.50 per person, children three through twelve are $3.50 each, and this includes admission to the museums and the fort. Call (915) 336-8052 or 336-2264 for reservations.

WHERE TO STAY

All thirteen motels are standard issue, and there are no historic hotels or full-of-character bed-and-breakfast places. Eleven motels are located on Dickinson Boulevard, around which I-10 loops on its way from east to west. Most offer the usual discounts for AAA, and AARP (please check with each motel individually and also for seasonal fluctuations on rates).

The following rates are for single and double, respectively, and a room tax of 13 percent needs to be added.

Top-Priced Motels

Best Western Sunday House. 3200 West Dickinson, 1-800-528-1234 or (915) 336-8521. With 112 rooms, it has a colorful restaurant, the Alpine Lodge, and an attractive blue-painted pool. Rooms are $42–$52. Discounts are available for AAA and AARP.

La Quinta. 2601 West I-10, 1-800-531-5900 or (915) 336-9781. Fort Stockton's second newest motel at Exit 257 has 97 rooms, a restaurant, lounge (for cocktails), and pool. Room rates are $45–$58. Discounts are available to AAA and AARP.

Days Inn. At Exit 257 and 1400 N. Hwy U.S. 285, 1-800-325-2525 or (915) 336-7500. It is Fort Stockton's newest motel with 50 rooms, rates from $40 (one person, AAA discount, low season) to $50 (double, no discount, high season). They also have a restaurant.

Econo Lodge. 800 East Dickinson, 1-800-424-4777 or (915) 336-9711. It has 87 rooms, with restaurant, lounge, and two pools and offers a free breakfast buffet. Room rates are $32–$44. Discounts are available to AAA and AARP.

Texan Inn. 3100 West Dickinson, 1-800-GO-HOJO or (915) 336-8531. It has 98 rooms and a restaurant, lounge, and pool. Rates are $27–$45.

Mid-priced Motels

Budget Inn. 801 East Dickinson, (915) 336-3311. $19–$28.

Motel 6. 3001 West Dickinson, (915) 336-9737. $23.95–$27.95.

Sands Motor Inn. 1801 West Dickinson, (915) 336-2274. $22.95 and up.

Budget-Priced Motels

Comanche Motel. 1301 East Dickinson, (915) 336-5824. $16.95–$21.95.

Deluxe Motel. 500 East Dickinson, (915) 336-2231. Colorful, close to Greyhound Bus Station, with lots of nonsmoking rooms; $17.95–$22.00.

Economy Inn. 901 East Dickinson, (915) 336-2251. $17.95–$27.95.

Gateway Lodge. 501 East Dickinson, (915) 336-8336. $16.30–$20.50.

Spanish Trail Lodge. 700 North Alamo, (915) 336-3381. $14–$16.

Town and Country Motel. 1505 West Dickinson, (915) 336-2651, $16–$26.

RV Parks

KOA. Four miles to the east on I-10, Exit 254, it has the most amenities, including cabins and a pool. Some of the others are rather sparse on shade or too close to I-10. (915) 395-2494.

Parkview RV Park. On Texas 285 to the southeast of town. Spacious and well shaded, it is well away from the freeway. (915) 336-7733.

The pamphlet, *Fort Stockton Restaurant and Accommodation Guide,* lists the eight campgrounds in or near Fort Stockton. As usual, you get what you pay for, and a $7–$8 per night fee usually reflects a lack of showers and other facilities.

WHERE TO EAT

Sarah's Cafe. 106 South Nelson. (915) 336-7124. For Mexican food, it has the history, a good site near City Hall, and an unmistakable pink exterior. Inside, Cleo Castelo continues the family tradition and has been widely written up. Daily specials range from $2.99 (beef tacos) to $4.95 (noon buffet). Combination plates are $3.25–$6.00. A change for dessert is the cinnamon buñuelo and ice cream for $1.35. Beer and wine are available. Sarah's is open Monday through Friday, from 11:00 to 2:00 for lunch and from 5:00 to 9:00 for dinner.

Also favorably noted and worthy of mention: **La Hacienda** at 1201 West Dickinson, (915) 336-5682, serving substantial portions (try the combination plates, $4–$5); and **Mi Casita** at 405 East Dickinson (915) 336-5368. Recently opened is **Bien Venido** at 405 West Dickinson, (915) 336-3615, open 11:00 A.M.–10:00 P.M. every day; plates are priced around $4.50.

On the steak front are the predictable **K-Bob's Steak House** at 2800 West Dickinson, (915) 336-6233, and the **Steakhouse** at 100 West Dickinson, (915) 336-5909. The former is mentioned for its salad bar, and the latter recommended also for breakfasts.

Just off I-10 at Exit 257 are the familiar golden arches of McDonalds, and the various other familiar names are variously scattered along Dickinson Boulevard: Sonic, KFC, Pizza Hut, and Dairy Queen.

For reliable and conventional full-scale menus, the four motels listed in the top-priced section have their own restaurants.

The **Alpine Lodge** at The Sunday House, 3201 W. Dickinson (phone [915] 336-8521), has a bright and airy decor and a varied, cosmopolitan menu. **El Corral** at La Quinta, 2601 W. I-10 (phone [915] 336-9781), offers a good Mexican selection and also has sandwiches in addition to the plate dinners.

The **Brazen Bean Restaurant** has recently opened at 3105 W. Dickinson, (915) 336-3070. Open seven days a week for lunch and dinner, it serves steaks, burgers, chicken fried steaks, and catfish, all with complimentary salad. The most popular dish is the chicken fried steak plate, including two vegetables, for $5.95.

There is one unusual restaurant in Fort Stockton, remarkable for a specific item on the menu: the truck stop at **Comanche Springs Plaza**. At Exit 257 on I-10, (915) 336-9713, this stop is behind the La Quinta. A brisk, efficient eating factory with personable waitress service well tuned to truckers' humor. The house special is "Big Chief Sitting Bull," the granddaddy giant cheeseburger. Five pounds of ground beef are served on a ten-inch bun with all the trimmings, including fries; it sells at $14.95 and usually satisfies four or more persons. It is also offered free to any person who can eat it alone within one hour. A successful attempt happens from time to time, and in 1993 a woman achieved the feat for the first time.

SHOPPING

Mesquite Tree. 1101 W. Dickinson Blvd. This shop has a varied and substantial collection of gifts, well displayed in twenty-five small booths. Some of the wood and ceramic items are locally made; others—of the knickknack souvenir variety—are bought from the wholesale market. The store is bright and attractive and is joined to Honaker's Antiques; it is open 9:00–6:00 on six days and 1:30–5:00 on Sundays.

The Red Barn. Three miles north of town on Texas 285. If the selection of collectibles at The Mesquite Tree does not satisfy, Pat Honaker has a much larger collection of varied items collected from around the region for sale here.

Comanche Tortilla Factory. 107 South Nelson. Owner Ben Gallego tells us, "You cannot live by bread alone; eat a tortilla." To prove this, he offers the public the chance to watch his tortillas being made and to have a sample before deciding whether to purchase any one of several different size packages of corn or flour tortillas; they also carry asadero cheese, spices, tostadas, and salsa. On Thursday, he sells regular and jumbo tamales.

WHAT TO SEE

Follow the Historical Trail and take time to visit the two museums.

The **Annie Riggs Memorial Museum,** formerly a hotel, is a substantial and handsomely restored building in the territorial style with a wide variety of items inside which do justice to the lady herself and the times she lived in. Open daily, year-round; hours change according to season. Admission is only $1 and well worth it. (915) 336-2167.

Of particular note is the guest room furnished much as it was in 1900, with a cast-iron bed costing $6.75 from Sears; room rental was 50¢ a night. The patio is cool and quiet, and concerts are given here during the summer. In the entrance hall, stern faces look down from their frames on the wall; old tunes are still played on the piano in the parlor, and on the dining room wall is a set of rules set by Annie Riggs. A lot of character is created in this house. It is open Monday through Saturday, 10:00 to 1:00 and 2:00 to 5:00.

Historic Fort Stockton, (915) 336-2400, has been painstakingly reconstructed after archaeological research and now offers the visitor a view of the Guard House, Officer's Quarter Number Seven and in Barracks Number One, the Historic Fort Stockton Museum. The $1 entrance fee includes the chance to see a fourteen-minute video about the history of the fort. Originally consisting of thirty-five buildings, of which only four remain, it housed the black soldiers and white officers of the Ninth Cavalry sent to maintain order on the frontier and to provide protection to the stagecoaches. The fort today is gradually being restored to its former state.

The black soldiers of the Ninth Cavalry were called "buffalo soldiers" by the Indians because of their dense, short-cropped hair. The fort, named after a naval officer who distinguished himself during the Mexican War, was established in 1858, was abandoned during the Civil War, and resumed service in 1867 to provide protection against Indian attacks on the roads and trails that carried the settlers westwards. By the early 1880s, these attacks had died down, and the fort was abandoned in 1886 as the frontier moved west.

Fuller details about each stop on the tour through the fort are contained in the pamphlet, *Fort Stockton,* and on the cassette.

WHAT TO DO

Ft. Stockton has an eighteen-hole golf course (see Chapter 4 for description), three swimming pools, and sixteen lighted tennis courts.

Temperatures are high in the summer, and the passage of traffic along Dickinson Boulevard is heavy. Get away from this noise by visiting the quieter refurbished downtown area containing the museums, Comanche Springs Park, Sarah's Cafe, and OQ8. The largest town in the area then seems like a friendly small town, where the washing hangs on a line right next to City Hall.

EXCURSIONS

Twenty-five miles east of Fort Stockton on I-10 is **St. Genevieve Winery,** a French-American success story. In the unlikely setting of the dry, bare, West Texas desert a one-thousand-acre, bright green patch of productive vineyard exists. This is the largest winery in Texas, the fifth largest in the United States, and a producer of prize-winning wines. Take a two-and-a-half-hour tour and visit this high tech winery; you will learn about the process of wine making, from harvesting to bottling; a tasting is included. The tour leaves from the Fort Stockton Chamber of Commerce at 1:00 P.M. on Wednesday and at 10:00 A.M. on Saturday. The cost is $8. Book by calling (915) 336-8052 or 336-2264.

EVENTS

Water was the original reason for an interest in this spot, so it was appropriate that during the Texas Centennial celebrations in 1936 the city decided to recognize this fact with a **Water Carnival.** Set to music and highlighted by spotlights, each year an original script is performed by the swimmers and dancers. The outdoor swimming pool at Comanche Springs is the setting, and as the sun sets, modern techniques and today's youth offer a pageant which reflects the history of yesteryear.

There is some special event happening most months and certainly all through the summer. But the most popular ones are:

June–August	Summer in the Patio; every other weekend a program of music, storytelling, and local entertainment is featured at the Annie Riggs Memorial Museum.
Mid-July	Water Carnival

October	Pecos County Fair
November	Women's Chamber Arts and Crafts Fair; Living History Day at Fort Stockton (first Saturday)

Lajitas

During the late 1970s, Houston businessman Walter Mischer bought a substantial tract of land in Lajitas in order to develop a resort. At that time, little was there, except for a modest collection of simple dwellings and the remains of a cavalry post. On the Mexican side, at Paso Lajitas, only a few simple houses stood.

Indian hieroglyphics indicate that humans had inhabited the area around Lajitas for hundreds of years, and around the turn of the century Lajitas enjoyed a boom as a port of entry into Mexico. A few years later, it became a major headquarters for troops combating Pancho Villa's incursions across the border. By the 1970s, nothing was going on, at least not legally. But Walter Mischer had a vision for the future—a desert development with all the facilities of a top resort—while remaining true to the history of the region, where he had a ranch for thirty years.

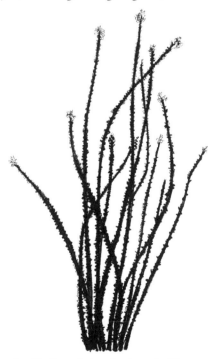

Today Lajitas on the Rio Grande is complete—a resort unique in the region offering a variety of accommodations and a selection of activities, such as golf, tennis, and horseback riding. In complete contrast to the lifestyles and living quarters of the inhabitants of Terlingua, only a few miles away, Lajitas Resort, with its own newspaper, suggests big money. Strategically located between the national and state parks, with a river crossing into Mexico and a landing strip for golfers or others who want to

Ocotillo, Fouquieria splendens. *By Elva Stewart.*

fly in, the resort has a presence. And the frequent tour buses are witnesses to its popularity.

The elaborate architecture on one side of the main building presents an Old West face with a boardwalk and on the other side features a mining town frontage. This choice of backdrops was made for the purpose of attracting movie makers. The first sight that greets the visitor is the Badlands Hotel, a re-created 1880s hostelry. The hotel reception area, where all accommodations must be booked, is decorated with red saloon-style wall coverings and has a high wooden ceiling. There are guest rooms in this building and also a delightful swallows' nesting place.

WHERE TO STAY

Other buildings nearby offer a good standard of comfort and upkeep with a variety of styles. The following four locations offer a total of eighty-one rooms and are all within easy walking distance from the main building.

Motels

La Cuesta Motel. Rooms have a traditional Spanish decor. Room rate for one person $59; two persons, $65; three persons, $75; four persons, $85. Rollaways are $10. All prices are plus tax.

The Officers' Quarters. These motel rooms are in military-style buildings, replicating those at Fort Davis, built around a courtyard. Room rates are the same as at the La Cuesta Motel.

Cavalry Post Motel. This motel offers a slightly different accommodation with the same standard of furnishings and level of maintenance. Room rates are the same as at the La Cuesta Motel.

Bunkhouses and Other Accommodations

This accommodation is supplemented by a bunkhouse, used by families or by small groups, with two separate seven-bed (single beds) rooms with their own bathrooms. There are also two cabins, one- and two-bedroom condos, and some houses for rent. With sometimes two to three buses a day at the resort during busy periods, Lajitas needs all this space. But the buildings are sufficiently spaced out so that families and individuals need not feel overwhelmed by the groups.

A cabin with a large combination living and bedroom (two double beds), efficiency kitchen, and bathroom rents for $40 a night.

A one-bedroom, fully furnished condominium, with TV, (four person limit) rents for $95 a night, or $475 a week. Two bedrooms (six person limit) are $148 a night, or $740 a week.

A bunkhouse, complete with fourteen twin-size beds rents for $244; or seven beds only, with kitchen, rents for $138; without a kitchen, the price is $106.

Houses rent from $155 to $185 a night, with six person limit.

RV Park and Tents

Down near the Rio Grande, next to the nine-hole golf course, there is an eighty-site RV park with hook ups, side-by-side parking with outside tables, and a well-organized management in a central office and lounge area. On a separate shady grassy area there are eighteen sand pads for tents. There are tennis courts and a swimming pool closer to the main buildings, but these are for hotel guests only.

An RV park space rents for $12 a night. A tent site (includes a shower) rents for $8 a night.

Weekly and monthly rates are available on all accommodations. There is also a 20 percent discount from June 15 through September 15.

WHERE TO EAT

Badlands Restaurant. Adjacent to the Badlands Hotel, this establishment, together with a saloon and a large meeting room, offers a substantial menu with standard American and Tex-Mex dishes—nothing very exciting but sufficient to satisfy the average bus traveler who has come a hundred miles from Alpine. With a tiled floor, wooden tables, and fans rotating on the ceiling, the large restaurant has a cool feel to it, and perhaps needs it when the tour groups come in. Pork chops ($8.95), lemon pepper chicken breast ($7.95), and New York sirloin steak ($13.95) complement other specialties, such as Lajitas fajitas ($8.50) and the Pancho Villa special ($6.95).

Frontier Drug Store. For those wanting a light snack or refreshment when the restaurant is closed, this place on the boardwalk has a soda fountain for ice cream sundaes and light snacks.

WHAT TO DO

Parks

In addition to driving to the **Big Bend National Park** (the entrance is 21 miles away, and you can also walk directly into the park from the RV campground), the **Big Bend Ranch State Natural Area** is nearby. The beautiful River Road winds its way for 50 miles along the Rio Grande to Presidio, and the Warnock Environmental Education Center provides an excellent introduction to the flora and fauna of the region, as well as the necessary permits. See Chapter 1 for descriptions of both parks, entrance fees, hours, and telephone numbers.

Golfing

The **golf course** is nine holes, but the tees can be moved to provide an alternative second round. The fee is $10 for all day, and $14 on Saturday and Sunday. Carts are available ($8 or $13), and clubs may be rented ($10). See Chapter 4 for a description of the course. Open 9:00 A.M. to sundown seven days a week. Pro Shop. (915) 424-3211.

Horse Trails

Lajitas Stables is a quarter of a mile from the boardwalk. Horses can be rented by the hour ($14), all day ($65), or for overnight trips (two days for $190 per person). All trips are escorted. The most popular ride is a three-hour excursion ($28), which takes in a quartz crystal field and an Indian camp. On overnight trips, a jeep provides support, and campfire meals are included. Saddle and paddle trips can also be arranged by the stables, using rafts and horses alternatively. (915) 424-3238.

River Trips

For river trips, the most popular of the recreational activities, see the section on the descent into Santa Elena Canyon under "River Trip Outfitters."

Shopping

A good selection of items is available in the various shops along the boardwalk. The **Lajitas Art Gallery** features a special exhibition that changes monthly and offers photographs and appealing jewelry pieces made from stone ($10). **Gloria's Last Chance Liquor Store** provides liquor and some groceries. **Lajitas Mercantile** has fashions and accessories for women, and some men's clothing, including the latest in Western gear. Mexican and Indian items can be found in the **Crow's Nest gift shop,** next to the Big Bend River Tours. At the other end of the boardwalk is **Frontier Drug.**

A short walk towards the river and next to the RV park is the **Lajitas Trading Post.** The sign outside reads:

Welcome and Bien Venidos. Established in the early 1900's, the Lajitas Trading Post has stood throughout the years as a center of community service and to provide both sides of the border with the essentials of survival in this harsh land. The Lajitas Trading Post has changed very little since the days of Pancho Villa and you are invited to step through its portals to relive its past.

Underneath this invitation, follows: "Lajitas Trading Post, Home to Clay Henry, the beer drinking goat." Sure enough, in a pen surrounded by empty beer cans and bottles, is Clay Henry, actually son of Clay Henry, Sr., since the latter died a short while back at the good age of seventeen. Inside the historic store, the source of the beer, is a wide variety of groceries, picnic supplies, ice, gift items, and some weary vegetables. A pleasant diversion is to take a beer outside, play pool, and hear what the locals have to say, which is usually plenty. Gas is available here also.

Right next door is Larry Harris, who makes items out of sotol (a plant of the agave family). One of the most popular items is a lightweight walking stick (around $7). A shortage of sotol has recently redirected him into other craft work, using sterling silver and silver plate to make wind chimes ($15) and flower vases ($20), and cutlery to make spoon and fork earrings ($15).

On the way back to the Badlands Hotel you might pause at the historic adobe church, used for Sunday services and occasional weddings.

Excursions—Crossing into Mexico

Car. Kiko García offers an all-day trip by road to San Carlos, 20 miles from Paso Lajitas on the Mexican side of the Rio Grande. You cross the river by rowboat, then Kiko drives you in his Suburban the rest of the way. The road is an unimproved dirt road which climbs 2,500 feet to the small town of San Carlos. There are two canyons to visit and the chance to swim. Lunch is at Kiko's mother's house, and you can eat all you want of her home cooking. The only shopping is for geodes and rocks, but you will get a glimpse of a small rural Mexican community and, more important, hear from Kiko about what life is like on the Mexican side of the border. The trip costs $50 per person, with a minimum of two people. Call (915) 424-3221 for reservations. For crossing by foot into Mexico, see "Crossings into Mexico."

Big Bend Adventures, c/o Lajitas Trading Post, offers trips into Mexico by horse or vehicle and to the Big Bend Ranch State Natural Area. (915) 424-3234.

With these diverse accommodations, unique setting, and varied recreational offerings, it is hardly surprising that Lajitas sees some busy times. Companies sponsor golf tournaments, hundreds of bikers meet in February for the Chihuahuan Desert Race and Festival, the Chili Cook-off Competition draws huge crowds in November for the food as well as the beer (see Chapter 4 for description); and professional groups take advantage of two different meeting rooms. On a recent occasion, Hallie Stillwell, the ninety-six-year-old moderator of the Big Bend Historical Association, addressed the group, while outside youthful bikers were holding a throw-the-bike competition. This is a complete resort, and although it is not world class, visiting groups can sometimes overwhelm the place. Don't be too surprised.

Marathon

Marathon (population 800) is the gateway to Big Bend National Park for most people driving from the east or northeast. Founded in 1881 by Capt. Albion E. Shepherd, a retired sea captain, the surroundings of plains and mountain reminded him of Marathon, Greece.

This area was directly in the path of the Comanche War Trail, the route out of the northeast which the Comanches followed when they raided settlements, ranches, and wagon trains in the Big Bend area and across the Rio Grande. In 1879 Camp Peña (known locally as The Post), part of a chain of outposts across the region, was established to contain these raids. Today, only a memorial marker remains, and the site has been converted into a shaded picnic spot and swimming hole 5 miles south of Marathon.

In the late 1800s, with the removal of the Comanche threat and the arrival of the railroad, the area began to thrive on cattle raising, and Marathon prospered as the shipping point. One of the most famous cattle barons in the region was San Antonio businessman Alfred Gage, whose name is better known today for the Gage Hotel, the premier attraction of Marathon and a state historical landmark.

Like other small towns in West Texas which prospered when ranching flourished, Marathon today is living in reduced circumstances, and the initial impression of the town is that it has been partially abandoned. But, despite the discouraging signs of neglect, there are still some worthwhile reasons to stop here, including one of the region's top hotels, to which many people would drive fifty miles to eat dinner.

Hotels and Motels

Gage Hotel. (915) 386-4205. Built in 1927 by rancher Alfred Gage, this hotel has become a destination objective, and no article on Big Bend is complete without full coverage of this finely restored landmark, stuffed with antiques (Western, Indian, and Mexican). A new section, Los Portales, was opened in 1993, doubling the number of rooms to thirty-seven. Here, too, careful attention has been paid to history: the Mexican tiles in the bathrooms, the hundred-year-old woven covers for the beds, and the numerous artifacts hanging on the walls—a living museum commemorating the ranching pioneers, the Indians, and Mexico.

By 1920 Alfred Gage, a prosperous banker as well as businessman, was making frequent trips from San Antonio to Marathon to check on his five-hundred-thousand-acre ranch. Since there were no accommodations in the area, he decided to build a simple, yet substantial, brick building to act as his second home. The original part of the hotel was built by the regional architectural firm of Trost and Trost, known for other work in the area, such as the El Paisano Hotel in Marfa and some of the early buildings at Sul Ross State University in Alpine.

Gage did not live long enough to make much use of his new home, since he died the year after it was completed. In later years, unsuccessful attempts were made to turn the building into a museum, but it was not until 1978, when the property was bought by J. P. Bryan of Houston, that thorough restoration was started. What has been achieved is a recreation of a frontier hotel, with saddles, ropes, and chaps prominently on display, and Indian fishnets, pottery, and baskets also liberally positioned throughout. Such is the careful attention given to the antiques and artifacts (many going back for one to two hundred years or more) that a complete list is available at the front desk specifying forty-three different items in the old building and eight different types of plants. Each bedroom has its own character, often highlighted by a fine piece of old furniture, bent with age and caringly polished each day. Where original matching furniture of the same period or from the same region was not available, custom-made reproduction furniture was handcrafted in Mexico.

Rooms in the main building (seventeen rooms) rent from $42 per room, with bath down the hall, to $60, with a bath in the suite. Charges are for double occupancy; there is a $5 charge per extra occupant. Each room has its own name. The old wood furniture, the natural fiber texture of the handwoven bedspreads, as well as the numerous artifacts, all give a sense of history in a simple yet stylish manner. No phones and no TV (except for one in the bar) are included in the rooms. There are different configurations of beds, so ask for details. Or, ask for the Room Description and Rates sheet, which describes the type of accommodation and rates for all thirty-seven rooms.

Los Portales (The Porches), the new section, provides twenty rooms and suites. All have a bath, some have a fireplace; they rent from $80 per room to $125 for a suite. A great deal of thought and creative effort has been taken with these rooms regarding their decor and comfort. All the buildings are made of adobe bricks; all the doors, no two of which are the same, are made from mesquite wood. The beams across the ceilings are from ponderosa pine, and the sticks (latillas) between the beams are from the local sotol plant. Some of the rooms have a one-page detailed description of the various furnishings and fittings. Modern services are not overlooked; water in the showers runs hot in three seconds. And outside you can lounge in the shade of the courtyard, where the sound of trickling water from the fountain offers relief from the desert sun, or you can take a swim in the pool. The hotel is attentively managed by Bill and Laurie Stevens.

Reservations are important. The hotel is often full, even with its capacity almost doubled.

Captain Shepherd's Inn. Adjacent to the Gage Hotel, (915) 386-4205. This bed-and-breakfast house, opened in late 1994, offers six rooms, all with a private bath ($80–$125). Bookings for the Inn are taken at the Gage. An extensive continental breakfast is included in the price. The Gage promotes special offers throughout the year, including a one-week stay (the traditional package is $435 for two persons), seasonal weekend packages (hayride and chuck wagon cookout, with music and stargazing introduction, is $299 for two), and float trips on the Rio Grande (two nights at the Gage, two dinners plus a day on the river, is $390 for two persons). For further details and reservations, call well in advance of your stay.

Marathon Motel. On U.S. 90 West, (915) 386-4241. This is a modest but clean motel; it was built in the early 1940s, and was where part of the movie *Paris, Texas* was filmed. It also had a poem written about it by M. Treace, which includes the line: "Make a point to stop by and chat a while/Mary and John are always ready to greet you with a smile." Mary and John Hoover, owner-managers, are in the process of renovating the eleven country cottages which form the motel. Its location on the western edge of town offers fine views of desert and mountain. The price per room is $31.80 for one person; for two persons, $37.10; for three persons, $42.40 (including tax).

RV Parks

Marathon Hotel RV Park. (915) 386-4241. They charge $11.50 for a full hookup with electricity, water, and cable TV. Showers ($2.00) and toilets are located in the office building. Tent camping is $8.00.

WHERE TO EAT

Iron Mountain Grill Restaurant. Located in the Gage Hotel, (915) 386-4205. Breakfast includes Gage Granola with fresh fruit ($4.25); three-egg omlettes ($4.50–$4.95), enchiladas montadas (two cheese enchiladas, topped with two eggs, with beans and flour tortillas for $5.25). Lunch typically includes homemade soup ($3.25) and salad with chicken fajitas ($5.95) plus cornmeal-battered chiles rellenos with red chile sauce ($6.50), or three enchiladas served with beans and corn chili ($5.50). The dinner menu is more ambitious and elaborate. Sample dishes include: charcoal-grilled quail with a warm apricot baste over house potatoes ($12.95); herbed Texas goat cheese chiles rellenos ($10.95); T-bone lamb chop with jalapeño jelly ($15.95); a fourteen-ounce rib eye steak ($15.95). For dessert, try Shirley's homemade buttermilk pie ($3.75) or blackberry cobbler ($3.95). Open 7:00 A.M. to 2:30 P.M., and 6:00 P.M. to 9.30 P.M. Call for reservations.

Gilda's Grill. At the junction of U.S. 90 and U.S. 385. Open from 9:00 A.M. to 9:00 P.M., Monday through Friday and usually on weekends. It is basic cafe fare, with a burger for $2.10 and a double jalapeño cheeseburger for $3.30. There is a nice sign outside; maybe the interior will come next.

INFORMATION

The Gage Hotel acts as a general information office for the Big Bend National Park, as well as for Marathon itself. There are plenty of brochures in the lobby, and the hotel staff will advise on the campground space availability during the peak season (spring break).

WHAT TO DO

There is a **walking tour** of Marathon outlined on a map at the Gage, where there is also all sorts of other tourist information about the region. The route of the walking tour is less than one mile and there are ten points of interest (or remains thereof), which are explained on the map.

Of unusual note is the site of the first and only factory (1907–26) in the United States that produced rubber from the guayule plant, which grows wild in the Big Bend area.

Shopping

Lovegene's. 21 South First Street, (915) 386-4366. Amid the gray dullness of Marathon, the bright sign of Lovegene's, directly across from the Gage Hotel on the other side of the tracks, catches the eye. This is a studio-gallery run by husband and wife team James Evans and Gene Krane. He takes photographs and makes soon-to-be-collectors'-items photo lamp shades; she makes pots. The attractive and cheerful place offers work by thirty-five different Texas artists; half of them are from the Big Bend area. Pottery, jewelry, masks, books, postcards, and a good collection of cassettes of local bands are also to be found here.

Haley's Trading Post. Just down from the Gage Hotel. Fancy a cow skull or a smelly old cowboy hat? A sign in the window of the Trading Post reads, "Any skull in this window $25, your choice." Step into this shop and you will find a hodgepodge of fascinating old stuff, with a character (Della Haley) to match. Old books, tools, milk-bottle tops, antique spurs, and handmade burro shoes are some of the items to be found here. Walk next door to the Marathon Emporium.

The **Marathon Emporium.** This shop sells more conventional merchandise like antiques and photos.

SERVICES

Shuttle. Scott Shuttle Service, P.O. Box 477, Marathon, TX 79842, located at 400 North East Street, (915) 386-4574 or 1-800-613-5041 (twenty-four hours a day). Mike Scott, operating since 1983, can get you and your boat to the river and have your vehicle waiting for you when you take out. He also rents camping gear.

Charges are $1 per mile on asphalt and $1 per mile (in each direction) on a dirt road. For example, to put in at La Linda, for the 83-mile Lower Canyon trip, which may take from three to seven days, depending on the state of the current and the energy of the canoers, and to take out at Dryden Crossing, would cost around $230. This fee includes maps left in the vehicle to explain the route out, a fee to the landowner on the way out, and the code for opening his gates. The actual mileage traveled by Scott in this effort is 340 miles.

Canoe rental. There are eleven canoes to rent, including the twenty-foot-long "Old Town Tripper" (useful for carrying kayaks). They cost $35 per day (minimum two days), or $150 per week, including paddles, life vests, and bailing bucket.

Rates for transfers in a 15-passenger van can be quoted for picking you up at the nearest airport, Alpine or Midland-Odessa, or at the train station at Alpine. The El Paso–Del Rio bus stops at Marathon. Mike also provides bunkhouse accommodations next to his office—a fully furnished house costing $40 per night for four persons, plus $10 for each extra person.

EXCURSIONS

Camp Peña Colorado. The Post, a country park, is 5 miles due south of Lovegene's Gallery in Marathon. Within this shaded, well-watered park, the natural, spring-fed watering hole was a favorite campsite for Comanche and Apache Indians. In 1879, to protect the area against the marauding Indians, a military post was established. It survived until 1893—the last active fort in Big Bend country. Today, it makes a nice spot to picnic, bird-watch, or swim; overnight camping is frowned upon.

Housetop Mountain Campground. (915) 345-6792. This site includes a cafe, store, and buffalo herd. Located 20 miles east of Marathon on U.S. 90, this unusual cafe and store is set in the wide open country. You can eat buffalo burgers here, taken from the herd of 150 which graze nearby. You can also buy the meat, frozen ($4.20 a pound). Homemade pies are available for dessert. It is open from 8:00 A.M. to 5:00 P.M., Monday though Saturday.

There is an RV park—$10.00 for a hookup—or you can pitch a tent ($3.00, plus $2.50 per person for showers). There are tours by jeep to see the buffalo herd (more accurately, bison) and a few burros and a zebra, or you can arrange a longer trip, including a picnic lunch, on this ten-thousand-acre ranch. It is a fascinating experience to sit in a jeep at close quarters to a large herd of these majestic animals, which are placidly staring back. Call Ben and Patsy Ratliff, who run this unusual endeavor, to book tours in advance.

Marfa

Marfa (population 2,424) is the county seat of Presidio County, an area of 3,970 square miles. The name comes from a character in Tolstoy's, *The Brothers Karamazov*. The wife of a railroad executive was reading this novel while the train stopped to take on water after crossing Paisano Pass, the highest point on the east-west line. When the question arose about what to call this stopping place, she suggested Marfa.

The town's economy has seen a sad decline since those confident days in the late 1800s when the railroad arrived. In the late 1900s, the greatest activity has been the building of the new county jail.

Back in the old days, cattlemen were attracted to the lush grasslands of the high country and by the ease of shipping cattle to market on the new railroads. Around that same time, silver was discovered in the Chinati Mountains to the south. There was fertile land for farming along the Rio Grande Valley. Traders moved along the Chihuahua Trail through Presidio County into Mexico. Marfa was at the hub of this activity.

Today, for the visitor, the town is still a useful crossroads and, despite the economic gloom, not without its attractions: an imposing courthouse, a small museum, and an important modern art collection. To the north, only 24 miles away, are Fort Davis and the Davis Mountains. Sixty-two miles to the south is the border town of Presidio. The train does not stop at Marfa; you have to go to Alpine. But buses from the east and west stop here, and there is daily service going north to Midland-Odessa, and south to Presidio.

In 1955, the filming of *Giant* took place in and around Marfa, and the huge false-front Reata ranch house in the movie bears resemblance, in its imposing architecture, to the actual Presidio County Courthouse, which you can visit today. The feature for which Marfa is best known, however, are the Marfa Lights, visible from a spot 9 miles east of town on U.S. 90. They are there alright, but no one has been able to figure out what causes them or to guarantee when they will appear.

But, even without the film crews (and Marfa still attracts current movie makers), and with or without the satisfaction of seeing the lights, Marfa still has an appeal. Most of that appeal comes from the past, in the form of a few historic buildings, such as the courthouse, standing grandly at the end of broad Highland Avenue and the El Paisano Hotel, previously the only classy hotel between San Antonio and El Paso. These, plus the small, tucked-away museum, manage to convey a sense of what the community was like in earlier times when cattle raising was booming, when the silver mine at nearby Shafter was prospering, and when the town had a vigorous life of its own. A beautifully bound, two-volume *History of Marfa and Presidio County* gives an indication of the sense of history within the community. But an important, if specialized, interest in Marfa today comes from the presence of the Chinati Foundation, a showcase for the school of minimalist design.

INFORMATION

Your first stop in Marfa should be the Chamber of Commerce at 131 East San Antonio Street. Among other pamphlets about Marfa and the region, one in particular to pick up is the *Marfa Historic Walking Tour.* The office is open Monday through Friday, and the telephone number is (915) 729-4942.

WHERE TO STAY

Hotel and Motels

El Paisano Hotel. 207 North Highland Avenue, (915) 729-3145. This historic building, dating from 1927, offers nine elegant suites, some with sunken baths, and all with fully equipped kitchens. The stars of *Giant*— Elizabeth Taylor, Rock Hudson, and James Dean—all stayed in the hotel during the making of the movie, as the exhibit in the lobby shows. Prices range from $70 for two persons, to $100 for a two-bedroom, two-bath suite with exercise room and library. Work is under way to convert fourteen other rooms to simpler bedroom accommodations, priced at $60 for two. The tiled, high-ceilinged lobby is a prime feature, with deep comfortable couches and photo displays of past filming activity on the walls. This is a cool and comfortable spot to sit and read through your tourist literature. There is a small arcade of gift shops at one entrance, and at the other entrance is a pleasant courtyard. The hotel is presently going through a period of slow restoration and uncertainty. But at least the small indoor swimming pool is functioning, and the restaurant is in operation again. With further professional attention, the hotel may start to regain the charm and justify the claim, made in 1929: "Of Spanish architecture, the exterior of the building as well as the interior is pervaded with a pleasing and restful atmosphere. You will rest, relax, and be refreshed at the Paisano." Call ahead for reservations.

Holiday Capri Inn, (915) 729-4326, and Thunderbird Motel, (915) 729-4391. On opposite sides of U.S. 90 near the downtown intersection, these accommodations offer a total of fifty-two functional, standard-issue rooms. Check in at Holiday Capri Inn; they fill up this motel first. The Thunderbird Restaurant, adjacent to its counterpart motel, offers standard West Texas fare. For a quieter room, request one at the back. A single rents for $32.50, a double is $38.95.

The Lash-Up Bed and Breakfast. 215 North Austin, (915) 729-4487. One block from the Presidio County Courthouse, this yellow-painted, two-story, turn-of-the-century house is in a quiet setting. There are three comfortable, carpeted, country-decorated bedrooms, with a homemade quilt dominating each room. The breakfast is extensive and includes homemade rolls and biscuits. Picnic lunches are offered. The cost is $50 per room.

RV Parks
Apache Pines RV Park. On U.S. 90 West, one mile from town. It has good views to the south over the countryside. With a full hookup and pull through, the rate is $12. There are also camp sites with water, but no showers.

Another RV park is opposite the Border Patrol headquarters on U.S. 67 South. It has toilets and showers and is located in a plain site. Hookup is $10, with a 20 percent discount for seniors.

WHERE TO EAT

Carmen's Cafe. On the left side of U.S. 90 East, just before leaving town. A sign outside says, "Tie your horse and come in." Inside, there are two rooms, one with colorful murals, the other with a short counter. It is open for breakfast (breakfast burrito, $1.60) from 7:00 A.M. until 2:00 P.M., and from 5:00 P.M. to 9:00 P.M. in the evening, but is closed in the afternoon and all day Sunday. There are Mexican plates ($4.15–$6.25), plus chicken-fried steak, Spanish steak, and burgers. Bright and attractive, it features consistent cooking and is family-operated. (915) 729-3429.

El Paisano Restaurant. In the El Paisano Hotel, (915) 729-3145. Open daily from 7:00 A.M. to 9:00 P.M. The lunch menu includes sandwiches, burgers, salads, and fajita burritos ($4.95, with black beans and rice). There is a more extensive dinner menu offering steaks, chicken, and seafood, all served with soup or salad, potato, or Spanish rice. Specifically, there are fourteen-ounce rib eyes and eight-ounce filets ($15.95 each), three soft corn tortilla chicken tacos or a barbecued chicken breast, and a rainbow trout ($8.95), or shrimp, sautéed with garlic and salsa ($12.95). The décor could use some freshening up, but there is the potential for a high-quality restaurant in this historic setting.

Thunderbird Restaurant. On U.S. 90 West, next to Holiday Capri Inn. The menu has been extended with the addition of soups and salads, barbecue, and steaks, in addition to a larger salad bar ($3.95) and lunch specials. A combination plate of brisket ($6.90), a rib eye steak ($10.15), and a Sunday prime rib special ($12) are all popular. They are open daily from 6:00 A.M. to 9:00 P.M. (915) 729-4391.

Mike's Place. 120 East El Paso. Overlooking the tracks, Mike's is small and cozy, a favorite with the locals. It features burgers and bowls of chili. It is open from 8:00 A.M. until 5:00 P.M., until 2:00 P.M. on Saturday, and closed on Sunday. Mike's sign says: "7 days without a Mike's burger makes one weak." (915) 729-8146.

Mando's. On U.S. 90 West. It is a clean and pleasant family beer joint, with a jukebox and games. It serves Mexican food, steaks, and burgers. It is open Tuesday through Saturday, noon to late, and on Sunday from 5:00 to 10:00 P.M.

WHAT TO DO

Take the **walking tour.** For an understanding of how things used to be in Presidio County, see the video in the museum. For how they are now, take the twenty-two-point walking tour, which takes place in just four blocks along Highland Avenue. A map and a description of each place are available from the Chamber of Commerce.

Visit the **Presidio County Courthouse,** the most prominent building, which is visible from all directions and has an even more impressive view looking out from the dome. This four-story building with cupola was built in 1886, and its impressive dimensions reflect the confidence of the times. Built out of brick, it was stuccoed in the thirties and painted a pinkish color with pale yellow edging and upper part. Visitors can climb the wooden stairs, passing the high-ceilinged courtroom and circular balustrades on each floor, then continue up a narrower stairway to the dome. But first they must get a key for the topmost level from the clerk's office on the first floor. There are two seats at the top, and also a pair of binoculars trained down Highland Avenue towards the Border Patrol headquarters. If you wrestle with the binoculars, you can redirect them further towards the south. Stunning views exist in all directions.

The **Marfa and Presidio County Museum,** three blocks west of the courthouse, is a modest building, staffed by volunteers, and offers a surprisingly complete picture of Marfa's past. Start by watching a first-rate thirty-minute video, with local voices on tape, detailing the history of the area. The presentation includes brilliant colored pictures and lots of details of life as it was. Then walk through four different rooms which reveal life in the old days. The mining section displays the ledger of the Marfa and Mariposa Mining Company; the railroad section shows a picture of twenty steam locomotives passing through Marfa, a promotional exercise in 1922 to boost confidence in the railroad.

There is a handmade leather pouch on display which was carried by a cowboy on his belt to hold medicine for him and his animals. The food preparation area at the end of a chuck wagon is displayed with all the utensils. The history of Camp Marfa and Fort Russell is covered from 1911 to 1946 (the Chamber of Commerce has a printed history and a map of the fort). This walk-through history is not complete without the additional personal observations from Mrs. Godbold or one of the other volunteers. Open only on Wednesdays from 2 P.M. to 5 P.M., or by appointment by calling (915) 729-4678. A donation is suggested. Don't miss this stop.

Henry C. Trost is considered Texas' first nationally significant architect. Sul Ross State University is one example of his work. In Marfa, the **El Paisano Hotel** is seen as one of his most successful achievements. He sought to synthesize many turn-of-the-century architectural concepts with decorative forms of the Southwest. The El Paisano Hotel shows finely cast Spanish Baroque "cartouche" work and Southwest Revival detail, within the concept of a modern concrete structure.

The **Chinati Foundation** is located at the railroad tracks, and just out of town to the south. Guided tours of the unique collection housed here are given Thursday through Saturday from 1:00 to 5:00 P.M. To see this varied internationally known collection, call (915) 729-4362. The philosophy of Donald Judd, who started the foundation in 1979, is expressed in the foundation's catalog: "It takes a great deal of time and thought to install work carefully. This should not always be thrown away. Most art is fragile and should be placed and never moved again. Some work is too large, complex and expensive to move. Somewhere a portion of contemporary art has to exist as an example of what art and its context were meant to be."

Tours of the Chinati Foundation collection take place Thursday through Saturday from 1:00 P.M. to 5:00 P.M. or at any other time when an appointment has been made. Two hours should probably satisfy the average visitor the first time. You will first need to go to the office of the foundation at the old Fort Russell site. You find this by taking U.S. 67 South from the intersection in the center of town, turning right after a quarter mile, at the Border Patrol headquarters sign. Pass the border patrol buildings and turn in left through a gateway marked Fort Russell.

After two hundred yards you will see the Chinati Office sign. If there is no one at the office, follow the map on the door and walk to apartment 13 or 9.

A young man from New Orleans was asleep in apartment 9 when I went, but he readily agreed to offer me a guided tour of the foundation. He had been there a year as a volunteer apprentice, after graduating in architecture in New Orleans. Part of his responsibilities was taking visitors around the foundation, perhaps two or three small groups each week. Most of the visiting groups are from Europe, where Donald Judd is widely known.

About six staff and artists are based permanently in Marfa, with two visiting artists usually on site, and one or two volunteers who lead the tours. The tour starts with a visit to the Artillery Sheds, two long brick buildings end to end. Following use as storage for artillery pieces, the sheds were converted into barracks to house German prisoners of war. A sign in German still remains, telling the prisoners not to enter a certain area. Judd added another sign, in German, saying: "Using one's head is better than losing it." Judd converted the barracks by putting on a new roof and by adding large windows with aluminum frames, which allow the desert light to come in and reveal the rows of box-like (4 feet-by–4 feet-by–3 feet) structures.

There are one hundred of these precise crisp-looking pieces of dense and heavy aluminum, which were milled in Switzerland. There is one piece that can be handled, but you are asked not to touch any of the other exhibits. These exactly engineered pieces, each one slightly different from the other, stand in shiny and orderly rows in contrast to the disorderly landscape outside. Every word spoken by the guide or exclamation by the visitor resonates against the concrete floor and lidless aluminum boxes. Across the windswept unkempt grass surrounding the buildings can be seen a row of seven-foot high concrete clusters built by Judd, stretching one kilometer in length on a north-south axis. Their function or appeal was not too clear to me when viewed from inside the artillery sheds.

After passing by several buildings which had been made half-ready for an exhibit that never materialized, the walking tour's next stop is a display of thirty-six small 10-by-6-inch pencil shadings on paper, mounted in a line on a wall in a room otherwise bare of exhibits. Blinds are removed from windows to reveal a sense of space. This work is by the Icelandic artist Ingolfur Arnasson (born 1956), who visited the foundation and created this work which is now a permanent part of the collection.

There are other equally interesting items on display at the old Fort

Russell exhibition. Three concentric rings of Icelandic stones are laid on the ground. More easily visible not too far away is a twenty-five-foot-high iron horseshoe entitled *Animo et Fide*, a monument to the last cavalry horse, by Oldenburg. The largest building on the base, where the majority of the old structures are untouched, is the Arena, previously used as a gymnasium, then as an indoor riding arena, and now used by the foundation for functions.

In the center of town the Chamberlain Collection, in two warehouses, includes smashed-up, sometimes repainted, automobile parts welded into a variety of shapes—an enormous, and to some provocative, difference from the exhibition at the fort. In the foundation office, back at the fort, books, posters, and postcards are for sale, including Donald Judd's *Architektur* ($25), a description of his work by the artist himself. Donations to the foundation are gratefully accepted.

Play golf at the highest **golf course** in Texas, one and a half miles from Marfa, at a nine-hole, airy course with low green fees, and clubs for rent. It has a great view towards the Davis Mountains. See Chapter 4 for a description of the course.

The **Marfa City Library** at 115 East Oak is a source of local pride. Drop by and take a look at the local newspapers or browse their book selection. There is a good collection of articles on the Marfa Lights and the Chinati Foundation. This is also a place to check out the *Big Bend Sentinel*, the active and forthright local newspaper, established in 1886, which covers a wider area than just Marfa. The May 14, 1992, issue is especially eventful. It reveals the arrest and sentencing to life imprisonment of Marfa County Sheriff Rick Thompson, who was convicted of smuggling 2,400 pounds of cocaine from Mexico in a horse trailer.

The **Marfa Gallery** on West El Paso Street, across the tracks at Highland Avenue, is a cooperative gallery displaying the works of six local artists. A bright and cheerful place, it offers a good variety of products at very reasonable prices. Copper enamel work (pendants are $14), hand-painted silk scarves ($22), Afghans ($30), one-of-a-kind jackets ($10–$30), pressed wool tortilla warmers, or hot pad, ($7.45), "crocodile undies" (from $14), and recipe holders ($5). The shop is presided over by cheerful and informative Margaret Anderson who also paints in oils and water colors.

The **Jamar Art Gallery,** 122 East El Paso, is a welcome new gallery specializing in art pieces from the interior of Mexico. It also displays contemporary art and artists from the region, such as Don Parkinson, and there are some antiques for sale. Hours are by appointment. (915) 729-4874.

Two miles west of town on U.S. 90 is the **Marfa Rock Shop,** with an extensive collection of rough rock, fossils, and arrowheads, and two informed and talkative hosts.

Events

The major event of the year for Marfa is the **Marfa Lights Festival,** which takes place over Labor Day weekend.

On the Friday night there is a street dance, with a live country and western band. Meanwhile up to 125 booths with arts and crafts displays and food to sell have been set up around the courthouse.

On Saturday there is the parade. Floats constructed by civic and school organizations, groups of horseback riders, and mariachi bands form the parade. There is also the ranch rodeo and a golf tournament. In the evening, the high point of the weekend takes place in the park. It is suggested that you bring blankets and chairs since this Concert under the Stars will run from 7:30 P.M. for three or four hours. A local group warms up the audience, then a nationally known entertainer takes over. On Sunday, the booths are open again, and any local group that wishes to play around the courthouse can have its turn. In the evening, there is a dance to live Tejano music.

Entrance to the Concert under the Stars costs $5. All the daytime activities are free, and up to three thousand people attend each year.

The **Marfa Lights** are the best known evening event in the whole region. These mysterious and unexplained lights that have been reported in the area for over one hundred years, have been the subject of many theories. The first recorded sighting of the lights was by rancher Robert Ellison in 1883. Variously explained as campfires, phosphorescent minerals, swamp gas, static electricity, St. Elmo's Fire, and "Ghost Lights," the lights reportedly change colors, move about, and change in integrity. Scholars have reported over seventy-five local folk tales dealing with the unexplained phenomenon. For more information, see Chapter 4, "Marfa Lights."

Monahans and Monahans Sandhills State Park

Stuck between I-20 and an oil field, Monahans (population 8,101) manages to present itself both as a state park destination and as an oil patch town. There's no mistaking the latter claim since there are working oil wells within the city limits, as well as the Million Barrel Museum. And even before you exit I-20 you can see, just to the east of town, the rolling white sand dunes of the Monahans Sandhills State Park.

In the late 1800s, the transcontinental railroad creeped across the dry Texas plains, a mile per day, and the lack of water was becoming a major, even critical, problem. But a Texas and Pacific railroad surveyor, Tom Monahans, looked out across the great sand dunes one day and, despite ridicule, decided to copy the Indians and dig a shallow trench. His well was eighteen feet in diameter and only fifty-three feet deep, but the water flowed freely, and the future of the railroad and the town of Monahans was assured.

The railroad came and stayed. Later, oil made its mark on the region and the city, and even with the downturn in the economic situation in the 1980s, Monahans has kept its reputation and position as the well service center of West Texas. The usual deprivations of many towns in the area, such as boarded-up windows or abandoned businesses, are not too evident here. Monahans is surviving all right and is making the most of what it has to offer. For visitors approaching the Big Bend region on I-20 or flying into Midland-Odessa, it might be worth a stop. The motel situation is just reasonable with two acceptable units, or camping among the sand dunes might be fun.

INFORMATION

The Chamber of Commerce is located next to the public library at 401 South Dwight Street, at the corner of East Fourth. It is open Monday through Friday, 9:00 A.M. to 5:00 P.M., and is closed from noon to 1:00 for lunch. Their telephone number is (915) 943-2187 or 943-6868. You can get a map of the town (not vitally necessary), an attractive pamphlet about Monahans, a separate one about Monahans Sandhills State Park (5 miles west), and any other advice you might want to ask for.

WHERE TO STAY

Motels

Best Western Colonial Inn. On the feeder road off I-20, (915) 943-4345. It has a pool and offers single rooms at $37, doubles at $43 (one bed) and $46 (two beds), all plus tax, with 10 percent off for AAA and AARP.

Texan Inn. Next door to the Colonial Inn, (915) 943-7585. It was previously the Howard Johnson's Motel, which opened in 1985. A single room is $30, a double with one bed is $36, and with two beds, is $42 (all prices are plus tax). There is a slight increase in rates June through September.

There are four **budget motels** in town with names like Rest EZ and Silver Spur, with rates in the high teens for a room. These place are mainly used by workers visiting the oil fields, and one has been used as background in a feature film.

RV Parks

Coleman RV Park. 4601 South Stockton, on Texas 18 South, (915) 943-5840. Well managed, with a laundry and showers. Full hookups are $10.

Monahans Sandhills State Park. To make reservations, call the Texas State Parks booking number (512) 389-8900. Accessed from Exit 86 on I-20, it has camping sites for RVs and tents, with electricity and water ($9), or with water only ($6); the entrance fee to the park is $3 per vehicle (free for Texas Conservation Passport holders). The showers and toilets are particularly clean. This is a pleasant, secluded setting for camping among the dunes, although the noise of freeway traffic can sometimes be distracting. The office at the entrance gate is staffed until 5:00 P.M.; after that you may self-select a site and pay into a box.

WHERE TO EAT

K-Bob's Steak House. On South Stockton, (915) 943-7498. A consistent and popular place, it offers a special on Friday consisting of an eight-ounce ranch steak with salad for $5.75, and on Saturday a fourteen-ounce top sirloin with a salad for $8.95.

Spotlight Restaurant. 2003 North Main (Texas 18 North), (915) 943-6751. More interesting than K-Bob's, it was formerly a TV studio and is making an effort to be distinctive with nightly specials like baked white-fish ($6.25), chicken-fried steak ($6.50), and pork chops ($6.75), which include a trip to the salad bar. The steamed vegetable platter ($5.50) comes as a surprise; this restaurant places emphasis on preparing dishes according to guidelines of the American Heart Association. There is a club adjacent.

Fermin's Restaurant. 400 North Main. It offers Mexican food and is recommended for Vicki's nachos supreme ($4.95).

Leal's Restaurant. Popular; try the Don Pablo special (burrito, cheese sauce, sour cream) for $3.95.

Bobby Joe's. 900 West Sealy. Serves Chinese food.

Big Burger. 1016 South Stockton. For a burger or a Coke, it provides a clean, attractive setting with collector's memorabilia of old Coca-Cola signs.

Fred's Barbecue. For a typical West Texas experience, take the time to search out this place; Fred has been making barbecue for many, many years.

McDonald's, Sonic, Pizza Hut, Dairy Queen, and **Subway.** A complete fast food assortment.

WHAT TO DO

The **Monahans Sandhills State Park** comprises almost four thousand acres of wind-scuplted white sand dunes, which form a small part of a dune field that stretches north and westward into New Mexico. Not apparent to the eye is one of the largest oak forests in the country, stretching over forty thousand acres of arid land. The forest is not apparent because the mature trees (Havard oaks) are seldom over three feet high, yet they send down roots as far as ninety feet to maintain miniature surface growth. These oaks, which are found only at this park, help to stabilize the dunes, some of which are up to seventy feet high; other dunes, which are bare of vegetation, constantly shift with the wind.

The Visitor Center explains the origin of the park and the history of the region. The large glass window in the museum serves as an excellent vantage point for viewing birds and mammals as they come to the feeding and watering station outside. A self-guided trail behind the center offers twelve points of interest, including a pack rat nest, cactus, sagebrush, and the Havard oak. On weekends during summer months, park rangers present campfire programs about the park and the region.

Kids can rent ($1 per hour) from the concession stand large plastic Frisbees for sliding down the dunes. There are also refreshments available at the stand. Adults can use the barbecue pits for picnics or the well-positioned camp sites for overnight camping. Good, clean rest rooms and showers are available. Admission to the park is $3 per vehicle. The park is 5 miles east of Monahans; there is an exit off I-20, prominently marked Monahans Sandhills State Park sign. Park information: (915) 943-2092; reservations: (512) 389-8900.

The **Million Barrel Museum** is situated between the Monahans Sandhills State Park and the town, on Business I-20, and is another curiosity. A fine refurbished house, which was moved from its previous site in town when the museum was opened in 1987, reflects life in the early part of this century. Its somewhat tenuous connection with oil is that the son of the

Monahans State Park. Photo by Blair Pittman.

owner eventually became president of Standard Oil Company of New Jersey. There are also exhibits of antique oil field equipment, a vintage caboose, and the old Monahans Jail.

The main source of interest is the huge circular concrete basin, which was built in 1928 by Shell Oil Company to hold oil. Apparently, it leaked and was only used for two years. The caretaker will talk and willingly speculate about the million-barrel useless tank. Today, it has some use apart from being a curiosity and serves as an amphitheater for performances. It is open daily except Monday (10:00 A.M.–8:00 P.M.) and Sunday 2:00–8:00 P.M., and there is no fee.

The **Pyote Museum and Rattlesnake Bomber Base** is another historical relic. Formerly it was a major air force training base and home to a World War II bomb group, which included the Enola Gay, the bomber that dropped the atomic bomb. Located fifteen miles west of Monahans on U.S. 80, the base was so nicknamed due to the large number of rattlesnakes in the area. The base no longer exists, but a small museum (entrance is free) displays area history artifacts and relics of the base.

Hardly worth a 25-mile drive, unless you were stationed there or at one of the numerous similar bases in West Texas; however, if you are nearby on a Saturday or Sunday and want a picnic spot in the shaded park, as well as the chance to see a detailed, if limited, slice of wartime history, drop in. Exhibits include a pair of dress trousers or "ones similar," worn by the base commander. The base includes a swimming pool and overnight camping of the simple kind.

EVENTS

Monahans has recently put itself on the events map with the imaginative and appropriate **Butterfield-Overland Stagecoach and Wagon Festival.** The Butterfield Coach passed close to Monahans on one of its longest and hardest runs, through loose sand. In early August, 1994, the first festival was held, featuring trail riders arriving with their chuck wagons from surrounding towns, bull riding, a 50-mile-long horse race, roping and penning, cowboy poetry, and a well-known Tejano singer performing in front of an audience of four thousand at the Million Barrel Museum. The event is scheduled to be repeated each year. Call the Chamber of Commerce at (915) 943-2187 for details.

Pecos

One of the largest towns in the region (population 12,122), Pecos also looks to be one of the most impoverished. It is a victim of changed economic circumstances and a town struggling to regain momentum. At the top of the triangle formed by the two interstates (I-10 and I-20) and Texas 17, Pecos is the center of the largest irrigated land area in Texas.

The arrival of large-scale fruit and vegetable (onion, green pepper) cultivation offers some hope for the Pecos economy. Each August Pecos has a cantaloupe festival to celebrate its best-known harvest. Now, new strains of cotton—green- and next, blue-colored—are being introduced in the area and look promising.

When I-20 was built, Pecos' main street (like that of many other towns in a similar situation) lost much of its appeal, at least to through-travelers. More recently, the closing down of major chain stores, as they relocated in malls elsewhere, added to the economic gloom. Today, approaching Pecos from the west on U.S. 80, a vista of boarded-up windows and closed-down shops greets the visitor. The funeral home is the most prosperous-looking business on this strip.

But, as with other towns, the center of activity has shifted, in this case along U.S. 285, which heads northwest to Carlsbad Caverns. And here Pecos, which has no fort to celebrate or spring to use, has developed an attraction which is worth making a good detour to visit—the West of the Pecos Museum, a fascinating and varied collection of pioneer artifacts of the region, housed in thirty rooms of a famous old hotel, which even has bullet holes in the floor of the saloon.

INFORMATION

Visit the Chamber of Commerce at 111 South Cedar (U.S. 285) next to the West of the Pecos Museum, for a map of the town, for the pamphlet *Pecos, the Visitor Check List*, and for all sorts of pamphlets on nearby attractions and information on local events. The telephone number is (915) 445-2406.

WHERE TO STAY

Motels

Best Western Sunday House Inn. Country Club Drive and I-20, 1-800-528-1234 or (915) 447-2215. It has a restaurant, lounge, and pool with 104 rooms. For two people, the rate is $46.00, plus tax. For AAA and AARP, the rate is $41.40 (for two), plus tax. A free continental breakfast is included.

Holiday Inn. I-20 and U.S. 285, 1-800-332-5255 or (915) 445-5404. It has a restaurant, lounge, and pool with 98 rooms. For two people, the rate is $44.95, plus tax. For AAA and AARP the price is $39.95, plus tax.

Motel 6. 3002 South Cedar, (915) 445-9034. Off I-20 at Exit 42, it has a pool and 130 rooms. The rate is $20.95 for one, with the second adult at $6.00 extra. The third and fourth adults are $3.00 each (plus tax, no discounts).

Laura Lodge. 1000 East Third Street, (915) 445-4924. It has a pool, budget rates, and good management. Rates are $16.95 for a single, $18.00 for two (one bed), and $25.00 (two beds). Prices are plus tax.

Town & Country Motel. 2128 West Third Street, (915) 445-4946. It has 34 rooms and a pool. The rate is $25 for one and $28 for two persons.

RV Park

Trapark RV Park. 3100 Moore Street, (915) 447-2137. It has 28 full hookups; the rate is $13.50. A tent site rents for $9.00. It is close to a swimming pool and park. All facilities are clean and quiet. It has pull-through and tent sites, and includes free morning coffee. The management is helpful.

WHERE TO EAT

Sunday House Motel Restaurant. (915) 447-2215.

Holiday Inn Restaurant. (915) 445-5404.

Cattleman's Restaurant. 425 West Third Street, (915) 445-3433. Well patronized by the locals and features a full-scale menu.

Chicken Charlie's. 1000 South Cedar, (915) 445-2511. Relocated from Balmorhea three years ago, it is prospering. Chicken-fried steak ($4.95 for the small size, $5.95 for the large) and 1¼- to 2-inch-thick steaks (a sixteen-ounce rib eye is $12.95).

La Norteña Tortilla Factory. 212 East Third, (915) 445-3273. This place features tamales (large, $5.00; small, $2.50); menudo (pint, $1.25; quart, $2.25); barbacoa de cabeza ($5.95). Take your tamales and have a picnic in Windmill Square, the downtown park, next to the museum, near the fountain, and not far from the grave of Clay Allison, the "Gentleman Gunfighter." If you don't feel like eating tamales in the park, you can visit La Norteña Restaurant at 802 South Eddy.

Tommy's Place. 1205 East U.S. 80, (915) 445-2641. Across from Laura Lodge, Tommy's has homemade Mexican food. It is nice and clean, reasonable, and just plain delicious, as it says on the menu. In its fourth year, Tommy's seems to be doing alright. Favorites are chile verde burrito for $1.39, and the chile verde plate for $5.25.

WHAT TO DO

The **West of the Pecos Museum,** 120 East First Street, an original two-story building, dates from 1896 and was built of red sandstone. Eight years later, a three-story building, the Orient Hotel, was built next door and continued in operation until the fifties.

On the ground floor as you enter is the lobby, with a pressed tin ceiling and wooden staircase. To the left is the dining room, and on the right is the saloon. Here, marked on the floor with two plaques, are the places where two men died in 1896 during a double killing, each shot by Barney Riggs, a local man. The story behind these shootings, and the subsequent movements of and ultimate shooting of Barney Riggs, are told in a booklet sold at the well-stocked museum shop ticket counter.

The rest of the two floors of the hotel are crammed with all sorts of memorabilia, each room featuring one aspect of life in the region. A display of a mummy found in the Chinati Mountains dates from early times; a display of cowboy hats, battered and stained, dates from only twenty years ago. There is a schoolroom, a telegraph room, and much information about Clay Allison, the Pecos "Gentleman Gunfighter." Each exhibit is displayed with care and attention to detail, and the whole building is spotlessly maintained.

The entrance fee is $3, and the museum is open daily, 9:00–5:00, and on Sunday, 2:00–5:00 (open till 6:00 in summertime). Call (915) 445-5076 for more information. Various other exhibits are in the immediate vicinity of the museum, including the jail, the hanging tree, and the Judge Roy Bean replica.

What impressed me about this museum is not just the rooms and closets crammed with artifacts or even the living history (or dying history) of the shoot-out in the saloon. It is also the energy and creativity of the enterprising museum committee and the volunteers who sustain this sort of cultural enterprise. A nice touch: during the cantaloupe season, visitors to the museum are served slices of cantaloupe.

A recent fund drive has raised enough money to open the third floor of the hotel, an operation which involves structural changes. The fundraising included putting on lunches, selling sponsor bricks to the public with the benefactors' names painted on, and also putting Sooie, the slue-footed pig, the museum's mascot, into action. Incidentally, Sooie is not a porcelain money box pig, but a real, live, grunting animal. In an aggressive fundraising effort, Sooie was taken to local stores likely to donate and kept there until the owners agreed to participate in the fundraising.

Maxey Park and Zoo is a surprising venture and, at first sight, perhaps a welcome relief for those traveling with children on I-20, Country Club Exit. This small, half-formed zoo, with zebra, bison, and other indigenous and exotic animals, includes two recently added, miserably confined mountain lions, a children's playground, a botanical garden, and a children's miniature version of the Alamo. Take Exit 40 on I-20. The admission is free; there is also a picnic area and nearby is the Trapark RV Park.

Toone's Grocery is easy to appreciate. This old-fashioned general store, still clinging on, just outside the city limits on U.S. 80 West, reeks of history. Look at the wood floor, the massive safe, the meat-cutting section, and the whole range of foodstuffs, household items, and clothing; buy something and help keep alive an independent small store. It is located at 2136 West Highway 80 (Third Street). (915) 445-3662.

June–July	West of the Pecos Rodeo. Pecos is proud that the first rodeo in the United States to offer prizes took place here. The rodeo takes place for three days in early July, with nightly western dances, a rodeo parade, and a Western art show. Contact the Chamber of Commerce, (915) 445-2406 for precise details.
August	Cantaloupe Festival. Pecos cantaloupes became famous throughout the United States because they were served to railroad passengers.
September–October	World Championship BBQ Cook-off. Meat is provided, bring your own firewood. Reeves County Fair and Livestock Show.

Presidio

"Nuevo Real Presidio de Nuestra Señora de Betlena y Santiago de las Amarillas de la Junta de los Ríos Norte y Conchos"—the name originally given to what is now Presidio, Texas (population 4,242), and Ojinaga, Mexico, by the Spanish when they built a settlement here in 1759–60.

This settlement was new ("nuevo") to the Spaniards, but an ancient Indian settlement had been here long before the Spanish arrived. Indians had chosen to live here because it was a fertile area at the junction ("junta") of two rivers, Río Conchos and the Río Bravo del Norte—to us, the Rio Grande, but to the Spanish, "the wild river of the north." Archeological evidence suggests human arrival here in this fertile area as early as ten thousand years ago.

The first Spaniard, Cabeza de Vaca, arrived at La Junta (the Spaniards' shortened name for the area) in 1535. De Vaca had been shipwrecked in Florida, rafted across the Gulf of Mexico to what is now Galveston Island, and from there trekked west. When he reached this area, he discovered a considerable population in perhaps a dozen villages, each numbering in the hundreds. These settled agriculturalists lived in an oasis surrounded by rugged desert; produced corn, squash, beans, and calabashes; and engaged in trading. Strangely enough, this ancient activity accurately describes modern Presidio, except that today's vegetable is the onion and today's fruit is the cantaloupe. Presidio is the onion capital of the United States, with claims to be the oldest continually cultivated region in North America, and the only cross-border link in the 450 miles between El Paso and Del Rio.

With the Spaniards came the priests. In downtown Presidio, Santa Teresa Church recently celebrated the 310th anniversary of the first mission.

With the westward expansion of pioneers and the forming of the border came violence too. Ben Leaton, employed by the Mexican government as a scalp hunter in Mexico (Apache scalps fetched twenty times the price of a horse), arrived at La Junta in 1846. He settled and built a massive fortress (today's Fort Leaton) on the site of a previous Spanish military post, or presidium. Since local people felt such resentment towards Leaton, then and now the fort retained the name of the old Spanish village (El Fortín). But the name Presidio lasted, and the town of that name was established in 1930.

Today, the visitor finds a working town engaged in agriculture and cross-border trade. "This is the real world," says John Ferguson, local community leader who is taking a lead in presenting Presidio as the gateway to northern Mexico to tourists. James Mitchener has said that Presidio is his favorite border town, and it would be interesting to know why. He must not have noticed the heat. Presidio is "America's Hot-Spot," states the Chamber of Commerce brochure facing the problem head-on. This hot and dusty working town with an expanding population provides attractions nearby, a place to stay in town, and at least two interesting restaurants; it also has the only major bridge to Mexico for 450 miles.

INFORMATION

For tourist literature and information about Presidio and Ojinaga (including a map of O.J., Ojinaga's nickname), visit the Presidio Information Center and Gift Shop, owned and run by former Mayor John Ferguson and his wife. Located next to the post office on U.S. Business 67, it is on the other side of the road junction from the Border Patrol headquarters. It is open daily from 8:00 A.M. to 8:00 P.M.; the telephone number is (915) 229-4478. The information office and gift shop exist to promote cross-border traffic with resources and information, and to offer reasonably priced Mexican souvenirs.

HOW TO GET THERE

Visitors on the Texas Mountain Trail will find Presidio at the start or end of one of the most scenic routes in North America, the 50-mile El Camino del Rio (the River Road). See "Big Bend State Natural Area and the River Road" for a full description of the drive.

There is daily bus transportation north to Marfa, Alpine, and on to Midland-Odessa. There is daily bus service (except Thursday and Sunday) southwest to Chihuahua City in Mexico. And there is more frequent service (several times daily) from Ojinaga (see the section on "Ojinaga").

WHERE TO STAY

Motels

Three Palms Inn. Old U.S. 67 North, (915) 229-3211. Near the Border Patrol headquarters, it has forty-two rooms, including twelve new units around the pool. This is the only sizable and modern accommodation in Presidio. Singles (old rooms) rent for $27 and (new rooms) $37. Doubles (old rooms) are $35 and (new rooms) $45, plus tax. It is strongly advised to book reservations in advance. The popular Cafe Rose's is next door.

La Siesta. U.S. 67, (915) 229-3611. This older establishment has six units. Rooms are compact, wood-paneled, and clean. A family-run business, it is charming, helpful, and has a small pool. It is close to El Patio Restaurant for breakfast. A single rents for $20.79; a double (one bed) rents for $27.50.

RV Park

Presidio Valley RV Park. 2 miles east on RR 170, (915) 229-3162. Located 3.25 miles from Fort Leaton. The rate is $10, with a full hookup. It is suggested you call in advance of your arrival to determine if the park is open.

WHERE TO EAT

Las Pampas. RR 170. A family from Argentina produces an attractive international menu of pizza, steak Milanese ($6.75), liver ($6.00), and churrasco (mixed grill). Open daily from 6:00 A.M. to 10:00 P.M.

La Escondida. Just out of town, across Cibolo Creek, heading north on U.S. 67, take a sharp left before the road forks left to Ruidosa. Follow a gravel road a quarter mile, then turn left for a hundred yards and enter a gateway on right. An unexpected surprise, a courtyard with a honeysuckle tree, awaits you. It has a separate, dimly lit bar. The restaurant, with distinctive waiters, offers jumbo shrimp, brisket ($7.50), a Mexican dinner combination, and tampiqueña, a strip steak with green sauce, enchilada, taco, and beans ($8.95). It has a tile floor, tablecloths, and for some reason, menus with reworked prices and Oil Flyer printed on the front. It is open from noon to 10:00 P.M. daily except Monday. (915) 229-3719.

Cafe Rose's. Next to the Three Palms Inn, on old U.S. 67. This popular and reliable cafe's thirteen years with the same management makes it a favorite of the locals. Spacious and cool with a bright decor and competent service. The menu includes chiles rellenos for $4.50, sirloin steak for $7.95, a four-layer banana pudding, and Schwann's ice cream and yogurt. Open daily 6:00 P.M. to 9:00 P.M. (915) 229-3998.

La Frontera. Opposite Las Pampas on O'Reilly Street. (915) 229-3284. Compact and clean, it features Mexican food well prepared by Ofelia Barrera, the owner.

El Patio. Just along from La Siesta Motel. (915) 229-4409. It features a breakfast buffet ($2.90).

Try the **Presidio Tortilla Factory** (opposite the Border Patrol headquarters) for fresh tortillas, or if you are buying drinks before traveling down the River Road toward Lajitas or north to Marfa, go to M B's Supermarket in downtown.

WHAT TO DO

Sights

Most of the things to do lie outside Presidio, such as Fort Leaton (see Chapter 1, "Big Bend Ranch State Natural Area").

Nineteen miles north of Presidio on U.S. 67 is the mining town of **Shafter.** In its heyday in the early 1900s, three thousand people lived here; it was the richest place in Texas.

Thirty miles along a paved road, RR 170, brings you to **Candelaria,** the site of a once bustling industry in this area—producing wax from the candelilla plant.

Shopping

Spencer's Famous Brands. This well-stocked store carries western apparel and accessories; it is near the old church downtown. (915) 229-3324.

Presidio Information Center and Gift Shop. For Mexican goods, check here for quality and prices before going to Ojinaga. (915) 229-4478.

The **Onion Festival** is celebrated each May. The previous winner of the onion competition weighed 2 lbs. 8 oz. There is an annual parade (with a prize for the worst tractor), an onion cook-off, and a Queen of the Onion Festival competition.

Ojinaga

Directly across the river from Presidio is Ojinaga, a regional center of thirty thousand people, that caters to the agricultural community of this part of the State of Chihuahua, Mexico's richest. Pronounced "Oh-hin-aga" in full and called O.J. in short, this is a pleasant, clean town. It scarcely goes out of its way to tempt tourists, but it also doesn't pester them. Visiting Ojinaga is like stepping back thirty years in time.

GETTING THERE

You can drive to the control point (on the U.S. side), park, and walk across the modern bridge, but it is a hot and lengthy hike, ending with an uphill stretch. Better, unless you drive across yourself, is to catch the blue-and-white Suburban shuttle, marked Ruta Presidio-O.J., outside M B's supermarket in Presidio; it leaves roughly every half-hour ($2). The shuttle takes you to the main square (*zócalo*) in Ojinaga, the best point for walking around. In Spanish, the shuttle is called *el chuco*, a useful term to know when you want to come back. Or, take a taxi returning to Ojinaga for $5; ask at the M B store.

If you drive across, check first that your U.S. insurance covers you for travel into the Mexican border area; some U.S. policies, particularly ones issued in Texas, cover you for travel up to twenty miles into Mexico. If your policy does not cover this, you will need to buy insurance (*seguro*) either from the Presidio Information Center, or from a small yellow office next to the duty-free warehouse, or just across the bridge on the right. It costs around $4 for minimum daily coverage.

A convenient aspect about this crossing point is that the bridge and facilities are new, there is little traffic, and little delay; there is a bridge toll of $2 payable on reentry to the United States.

Tourist information and secured overnight parking in Ojinaga are available at Delegación de Transito, near the museum on Hidalgo, one block south of Independencia, if you have not already got all your information in Presidio at the Information Center and Gift Shop, next to the Post

Office, which also sells maps of OJ for $1.00. Open daily from 9 A.M. to 6:00 P.M. (915) 229-4478. OJ telephone code from the United States is 01152-145 + five-digit number.

WHERE TO STAY

If the motels in Presidio are full, or if you are curious to see a bit of Mexico, consider spending the night in Ojinaga.

Motel Ojinaga. This imposing, modern full-service motel stands one-half mile west of the International Bridge. It has eighty rooms, an ambitious restaurant, and a pool. A room for two rents for $40. Phone: 3-01-91 or 3-02-51.

Motel Diana. On Libre Comercio, two miles west of International Bridge. It offers no frills and has quite adequate rooms; the rate is $29 for two. Phone 3-16-45.

Hotel Rohana. In the town center. A good place to stay, where singles are $20.60; doubles are $28.00. It is clean, well managed, and has safe parking.

WHERE TO DRINK

If you want a beer, try the **Bikini Bar,** off the Plaza, a typical drinking place. For a cocktail you might go upscale to the bar at the Hotel Rohana.

WHERE TO EAT

There are two restaurants which are well worth the trip.

La Fogata Steak House, on Calle Juarez. This place offers cabrito (goat) and good steaks in a plain, clean setting. The owner speaks English. Phone: 3-06-04.

Los Comales Grill, on Calle Zaragoza. More upscale, it offers a three-course menu (soup, bass, dessert) for $8. For a splurge, you might try machaca, a very generous chile con queso ($7) for two, followed by a steak ($6–$7) or shrimp.

WHAT TO DO

Once you are in Ojinaga, nothing much is going to happen, since it is not that sort of place. It is an agriculturally oriented working town, with plenty of pick-up trucks, which has not yet geared itself toward tourists; the souvenir shop (Artesanias de Mexico) is a disappointment. Shop in Presidio, Lajitas, or Terlingua.

The dentist trade is flourishing in Ojinaga, as in all border towns, and related to that there are all sorts of prescription and non-prescription drugs available at the pharmacists at much reduced costs, compared to prices in the United States. What is much more rewarding is to go over on Sunday and watch the *paseando*, the ritual of cruising around, of seeing and being seen. (The maximum number of passengers I observed in the back of a pickup was twenty-eight!)

But, if you arrive and there is no special event or paseando taking place, there is still enough to see. Around the *zócalo*, there is the picturesque old mission-style church down at one end and the stately *presidencia* (city hall) along one side. Inside the gates of the presidencia are large striking murals. Walking down a side street across from the church, you will pass in front of the old Guarnición de la Plaza, the former location of the military garrison, and the objective of Pancho Villa and his revolutionary soldiers during the Battle of Ojinaga in 1913. Just around the corner on Zaragoza is a bakery, Panaderia La Francesco, where you can buy Mexican loaves, *bolillos*, straight from the oven. Stand in line with your tray and tongs for handling the hot loaves, sweet empanadas, and other baked goods. There is a small museum attached to a secondary school near the town center, at the corner of Independencia and Hidalgo, and it is open Monday–Friday, 9:00–5:00. The charm of Ojinaga is precisely that it has remained local and unchanged—slightly dated, like an elderly aunt. What is worth seeing is any event (sporting, rodeo, a parade) where the local people are participating. Inquire at the Presidio Information Center, or look in the local paper, to see what is going on.

The Mexican Revolution of 1910 started not far from here, when Father Hidalgo raised his banner of protest. Pancho Villa was later prominent along this part of the border. More recently, a local drug boss, Pablo Acosta, fought a gun battle outside OJ. But today Ojinaga is about as unthreatening a place as you could find. Be sure to get a map before you leave Presidio, and make sure you know where to pick up the shuttle when you are ready to go back.

SERVICES

General information. For tickets for the bus to Chihuahua, or for the Copper Canyon excursion leaving from Presidio, and for car parking ($3 per day), see Stella McKeel, a reputable agent of long standing, in her agency on U.S. 67, opposite the Border Patrol headquarters, near Three Palms Inn. Call (915) 229-3221 for reservations for the bus to Chihuahua. The direct bus, the Presidio-Chihuahua, runs on Monday, Tuesday, Wednesday, Friday, and Saturday, leaves at 1:30 P.M., takes three and a half hours, and costs $11 one way.

Bus. Several buses leave daily from two bus stations for Chihuahua, traveling time three and one-half hours; fares are around $7.50, a little more for the extremely modern Futura buses.

Personal car. If you have driven across in your own vehicle, and if your insurance is good (or you have purchased one-day coverage in Mexico from an agent in Presidio), you might think of a picnic excursion to the spectacular Cañon de Peguis.

Here, fifty minutes along the highway to Chihuahua (Mexican Federal 16) before the Mexican immigration checkpoint when you need a tourist visa, the road winds up to a high point, and far below you can see the green Río Conchos thrusting through the canyon. You can look back to the north, across Ojinaga, and see the water tower of Presidio, a symbol of civic pride, standing tall and white. This is a good spot to picnic and a fast two-lane road to drive.

Closer, about eight miles only from the border bridge, is Presa Tarahumara, a small dam on the Río Conchos that is a favorite for bird-watchers and picnickers. Look for the Presa Tarahumara sign on the Chihuahua City highway, about fifteen minutes from OJ.

EXCURSIONS

Details of this trip to Chihuahua and the remarkable Copper Canyon are offered by many agencies, or you can see it on your own. Getting to Chihuahua from Presidio-Ojinaga is closer and easier than from El Paso–Juárez. The distance is only 147 miles, and the journey takes three and a half hours. See a travel agent or the Presidio Information Center about various trips to Copper Canyon.

Ruidosa and Candelaria

From Presidio, RR 170 takes you northwest for 36 miles to Ruidosa, and from there a 48-mile drive on FM 2810 through Pinto Canyon in the Chinati Mountains will bring you to Marfa. Or, continuing to Candelaria for another 12 miles, you reach the end of the highway. The only way forward from here is a dirt road, which leads to an unofficial fording point of the Rio Grande and a questionable road to Van Horn.

At Ruidosa, if you have come from Marfa and have finished the unpaved section of the road through Pinto Canyon, you can sit outside the general store, have a drink and watch the kids playing in the street. If you are heading towards Marfa, turn to the right immediately after the general store. You then have about 15 miles of gravel road, somewhat steep at times, but manageable by any auto with a normal clearance. There are some creeks to cross, and you pass an abandoned mine and a horse corral, before the road climbs steeply and resumes an asphalt surface as state maintenance begins. It is then 32 miles to Marfa.

If you continue to Candelaria, you will find a quiet, end-of-the-road place with a school and church and a store which is owned by two old ladies. The paved road stops here although it is possible with the right sort of vehicle to continue on a gravel road to Van Horn; the border patrol and the people they are chasing are the main users of this stretch. In Candelaria the main attraction is the footbridge across the Rio Grande. Here, it is less than fifteen paces across, a not very wide expanse of the Rio Grande. This is because almost all of the water has been dammed or diverted far upstream from El Paso in New Mexico, and the Rio Grande remains little more than a stream until the Río Conchos flows into it farther downstream, just before Presidio. Crossing the footbridge and walking a little less than a mile along a dirt road will bring you to a sleepy Mexican village little changed over the years. But tread carefully here, figuratively speaking. This whole border area is rife with smuggling activity, and discretion is the best attitude to have.

Shafter and Cibolo Creek Ranch

Eighteen miles north of Presidio on U.S. 67 is the former mining town of Shafter. In its heyday in the early 1900s, three hundred men worked in the silver mine and ten times that number lived in the town, which was the richest place in Texas. For sixty years the community prospered, a lively place after work hours when the Irish and Mexican workers patronized the saloons and the brothel.

But, in the early 1940s, "that Friday in 1941," as the local people called it, events changed abruptly, as often happens in the mining industry. The price of silver fell and pockets of water were discovered underground. The labor force also started to organize itself. These factors, all developing at the same time, led to a sudden decision by the company to close down the mines.

Silver remains in the ground, and when the price reaches fifteen dollars per ounce, it will become economically feasible to pump the water out of the miles of tunnels and restart mining. Until that time, Shafter is likely to remain very quiet, a near ghost town with a population of around forty, with a lovely creek flowing through it and the Three Sisters Mountains behind.

There is little sign from the highway of anything going on, and in fact nothing much is. But, it is still worth a detour to get the feel, more easily than at Terlingua where reconstruction has begun, of what was previously an active mining town with a vigorous life of its own. Turning off the highway, you will pass the prominent Sacred Heart Catholic Church, effectively floodlit at night, which has been restored and was rededicated in 1990 on its centennial. It is clean and carpeted, with a high wood ceiling. Next to it is the post office, open for two hours daily.

Farther on, next to Cibolo Creek, there is an RV Park, quiet but apparently in business. Full hookups are $12, tent sites are $5. Across the creek, after pausing at a curious number of Stop or Yield signs, one arrives at the Shafter Memorial and the extensive graveyard. The Memorial, a historical pictorial display, takes the form of a red-roofed display stand, with notice boards on each side detailing the history of the town through its principal families. There are pictures of tennis games in the old days and of early pioneer Anita Brooks Hughes at the age of 104.

There is a pleasant, forgotten feel to Shafter, at least to the visitor; the history of the place is all around, and the winds of change have not yet blown much economic improvement to the community. For the locals, the closing down of the cafe on the highway and then the store may have been a blow. But, since most of them work in Presidio, the quiet and relative coolness of the place may be compensation enough. It is a great place to stop for a while, take a stroll around, cross the creek, and look at the pictures of life in earlier, more prosperous times.

FORT CIBOLO

Nine miles farther north on U.S. 67, and well into the mountains, is an entrance gate to the restored Fort Cibolo. Here, at the end of a comfortable 5-mile gravel road, rising like a fortified village, and outlined against the stony mountainside, is the meticulously rebuilt and refurbished adobe headquarters of the Faver Ranch, a memorial to larger-than-life pioneer Milton Faver (called respectively by the Spanish title "Don"), who dominated the area and his times.

It reads, "Of the many colorful characters listed in the early history of Texas, none of them rank[s] higher than Milton Faver. His life was not only an eventful one, but was made more intriguing because of the veil of mystery that defied penetration to the very end. Occasionally the winds of chance lifted it up, for a hurried peep on his early life, and this served to further excite the imagination and add zest to the romance."

Milton Favor, or Don Meliton, "Lord of the Three Manors," as he was known to his Mexican workers, was small in size but larger than life. His background was as obscure as his lifestyle was independent. He married a Mexican woman, employed only Mexicans as soldiers, and established, in the 1850s, the first Anglo American owned ranch in Big Bend. His tomb is on a hill overlooking Fort Cibolo, and the epitaph, including the exact hour of his death, is in Spanish.

Much about this man's life is intriguing. Rumors about him were rampant—was he a fugitive from justice in Independence, Missouri? what was his background (possibly English stock)? And did his unusual formality of receiving visitors at the fort indicate an old-world lifestyle? Despite his eccentricities, he was certainly a successful businessman. After an earlier and profitable career in the freight business in Chihuahua, he arrived in the Big Bend and purchased three ranches, all with good

water sources (Cibolo, Cienega, and La Mora). His stock increased to twenty thousand head of cattle, plus thousands of sheep and goats. He sold the cattle and fruit from his peach orchards to Fort Davis. In the hot, desolate countryside below the Chinati Mountains, he built a veritable fortified headquarters, with three- to four-foot-thick and twenty-foot-high adobe walls, circular watch towers with gun positions and heavy gates which could be barred against Indian attackers. So independent and powerful did he become that he was "almost a nation to himself," said the *Fort Worth Star Telegram* in 1893. He refused to ride the train and would disappear on horseback for days or weeks at a time. He died, a mysterious old man with a long white beard,

Cholla, Opuntia ibricata. *By Elva Stewart.*

on December 23, 1889. His adventurous spirit and wide-ranging interests matched well the country in which he lived.

John Poindexter, a Houston businessman, fascinated by the story and achievement of Faver's life, bought the Cibolo Ranch, (and the two adjoining ranches, La Cienega and La Marita) four years ago and set about rebuilding them accurately, down to the last detail. A researcher was hired to study the written records, and the surviving elderly people who had worked at the ranch were brought in to confirm the restoration. Square nails like those used in the late 1800s were made for the rebuilding project. A peach orchard was planted since Faver had grown peaches, shipped the fruit to the soldiers, and made peach brandy.

At the entrance to the fort, a museum has been created. Every document and book owned by or about Milton Faver has been collected for the library. Antiques from Mexico have been bought to furnish the dining room, and the oil paintings are originals. A tiny chapel with a Mexican altar offers a cool and quiet sanctuary. During excavation and rebuilding, great care was taken to protect the original structure, and the old adobe wall and foundations have been exposed. A collection of arrowheads can also be viewed.

The restored fort, now operating as Cibolo Creek Ranch, is open to the public and has been appointed one of the Small Luxury Hotels of the World. Rates run from around $325 per person per day (single) to $470 double for a deluxe room. Included in the price are: pickup from Alpine, three gourmet meals, free beverages (alcoholic and nonalcoholic), swimming at the ranch, horseback riding, and a vehicle tour of the ranch. The same rates apply to La Cienega, the sister ranch. A 10 percent service charge and state sales tax needs to be added to these prices. The quality of the accommodations, the dining experience, and the all-important activities are described in the handsome brochure, *Cibolo Creek Ranch, a Texas Legacy.* A highlight each year is the annual Trail Ride, open to the anyone with $800–$1,200 to spend on the event (the price depends on whether or not you supply your own horse), which leaves from Marfa in late June and arrives at Cibolo Creek Ranch on July 4. For information on this unique ranch, call (915) 358-4696 or 1-800-525-4800.

Study Butte and Terlingua

Located at the junction of Texas 118 and RR 170, about 3 miles from the west entrance to Big Bend National Park, Study Butte offers the visitor motel and RV accommodations, fuel, restaurants, groceries, souvenir shopping, and information. Also available are trail rides (horse or wagon) and river trips.

Named for early miner Will Study (pronounced "Stewdy"), the Study Butte Mine was located behind the present Study Butte Store. Today's Study Butte presents a half-finished appearance. Buildings are scattered here and there, some painted an odd color, others partially built.

Terlingua Ghost Town is located 4 miles west of Study Butte on RR 170. It is an area undergoing change, but in this case, a change planned by the sole owner. It is an area of extensive deposits of cinnabar, a red stone containing mercury, which was mined between 1900 and 1942. Places of interest include the old cemetery, protected mine shafts, and the restored theater-restaurant. While here, tourists may visit a landmark restaurant and night club, a first-rate gift shop, a river-trip outfitter and tour organizer, and a useful daytime eatery.

Behind this simple listing of the origins and current services of these two side-by-side communities lies a much more interesting story of alternative lifestyles and the nonconformist people who lead them. Between the huge, open spaces of the Big Bend National Park, and the nearly as huge spaces of the Big Bend Ranch State Natural Area, and not too far from the resort of Lajitas, exists this mixture of folk who regard Alpine as a big city and relish their different way of life.

The people attracted to this area of striking scenery, low population, and few regulations are artists, boat people who guide the rafts on the river, and those who simply find the lifestyle such a pleasant relief from the big city that they will put up with a lack of amenities. Many of the residents live in simple fashion, some in the remains of the buildings in the ghost town, and earn their living by selling their art or working in the tourist business.

WHERE TO STAY

Motels

Big Bend Motor Inn, at the interesection of Hwys. 118 and 170. 1-800-848-BEND or (915) 371-2218. This seven-year-old inn has forty-five rooms, of standard comfort and adequate taste. There is a small pool. Advance booking is recommended and at busy times, essential. This is the most modern motel in the area and includes TVs in the rooms. Doubles are $63.55, including tax. Meals can be taken at the cafe next door, also owned by the motel.

Mission Lodge. Across the highway from Big Bend Motor Inn, 1-800-848-BEND or (915) 371-2555. This newer, four-year-old lodge, with thirty-six rooms, is owned by the Motor Inn. There is nothing much in either of these two motels to keep you in your room or on the premises. But they are strategically sited and adequately managed. A double is $52.95. A TV is included in the rooms and you have use of the pool at the Motor Inn.

Chisos Mining Company and the **Easter Egg Motel.** Both located a mile further on the highway towards Terlingua, (915) 371-2254. This older, prefabricated property has twenty-four rooms that are small but clean, but the prices are low. Cabins are also available for longer rentals. A double is $35, plus tax.

Further north on Texas 118 (33 miles) are more pleasant, if isolated, new motel accommodations: **Longhorn Ranch Motel** (12 miles); **Terlingua Ranch,** with thirty-two cabins 16 miles off the highway; and Wildhorse Station, 6 miles north, with three furnished mountain cabins, each sleeping four to eight persons. For more information on these three alternatives, see Chapter 4, "Texas 118."

The only other accommodations in the area are within the park or in Lajitas.

RV Parks and Camping

Big Bend Travel Park. 1.5 miles west of Study Butte, (915) 371-2250. Forty-nine well-shaded spots are down by the creek; the rate is $10 for full hookup. A laundry is available and they also have showers (25¢ per minute). Tent camping costs $2. The subterranean La Kiva restaurant is located within the campground.

B J's. 2 miles further west on RR 170, (915) 371-2259. It has the lowest rates—$8 for a full hookup, with a recreation room and showers, but without shade covers.

Terlingua Oasis RV Park. In the rear of the Big Ben Motor Inn, 1-800-848-BEND or (915) 371-2218. Its sites have partial shade. Full hookup is $12.50 for two people. There are twelve two-person cabins that rent for $18.50 each. Tent sites (six) are $10.00 for two and $2.00 for each additional person. Use of the pool and showers is included. The cafe and grocery are nearby.

Study Butte RV Park. Next to Study Butte Mall, (915) 371-2404. Charge is $8 for hookup, showers available.

Ocotillo Mesa RV Park. Six miles north of Study Butte, off Texas 118,

1-800-729-1406. This is a plain-vanilla site, with no showers and no rest-rooms. Check in is at Wildhorse Station. A full hookup is $10. Drive three-quarters of a mile from Texas 118 on a good road. There is a walk from the RV park up to the saddle in the mountains which affords a remarkable panoramic view.

SERVICES

Half a mile from Study Butte on RR 170 is the post office, with a useful bulletin board outside. The *Terlingua Moon*, the local newsletter, can be picked up here. One mile farther on the left is the new Big Bend Family Health Clinic.

WHERE TO EAT

Starlight Theater. In the Terlingua ghost town, (915) 371-2326. This relatively new arrival gets the awards for enterprise, imagination, and style. Converting an old movie theater, which had become a roofless refuse dump, into a stylish and fun eating place and night club took some courage, and it has been enormously successful. What you find when you enter is a long room preserving the original adobe walls, with the modern additions of pastel-colored tablecloths, a high ceiling with rotating fans, and a colorful central bar, above which are suspended some cattle horns. At the far end, where the screen previously hung, Angie Dean, owner and manager, had the brilliant idea of putting a mural of a stage across the whole wall, with curtains on each side, local characters in the foreground, and a landscape behind.

The menu offers a good variety of main courses (a "feature presentation") chicken, steak (including the sixteen-ounce T-bone), chiles rellenos and a burger ($5–$15), all with potatoes, salad, and tortillas. The fresh salads are a welcome part of the meal. There are weekly specials: tortilla soup ($3.50) on Sunday, Mexican special ($6.50) on Monday, chicken street tacos ($6.50) on Thursday, shrimp Mexicana ($8.75) on Friday, and pork chop chipotle ($8.75) on Saturday. The restaurant is open nightly from 5:30 to 9:00; the bar does business until midnight, later on week-ends, and there are frequent events and music. This is a pleasant surprise for visitors, and a great place to meet the locals standing at the well-stocked bar. There is a regular supply of first-rate, live music by such locals groups as Just Us Girls (see "Music in the Big Bend").

Terlingua Cafe. In Terlingua ghost town, (915) 371-2465. Comple-menting the evenings-only Starlight Theater is the daytime-only Terlingua Cafe specializing in North Mexican cuisine. There are some fine views over the old mine workings and across to the Chisos Mountains in the national park; this restaurant has been taken in hand, enlarged, and upgraded by Pat Brown, whose previous experience as a chef and as a river rafting businessman makes him well suited for this spot. Breakfasts (6:00 A.M. to 5:00 P.M.) prominently feature traditional egg breakfasts, breakfast burritos (design your own), and some fancy options, like hangtown fry, the condemned man's last request. For lunch, there are salads, burgers, more substantial plates, Texas traditions, enchiladas, liver and onions, and locally popular pan-fried oysters. Sunday brunch is popular, with the option of champagne to lift morale and sometimes a jazz ensemble to listen to.

La Kiva. In the shady RV park down by the creek 1.5 miles west of Study Butte, (915) 371-2250. La Kiva has been around a long time and is a different sort of surprise. Partly underground, it is modeled after an Indian kiva. Exposed rock, gnarled wood fixtures, Indian chairs, bone door handles, copper basins in the restrooms, an outside patio, and a solid looking bar make this cave-like fantasy a lot of fun. Steaks are the main feature (eight-ounce filet mignon, $9.50), a veggie plate ($3.50), and barbecued chicken (a half-chicken, $6.00). Open from 5:00 P.M. daily. An extra attraction is the Romantic Evening Package for two persons for $50, which involves two steak filet dinners, a bottle of wine or champagne, and the use of the hot tub. Call for reservations.

Desert Opry. Opposite La Kiva, 1.5 miles on RR 170 west of Study Butte, (915) 371-2265. This vegetarian cafe and art studio has live original music. This is a creative place, and the whole family of owners plays guitars, while Alice sings her own songs as well as plays. She also paints, and the walls display some of her portraits and other paintings; there are also pots and rugs for sale, and a mix of Mexican and Indian items. The food is tasty (pizza, vegetarian chili, and much more). Open from November through May only.

Road Runner Deli. At Study Butte Mall, (915) 371-2364. This sophisticated, gourmet eatery and take-away is a welcome addition to the food scene. The coffee is particularly good, freshly ground and made with distilled water, with a different blend featured daily. The sandwiches are generous, with a good choice of breads, and lots of salad ingredients, in addition to the choice of meat. The kitchen is spotless, the menu imaginative, and some of the dishes are exotic. Tabouli salad ($1.50), Indonesian rice salad, quiche, or large pastrami sandwich ($4.50), bagel with cream cheese ($1.50), and raspberry chiffon pie ($2.50). Consistency and creativity are the key, and locals and visitors alike seem to go for it. Breakfast, in particular, is becoming popular. Open 7:00 A.M.–3:30 P.M. daily.

Long Draw Saloon. On RR 170, 3 miles from Study Butte, (915) 371-2608. Pizzas, made on the premises, are available here. They are open seven days, 5:00 to 10:00 P.M. The pizzas come in two sizes, twelve or sixteen inches. Among the popular ones are the six-shooter (six toppings, twelve inches, $9.95) and the Pancho Villa (sausage and jalapeños, $8.95).

SHOPPING

At or near the Junction of Texas 118 and RR 170

Gas and groceries are available at Study Butte Mall and at the Big Bend Motor Inn. There is also a laundry next to the Motor Inn.

Study Butte Mall has ice, beer, Gloria's Last Chance liquor store, groceries, and a book exchange (behind the store). There's a rock shop further along on Texas 118, and on the same side of the road the **Desert Dragon Gator Farm,** where you can donate towards the food for the caged alligators, as well as getting a whole lot of information about 'gators, which may cause you to change your mind about them. There are also Paleontology Tours to fossil excavation sites. (915) 371-2499 or 371-2455.

In Terlingua is **Bill Ivey's store.** The Ivey family own the ghost town and are in the process of restoring it. The most recent success was the Starlight Theater, the next and greater challenge will be the Perry house, to be converted into a bed-and-breakfast. The store is large, well laid out and packed with goods. Beer, postcards, and T-shirts all sell well. But there is also an excellent book section, a large quicksilver jewelry gallery, the Dos Amigos Art Gallery, and all sorts of Mexican and Indian items. Raft rentals (do-it-yourself, with no guide) can be arranged here for $15 per person per day, with an extra charge for putting the raft into the river. Visiting this store is a must. (915) 371-2424.

WHAT TO DO

Try **river rafting.** At the junction of the two highways (Texas 118 and 170) is Outback Expeditions, a river rafting company. Far Flung Adventures is located in Terlingua. Big Bend River Tours, the third company, has its office on the boardwalk in Lajitas. Texas River Expeditions, the newest arrival, has its office in the Study Butte Mall opposite Outback Expeditions. See Chapter 4, "River Trip Outfitters," for a description of the various river trips available.

At the "Y" (junction of the highways), in a small line of shops, is Turquoise Trail Riders, who offer hourly accompanied **trail rides** around the mine area for $10–$15 per hour, depending on the length. There are also chuck wagon suppers, half- and full-day trips, and overnight horse trips. These are thoughtfully planned and carefully guided trips. There are bicycle rentals for $15.00 (4 hours) and $25.00 (8 hours). Before deciding which trip to take, read through the sheet "Description of our hourly rides." You will get more value for your dollar if you choose to take a longer ride, such as the Payne's Waterhole Excursion, where you will see numerous cave paintings, hidden pools of water, and a petrified skeleton of an ancient fish. This ride takes five to six hours and costs $66. Call (915) 371-2212 or 1-800-TTRIDE-1 for reservations.

INFORMATION

Jacque's Creations at the "Y" offers shirts, shorts, hats, hand-crafted items, and jewelry; but they also offer all sorts of sensible travel advice, and can make river and other bookings. Call (915) 371-2370.

SERVICES

Shuttle. The Big Bend Shuttle Service offers to pick you up from Alpine, or anywhere else, and bring you to Study Butte, Terlingua, or Lajitas. Or they will take you to the river and take you out, with your own raft or canoe and using your own vehicle or not. For more details, see Chapter 1, "How to Get There—Shuttle," or Chapter 4, "River Trip Outfitters." 1-800-729-2860 or (915) 371-2523.

Guide. Bill Bourbon, a weathered, knowing man, is a geologist, birder, and former park ranger. He is the first to suggest that as many people as possible should take the free interpretive services (guided walks, slides shows, talks) offered by the park service. Bill says, "A great deal for nothing"—all are free. A weekly list of talks and walks is posted throughout the park. He also recommends the seminars put on by the Big Bend Natural History Association, ranging from $20 for a half-day up to $338 for four days, including lodging.

Sometimes, usually because of timing, the dates of these activities are not suitable for the visitor. That is the time to call on the services of Bill, who can make all the difference in the world in interpreting what you see or, more probably, what you may miss without his expert guidance. He may suggest that a half-day river trip is not enough time after the journey to the put-in point, to "weave the web of the interactions between the lushness of the riverside, and the dryness of the desert."

"Let the country speak to you," he says, and he offers to be the interpreter. At $150 a day, the price for this knowledgeable and good-humored interpreter (he works regularly with tour groups and on the seminar program) is a bargain. He gives tours by appointment only; call (915) 371-2202. If you are undecided on your overall plans and have no accommodations booked, Bill will take care of the accommodations, as well as provide the guide service.

Other services: Big Bend Touring Society Guided tours of individuals or groups: history, geology, flora, fauna, archeology; Sam Richardson (915) 371-2548; Desert Walker Guide Service Hiking and Backpacking Guides; Step-on Guides for Park Tours (915) 371-2533.

Van Horn

Situated 121 miles east of El Paso, and 47 miles from where I-20 joins I-10, Van Horn (population 3,102) is a busy place. The 17 area motels provide 526 beds, the 3 RV parks offer 154 sites, and there are 20 restaurants. Most of these services, plus gas stations, are found along West and East Broadway, the 2-mile strip that parallels the interstate. The services offered are for the I-10 travelers, numbering 8,000 vehicles and 20 Greyhound buses daily. Van Horn is also at the crossroads of the Texas Mountain Trail.

The town's name comes from Lt. James Judson Van Horn, who was in command of the U.S. Army garrison at the nearby Van Horn Wells when he was taken prisoner and held for two years by Confederate forces. When a town was founded twenty years later, in 1881, they named it after the lieutenant.

It might have been more appropriately named Van Horne, since Maj. Jefferson Van Horne reportedly discovered the wells, located twelve miles south of the town. The wells had undoubtedly been known to the Indians for centuries, and since water was so vital in the early days of pioneering, a community inevitably developed here to serve the railroad.

INFORMATION

The first stop for anyone requiring tourist information should be the Convention Center and Visitor's Bureau at 1801 West Broadway, open

8:00 A.M. to 5:00 P.M., Monday through Saturday. Pick up the useful *Visitor's Guide*. Their telephone number is (915) 283-2682.

HOW TO GET THERE

Van Horn is well served by Greyhound Bus Lines. There are numerous daily westbound buses, and the eastbound schedule goes to Dallas, San Antonio, and Houston. One bus daily goes south and east to Marfa, Alpine, and Del Rio. The closest airport is in El Paso (120 miles away), where there are also various car rental companies.

WHERE TO STAY

A wide variety of prices between the high teens and the high thirties to low forties exists in accommodations, which for the most part, are strictly functional. The old Clark Hotel is now a museum, and the impressive-looking former El Capitan Hotel is now a bank.

Motels
Room rates for this group of motels are $30–$40, plus tax, for two persons:
Best Western American Inn. 1309 West Broadway, (915) 283-2030. Has pool.
Best Western Inn of Van Horn. 1705 West Broadway, (915) 283-2410. Pool, club, and restaurant.
Comfort Inn. 1601 West Broadway, (915) 283-2211. Has pool.
Days Inn. 600 East Broadway, (915) 283-2401. Pool, club, and restaurant.
Friendship Inn. 1805 West Broadway, (915) 283-2992. Has pool.
Super 8. 1807 West Frontage Road, (915) 283-2282. Van Horn's newest motel; next to McDonald's.
Howard Johnson Lodge. 200 Golf Course Road, (915) 283-2780. Van Horn's largest, with 98 rooms, pool, club, and restaurant.
Room rates for these motels vary between $20 and $30:
Country Inn. 1201 West Broadway, (915) 283-2225. Has pool.
Economy Inn. 1500 West Broadway, (915) 283-2754.
Freeway Motel. 502 Van Horn Drive, (915) 283-2939.
Sands Motel. 805 East Broadway, (915) 283-9247.
Seven Kay Motel. 1303 West Broadway, (915) 283-2019.
Sun Valley Motel. 901 West Broadway, (915) 283-2259. "A very nice medium price hotel," claims the sign outside. With a pool, thoughtfully provided tepees for shade, an owner who doesn't mind giving his opinion

on where to eat, an attractive exterior, their sign seems like a reasonable claim.

Village Inn. 403 West Broadway, (915) 283-2286.

Room rates for this group are up to $20:

Bell's Motel. 401 East Broadway, (915) 283-9030. On the east side of town.

Gateway Lodge. 1403 West Broadway, (915) 283-9210.

Royal Motel. 300 East Broadway, (915) 283-2087.

Taylor Motel. 900 West Broadway, (915) 283-2266.

RV Parks

Eagle's Nest. 1701 West Broadway, (915) 283-2420. In the middle of town, with a very visible sign, it has forty-six all-gravel shaded sites and a pool. Discounts are available at Phillip's 66. Rates are $12.50, with $1.00 off for AAA and AARP.

El Campo. 404 East Broadway, (915) 283-2427. On the east side of town, it has forty-eight sites and includes a laundry and showers. Rates are $11.10, with a 10 percent discount to club members.

K.O.A. U.S. 90 and Kamper Lane, (915) 283-2728. Set back from I-10, it has grassy sites and views across to the mountains. There is a pool, game room, and laundry. Rates are $12.50, with 10 percent off to club members.

WHERE TO EAT

Smokehouse Restaurant. 905 West Broadway, (915) 283-2453. Mitch and Glenda Van Horn not only run a full-scale restaurant but also offer the visitor the chance to visit (free) their Classic Car Museum in the same building (fifteen immaculately restored automobiles from the 1920s to 1960s), and read their informative and entertaining *Smokehouse News* (25¢). Not surprisingly, the Smokehouse special ($7.95), a combination plate of smoked brisket, ham, and sausage, with all the extras, is a highlight. It is open from 6:00 A.M. and is closed on Sundays. In addition to the variety on the menu, the walls of the restaurant are well covered with baseball and football memorabilia, another room has an air force motif, and the third one has household knickknacks all over.

Papa Chuy's Spanish Inn. 1200 West Broadway, (915) 283-2066. Papa Chuy's ads greet you coming from the highway: "Praise the Lord," or, if you have driven too far, they tell you so. Patio dining is offered along with the choice of smoking or nonsmoking sections inside. Outside a large sign reads, "John Madden Haul of Fame," recognizing the contribution of the hefty football announcer towards the restaurant's recognition by his compliments in *Time* magazine. Nineteen special Mexican dishes are the main attractions: three beef tacos ($4.10), three rolled enchiladas ($5.95), gorditas (two thick corn patties filled with meat and avocado) and machaca (chopped beef cooked with fried vegetables and cheese sauce, with beans and rice), chile verde plate ($6.10) and fajitas ($7.25). They are open 9:00 A.M.–10:00 P.M.

Toni's Place Cafe. 511 Rivas Street, (915) 283-2132. Although it lacks the high visibility of Papa Chuy's or the other West Broadway restaurants, this family-run Mexican restaurant offers food which has been pleasing the locals for twenty-one years. The favorite dish is the chile con carne plate ($5), and the menu includes all the usual Mexican dishes. Open Tuesday through Sunday from 11:00 A.M. to 8:00 P.M. No food is cooked until the customer orders it.

Westerner Restaurant. 1703 West Broadway, (915) 283-2249. It features a salad bar ($4.95), smothered burrito ($4.95), chiles rellenos plate ($5.95), pork chop ($5.95), and chicken-fried steak ($6.95). It is open from 6:00 A.M. to 10:00 P.M. daily. You will find good food, no hoopla.

Van Horn Cattle Company. Behind the Westerner Restaurant, 1703 W. Broadway, (915) 283-9902. The most stylish restaurant in town is also the newest. Tastefully decorated in Southwestern style with a view through large windows towards the mountains, the restaurant is open from 5:00 P.M. to 11:00 P.M., Monday through Saturday; the bar is open until midnight, and it is also open for lunch on Saturday. Prime rib and rib eye steak are popular, and so is the lemon pepper chicken. The stylish interior includes a long bar, and one side of the restaurant looks out over a pool.

Inside the motels are the Flamingo Restaurant and Pizza Palace at Days Inn and the Chaparral Restaurant (Sunday buffet) at the Plaza Inn. Chain restaurants are Dairy Queen, McDonald's, and Pizza Hut. For Mexican, try Los Pinos on U.S. 90, and Rosa's and Chemo's in town.

WHAT TO DO

There is not a great deal to do in Van Horn; in fact, the main service the town has to offer is to offer supplies to travelers passing through. The dozen reasons to stay in Van Horn listed in the Chamber's *Visitor's Guide* reads a bit thin, but the **Culberson County Historical Museum,** in the former Clark's Hotel, has a fine old saloon bar and is worth a brief visit. 210 Broadway. Open: 9:00–12:00 and 2:00–5:00 Monday, Tuesday, Wednesday, and Friday.

There is also an interesting new shop, **Los Nopales** (Prickly Pear), at 1106 West Broadway, next to Chuy's Restaurant. On sale here are antiques and collectibles, eclectic folk art, and desert plants. They are open 6:00 to 8 P.M. daily. Call (915) 283-2923.

The nine-hole **golf course** charges $5 for green fees and $7 for a cart. There is no waiting in line here, but there are great views of the mountains and some fresh clean air at 4,100 feet elevation. See Chapter 4, "Golf Courses of the Big Bend Area," for a description of the course.

To the north of Van Horn are the **Sierra Diablo Mountains.** Here in 1881, in the Vitorio Canyon, the last Indian battle was fought. A party of eighteen rangers followed and surprised a band of Apaches, whose leader, Vitorio, had been killed in Mexico the year before. This was also the last battle in the State of Texas.

Van Horn takes pride in the fact that it was designated by the Texas Department of Transportation as the **"Crossroads of the Texas Mountain Trail."** Indeed, it is the only spot where the trail crosses itself in the 925-mile figure-eight loop which takes in, at its extremities, Big Bend National Park and El Paso. Page six of the Van Horn *Visitor's Guide* suggests a four-day breakdown of the whole itinerary. There is so much ground to cover and so many varied sights to see that only those with very little time who never intend to return to this area should try to do this whole circuit in such a short time. Better to spend eight days doing the whole loop, or do half the circuit one year and the other half at a later date. GMC Truck has done a reprint of an article that appeared in *Texas Monthly* (August, 1991), entitled "Texas Mountain Trail." It is a high-quality printing job with a mass of facts and an excellent map. Your GMC Truck dealer may have a copy.

EVENTS

January	Culberson County Livestock Show
June	Frontier Days and Rodeo Celebration
August	Eagle Mountain Bluegrass Festival
November–December	Trans-Pecos Big Buck Tournament (deer hunting)

Whites City

Shortly after leaving Carlsbad on U.S. 62/180, thirty signs, one after the other on the roadside, advertise the delights and services of Whites City.

An additional five larger signs reinforce the message shortly before arrival. On arrival, the traveler finds that the entrance to Carlsbad Caverns is a gimmicky, touristy, company town with high prices and few redeeming features. The staff, all of whom wear Whites City shirts, are pleasant and helpful, but the overall impression is one of crass commercialism on the doorstep of one of the natural wonders of North America. The whole development, owned by the White family (unrelated to the family of the original discoverer Jim White), is stretched along a few hundred yards of both sides of the highway, which turns off U.S. 62/180 towards the park.

HOW TO GET THERE

Whites City is 20 miles southeast of Carlsbad, New Mexico, on U.S. 62/180. The entrance to Carlsbad Caverns is a further 9 miles from Whites City.

Bus. There are three daily buses leaving from Carlsbad at 4:40 A.M., 10:50 A.M., and 11:15 A.M., each taking thirty minutes. Buses leave El Paso at 3:00 A.M., 1:45 P.M., and 7:25 P.M., taking two hours and fifty minutes to reach Whites City, passing by the Guadalupe National Park entrance en route. The Whites City stop and the Guadalupe National Park stop are flag stops. Call the bus line to confirm the times. In Carlsbad, the telephone number is (505) 887-1108. In El Paso, the number is (915) 532-2365.

For those arriving by bus at Whites City, there is a twice daily shuttle to the caverns, departing around 8:00 A.M. and 11:00 A.M., and returning late afternoon. The cost is $15 for up to three persons, then $5 per person thereafter. Inquire about times and reservations at the Tourist Information counter in the souvenir shop at Whites City.

WHERE TO STAY

For reservations and information the following accommodations and camping, contact Best Western, 17 Carlsbad Caverns Highway, Box 128, Whites City, NM 88268, or call 1-800-CAVERNS.

Best Western Cavern Inn. Southwestern decor, with a pool and spa. Sixty-three units, which also feature Jacuzzi tubs, have rooms with two queen beds from $60–$75 from May through September, and $50–$65 for the rest of the year, single or double.

Best Western Guadalupe Inn. Also Southwestern decor, pool, and spa. Forty-two rooms, with two queen or one king-size bed for the same rates and for the same periods as the Cavern Inn. Both inns have

Aerial view of domes. Photo by Frank Armstrong. Courtesy McDonald Observatory.

Top: *El Capitan, Guadalupe National Park. Photo by Peter Marbach.*
Bottom: *Sierra del Carmen. Photo by Charles Bell.*

Top: *Mule Ears Peak. Photo by Charles Bell.*
Bottom: *Coyote at Big Bend National Park. Photo by Peter Marbach.*

Santa Elena Canyon on the Rio Grande. Photo by Blair Pittman.

South Rim, Chisos Mountains. Photo by Charles Bell.

View from the end of Lost Mine Trail, showing the edge of the South Rim on the right and Elephant Tusk Mountain in the background. Photo by Blair Pittman.

Top: *View of the Chisos. Photo by Blair Pittman.*
Bottom: *Sunset on the Rio Grande. Chisos Mountains in the background. Photo by Charles Bell.*

A rainbow spans the mountains of Big Bend. Photo by Blair Pittman.

nonsmoking rooms. In each case, an extra person costs $6. Tax is extra, and there are no discounts for seniors.

Walnut Canyon Inn. This older motel, with twenty-five rooms, is used when the first two places are full. Prices are $50–$60, year-round, single or double, with pool and spa privileges.

Hostel and Camping

For those carrying American Youth Hostel or International Hostel cards, there are accommodations in six-bed **dormitories** for $9.00 a night, plus tax.

An **RV Park and tent camping,** with pool and spa privileges, is $15.00–$20.00 per vehicle or $2.50 per person, plus tax. A 10 percent discount is available for AAA or Good Sam members.

WHERE TO EAT

Fast Jack's. It promises breakfast, lunch, and dinner—"Always Fast, Always Good." It is clean and efficient. A hamburger (one-quarter pound) is $3.49; a BLT, $2.95; three tacos, $3.95; chef's salad, $3.95; carrot cake, $1.50.

Velvet Garter Restaurant and Saloon. Offers one-half chicken for $7.95; trout, $8.95; fajitas, $8.95; rib eye steak, $10.95; and prime rib (eight ounces), $9.95, (ten ounces), $11.95.

WHAT TO DO

There are three gift shops on the same side of the street, **Patti's Western Collectibles, Scott's Indian Jewelry and Pottery,** and the **Green Turtle** for gifts, miniatures, and collectibles.

On the other side of the street, where all the accommodation reservations are made, there is a post office, a grocery store with high prices, a gift shop with the usual T-shirts, and some unusual items like Chilean rain sticks (bamboo sticks filled with pebbles, which give the impression of running water when tilted); the gift shop attendants are very helpful with tourist advice.

Next, there is an **arcade** with a shooting range, and game machines. After that is the twelve-room **museum** filled with thirty thousand items, ranging from cars, guns, dolls, Western memorabilia, and six-thousand-year-old mummified Indians. Admission is $2.50 for adults, $2.00 for seniors, and $1.50 for children, age six through twelve.

Of more creative interest, and appealing perhaps as a novelty to kids during the evening after a visit to the caverns, is a melodrama at **Granny's Opera House.** Carol Modrall and her fellow actors put on a one-and-a-half-hour production called *The Fatal Necklace, or Dastardly Deeds and Dire Consequences.* Shows are nightly during the summer, otherwise when there is sufficient demand (an audience of twenty is needed). You are encouraged to "cheer the hero, boo and hiss the villain!" Admission is $5.50 for adults, $3.50 for children under twelve. You must have reservations, so call (505) 785-2291 or 1-800-CAVERNS.

Chapter 4

◆

Special Features and Flavors

The Big Bend area is an interesting stew of spicy flavors, music, characters, and sights. Here are just a few samples to whet your appetite.

Chili Cook-Off

If you have an interest in attending Terlingua's annual chili cook-offs in early November, an event that draws up to 10,000 visitors, be advised that since 1983 there are two of them, neither of them in the old ghost town.

One is called the "Annual Original Frank X. Tolbert-Wick Fowler Memorial Championship Chili Cook-Off" and is held "behind the store," meaning the store on RR 170 (between Study Butte and Lajitas) operated by Arturo and Carolina White. Tolbert and Fowler (both since deceased) were prime instigators of the original cook-off.

The other cook-off is run by the Chili Appreciation Society International (C.A.S.I.) and is called the "Terlingua International Chili Championship." The organization has purchased its own site, off RR 170, several miles west of White's store.

The split came about in 1982 over entrance qualifications for the contending chili cooks. Tolbert vowed to start his own chili cook-off the next year, which he did. He also sought the legal right to trademark the name Chili Appreciation Society International but did not live to see it awarded to the opposition party.

Today the C.A.S.I. contingent has grown to perhaps five times the number who attend the more traditional group and is a lot more strict about a cook's qualifications. All cooks at the Terlingua event must already have qualified in a local cook-off—of which there are now hundreds around the state and even farther afield.

A visitor to a recent Tolbert-Fowler Cook-off noted that the entrance fee was $10.00, the atmosphere was very down-home and casual, visitors for the whole three days spent the nights in tents or trailers, and a great deal of beer was consumed. In addition to the actual cooking and tasting, there was a theme or skit connected to each of the competitor's cooking efforts, music to listen to, and a ladies' Wet T-shirt Contest to watch.

Pick your group, or sample chili from both. Well-known folks and esteemed locals have been associated with both cook-offs as cooks and judges and as participants. You may want to do your homework before you go there by reading Joe Nick Patoski's article "Chili Relations" in the November, 1992, issue of *Texas Monthly* and also Kirby F. Warnock's article in his *Big Bend Quarterly* in the fall of 1990. Or read Frank X. Tolbert's *A Bowl of Red*, whose first edition (1953) was partly responsible for it all.

The following is reproduced from *The Desert Candle*, a free bimonthly newspaper of the region, and provides more information about this spicy event:

> One of the well-known folks and esteemed locals referred to above offered his brief comments on the event where he was a judge. 'The wilder boozy excesses of earlier years had now been largely contained due to very efficient policing by the organization's own members. The organization of the preliminary cook-offs, and the efficiency of the judging of the Terlingua event, was generally first class. These events were primarily for chili heads or party people. But a modest entrance fee would enable you to judge for yourself.'

Crossings into Mexico

FROM LAJITAS TO PASO LAJITAS

At Lajitas, upstream from the RV park, you may go across the Rio Grande to Paso Lajitas. A $1 fee, payable when you come back, is charged for your brief passage in the metal rowboat, and after a three- to four-minute walk, you are in the quietest village on the Mexican side, all the more noticeable in its difference since it faces the Lajitas resort across the river.

Nowhere else do you find both such an abrupt or smooth transition from First to Third World. On the U.S. side, golfers are out on the course, RVers are chatting in the shade, and bikers in their special clothing are starting out on a desert trail.

By contrast, on the Mexican side, stray dogs are lying in the shade, roosters in their pens are crowing noisily, one man is making adobe bricks, and a woman is doing household chores. But looking through the dust and beyond the auto carcasses, there seems to be a real sense of community here.

There is one small, low-ceilinged church (with sixteen seats), a general store selling standard grocery products and avocados, and two restaurants. The first one, Dos Amigos, greets you only three minutes from landing; it is open 9:00 to 8:00. An outside table under an awning next to a shade tree offers a good view back across to the U.S. side. The menu offers breakfasts (ranch omlette, $3) and a variety of Mexican dishes (enchiladas montadas, $3.50; chiles rellenos, $4; Mexican plate, $7; beer, $1). Since the food is always specially made, it may take a little time to appear on the table. There are four seats outside and seventeen inside.

Farther down the street is Garcia's, a more substantial place, with all interior seating (twenty-two seats), and fans and sombreros on the wall. Compared to Dos Amigos, it has a similar menu, similar prices, but it's just a bit bigger and lacks the outside seating and the view. It is clean and popular.

FROM CASTOLON TO SANTA ELENA

Although there is a campground (Cottonwood) nearby, this crossing does not get much visitor traffic except for locals from Study Butte and Terlingua who go to Santa Elena to eat at Maria Elena's Restaurant. The row boat here costs $1.50 per person round-trip, and a four-minute walk brings you to a pleasant, quiet village of 240 inhabitants. There is a town plaza and an orderly look to the place; there are two churches and a school where fifty children attend grades one through six. In the square is a small grocery shop, and next to it a second restaurant. There is a curio shop next to Maria Elena's Restaurant. If you ask around, you may be able to hire horses for about $4.50 per hour.

FROM RIO GRANDE VILLAGE TO BOQUILLAS

The existence of a large RV park coupled with the easiest access from park headquarters at Panther Junction has made this crossing the most popular and the most exploited.

Before you even leave your car in a parking lot, a self-appointed attendant lets you know he will look after it for you. In the rowboat ($2 round-trip

Manuel, resident of Lajitas for over sixty years. Photo by Blair Pittman.

and you pay during the first crossing), the oarsman is encouraging you to tip his assistant. On the other side, burros and horses are for hire and are actively promoted for $3 round-trip to the village. Or a pickup truck will drive you for a fee. The walk is a little longer here, through sand, but is manageable in fifteen minutes.

Boquillas presents a different image on arrival than the other Mexican border towns. There is an impressive store and restaurant (Falcon's) with a helpful American waiter. The store is well stocked, and the prices are rather high. T-shirts are $10; blankets, $20; Guatemalan vests, $19.75. Rum is $9.25 and tequila, $7.50. The restaurant prices (three bean and cheese tacos, $1) and the prices in the nearby clean and colorful Park Bar, which has a pool table, are reasonable.

There is a schoolhouse, two churches, and two rock shops here, and excursions are possible by four-wheel drive or on horseback into the mountains or to a mine five miles away. Back of Beyond Tours provides the four-wheel drive trips for around $50–$60 per person per day with a four-person minimum. Longer or more interesting horseback trips into the mountains may be taken for around $70 per day, including all food and camping. You may write Back of Beyond Expeditions at P.O. Box 97, Big Bend National Park, TX 79834, but the two American owners, Zack and Rawls, are usually to be found in Boquillas, where their base is.

With a population of 225, Boquillas is no bigger than Santa Elena, but it presents a completely different image. The well-stocked tourist store, the availability of all sorts of walking, riding, and driving tours, and the general attitude of the inhabitants, alert to the possibility of tourists' money, all indicate that this is no longer just a quiet border village. There is even bus service here on Tuesday and Saturday at 8:30 A.M. to Melchor Muzquiz, 150 miles south.

FROM HEATH CANYON RANCH (FM 2627) TO LA LINDA

There is a bridge here and two Mexican guards, but no toll. On the other side there is very little; now only one family remains living in this town where formerly three hundred worked. There is a forlorn chapel, at some distance from the abandoned village, with birds flying in through the roof. On the way out of town, a man sells beer and sodas. The remains of the mine processing plant dominates the abandoned town, and rock hounds can sift through piles of rock. Horse rental is available from the sole remaining family for $4 per hour. It is with relief that most people return to the U.S. side and the warm greetings at the Open Sky Cafe.

GUIDED TRIPS INTO MEXICO

By horseback into the Sierra del Carmen. For fifteen years Marcos Paredes has been leading small groups on fully outfitted pack trips into the high country of the Sierra del Carmen. A minimum of four and a maximum of eight persons comprise the group, accompanied by Marcos and his guides, and the trips take 5–7 days, depending on the agreed itinerary and the time available for the group. The tour passes through logging areas and conifer forests and ascends to pristine wilderness at 9,000 feet. This area has just been declared a wildlife reserve, which adds to its appeal. Marcos charges $100 per person per day, a fee that includes transportation from the Rio Grande, horses, tack, camping equpiment, and all food and medical supplies. This is a strenuous trip and not for the feeble. About eight trips are run each year, and advance booking is necessary. (915) 477-2233.

By vehicle from Lajitas to the small town of San Carlos. This one-day excursion costs $50 per person. See Chapter 3, under Lajitas, for a description. (915) 424-3221.

FLYING DOWN TO MEXICO FOR BREAKFAST

George Merriman was pulling his airplane out of its hangar when we arrived at Alpine's airport for our morning excursion. George is the owner of Skies of Texas, the only charter flight operator in this area. He had suggested a short trip to me and to David Busey of the Chamber of Commerce so we could get an idea of the landscape from the air and appreciate the advantages for tourists of small-plane flying.

The sign outside the gate leading to the runway set the tone for flying in these parts: "Give way to airplanes." The office itself, in anticipation of a resumption of daily commercial air service into Alpine, had been newly decorated and furnished with comfortable couches. The runway (twelve hundred feet long) had been surfaced in 1992 and could accommodate four-engine cargo planes. Air traffic control is handled by San Angelo, Texas.

The single-engine Bonanza plane with its distinctive V-shaped tail had flown many hours but looked immaculate. We climbed into two of the three passenger seats, buckled up, and put on headphones so we could talk more easily in flight. After taxiing on the runway, it seemed only a matter of seconds, with a speed of sixty miles per hour, before we were airborne and climbing sharply to clear Twin Peaks mountain just south of Alpine.

Once at an altitude of around 7,000 feet, or 3,500 feet above the ground, we leveled off at a cruising speed of 165 miles an hour. The plane bobbed around a little, like a rowboat in a lake, and occasionally an updraft of air rising from the mountainsides would move us slightly more abruptly. To George, constantly correcting the trim of the plane and pointing out the features below, this was an entirely routine flight on a beautiful day, and the only difference was that he was not charging money.

As we looked below, headed due south, the landscape looked predominantly gray with some streaks of green. More interesting than the color were the rock formations, clearly defined mesas, steep-sided tables rising from the flat land, with bushes and small trees on the top. Ahead, in the distance, the higher mountains (the Chisos in Big Bend National Park and the Sierra del Carmen range stretching into Mexico) defined the horizon.

There were various signs of civilization in the high desert landscape we were flying over—dirt roads wound here and there with no apparent destination. And an occasional ranch with fencing and outbuildings could be seen to the right or left.

This ranching country had not always seemed so desolate and dried up. In 1909 J. D. Langford, having first cashed a check in Alpine with a cowboy on the sidewalk, headed south sight unseen to a homestead on the Rio Grande. Accompanied by his pregnant wife and his eight-year-old daughter, his possessions on the backs of mules tended by two Mexican men, Langford accomplished the trip in eight days that we were making in thirty-five minutes. He noted then the abundance of tall grasses and wildflowers swaying in the wind.

But returning to his homestead after an absence of almost twenty years, Langford found "just bare, rain-eroded ground . . . sun baked sand and gravel. Somehow, a brightness seemed gone from the land." Spurred by a wartime demand for beef, the ranchers had crowded too many cattle onto the sensitive land and had worn it out.

The ground soon gave way to more imposing rock formations as we approached our landing at Lajitas. Underneath us now was the Solitario (Hermit) of the Big Bend Ranch State Natural Area (BBRSNA). This ribbed and circular upthrust from the surrounding broken ground stretches nine miles across and resembles a vast soufflé. There must have been a fearsome explosion of energy to cause this widespread disturbance. Only from the air, or from aerial photographs, do you get to appreciate the huge size of the Solitario and to see its shape. It is the star attraction of the recently acquired BBRSNA, which is larger than all the other Texas state parks combined.

George now took us on a slow, wide turn over the Rio Grande, briefly into Mexico, before approaching the gravel runway, deserted of aircraft, at Lajitas. Light as a feather, we touched down, then taxied to a hangar to park the plane. After placing chocks under the wheels, more a gesture of habit than a precaution against rolling, we started out on a twenty-five minute walk past the Lajitas resort boardwalk to where we would find a boat to cross the Rio Grande.

The river is only twenty paces wide at this point, but deep enough that you need a boat. The Mexicans from the other side have just such a boat for tourists, a four-passenger metal rowboat, and you pay the oarsman $1 per person on the return trip. A few swift pulls on the oars, probably about 25¢ per pull, and we are across.

We now face a few minutes' stroll along a dirt road to find a restaurant for breakfast. To one side lies an abandoned and stripped automobile, goats are tethered to posts, dogs scavenge, and burros roam. It's not tidy, but it's different—the pace and purpose of life already seem slower.

The Dos Amigos Restaurant chooses itself for us, not because it is the first one we come to after three minutes (there is another, larger cafe in the village), but because of the sign. This is large and new, with red letters on a white background. It is hung crookedly, and the artist had not measured his space too well, so the result is that the final "n" and "t" of restaurant are squeezed into the top right corner. Outside there's a single table, with a white plastic tablecloth, shaded by a tree to one side and with an awning above. We get a view back across the Rio Grande to the RV campground and the golf course on the United States side.

A teenage girl comes out promptly and gives us menus written in English. Our Spanish is adequate for this sort of thing, and it gives a better feeling to be talking in their language, or at least trying to as a friendly gesture. Beer, soft drinks, and instant coffee are the drinks we go for, plus three different Mexican plates each costing the equivalent of $3.

We sit in the shade, the food arrives after a while. Nothing much happens, and perhaps that's the whole point of coming here. Some villagers are building a small house, but they take no notice of us; we are no novelty; the slightly run-down look of the place is not news to any of us, and it doesn't seem to worry the locals. Stray dogs roam, a donkey wanders past, the sun reflects off the car wreck. We finish our huevos rancheros and enchiladas montadas and walk back to the boat.

Back at the airstrip, we buckle in and taxi off. At busy times, such as during the famous chili cook-off, there are plenty of small planes here, but today we are the only one. George tells the San Angelo air traffic controller that we are taking off, and the next minute we are in the air again. A little over half an hour later we are circling over Alpine and the dominant McDonalds sign reminds us of a different type of food service. George gets the plane gassed up for his next passengers (a businessman or a hospital patient perhaps) and we say good-bye.

Charter prices for the three-passenger Bonanza plane, round-trip to Lajitas is $60 per person (three passengers), or $75 (two passengers). Allow three hours, plus $1 for the boat and $3 to $4 for breakfast. George Merriman is the pilot and owner of Skies of Texas. He owns two planes, the three-passenger Bonanza and a five-passenger twin-engine Barron. He offers aerial sightseeing tours around Alpine as well as point-to-point charters. Some of the local scenery is simply ideal for this sort of above-ground viewing: for example, the Solitario, which cannot be appreciated from the ground, or the upward sweep of the Chisos Mountains set against the deep cut of the river canyons. The Bonanza costs $120 per hour to charter, the Barron, $240. Depending on baggage, the planes can seat from three to five passengers. A sample trip, for someone with really limited time, could be to fly south from Alpine, cross over the Solitario in the Big Bend Ranch State Natural Area, turn east and fly at 2,000 feet above the ground over the Big Bend National Park to view the Chisos Mountains, the Basin, and the Rio Grande. Turn north and proceed via Marathon to circle over Fort Davis and view the Davis Mountains and McDonald Observatory. The flying time, depending on the aircraft type, would be around one hour and fifty minutes. The price per person, depending on the size of the group, would be around $85—in the deserted skies, with a clear view in all directions, it would be an unbeatable experience.

Other rates, for those wanting a Skies of Texas charter from the nearest major airport to Alpine are: from Midland-Odessa, $112.50 per person (two passengers with baggage) or $84 (four passengers with baggage); and from El Paso, $150 or $110, respectively. For information and reservations, call (915) 837-2290.

Marfa Lights

Lights and Marfa seem to go together, and for most people this unexplained phenomenon is the most common identification with the town.

Aerial view of Solitario, looking south toward Rio Grande. Photo by Blair Pittman.

Many studies have been done by scientists in different fields, and many books and papers written about the subject. But no one has satisfactorily convinced the scientific community, nor have the scientists themselves produced a theory to explain the cause of the lights. This mystery leaves lay visitors with the nice feeling, if they are interested and patient, of observing the unknown. The best estimate is that two times out of three, you will be lucky and see the lights.

Descriptions abound concerning the size, shape, color, movement, and general behavior of the lights, sometimes because the observers were not looking in the right place or were picking up lights for which there was a known cause (for example, the headlights of vehicles).

In 1988 one account described the phenomena this way: "Poof—there's the first one, a tiny round ball of white light, not exactly still. Then, poof, it splits and becomes two slightly wavering, shimmery spheres. In a minute, poof, another light appears to the right of the other two. And so on. Sometimes only two lights are present, sometimes six."

Another account, this time in 1963, claimed that: "as if on cue, a light appeared far off on the southern horizon. It was a pinprick of light. When I looked at it through a small telescope I had brought for the occasion, I found it was still a small point of light; yet, it looked different. It wasn't a star or a planet, and it didn't look as light bulbs do at a distance. Soon, the first light was joined by a second; then a third; then a fourth; until, finally, we were treated to eleven lights bobbing and bouncing just above the horizon."

But these accounts were by no means the first. In 1883 Robert Ellison, an old-time rancher near Marfa, reported seeing lights. He thought they were Apache campfires. About that same time, shepherds would gather around their fires at night and would tell tales about the lights: "Alsate, the last of the Apache chieftains of the Big Bend, was roaming the mountains lighting signal fires trying to guide his people home."

Through the years, various serious and sometimes professional attempts have been made from the air and on the ground to explain the mystery. The existence during World War II of a U.S. Army air force base near the place where the lights appeared provided an opportunity for aerial observations. On the ground, ventures ranged from painstaking attempts to triangulate the area in order to pinpoint the exact location (a failure, since the lights kept moving), to a huge ground "dragnet" effort, conducted by students from Sul Ross University, using jeeps on the ground and an airplane overhead. This attempt also failed. The lights kept moving, could not be pinpointed, and seemed to evaporate.

Sometimes, even for special efforts made at great expense, the lights didn't even show. Marfa residents tell of a recent visit by a Japanese group that arrived with all the necessary camera equipment and the funds to pay for a detailed study; they even had a priest to light candles. But no mysteries were solved. It appears that local residents take some pleasure when high-powered scientific groups can't find an explanation for their flighty neighbors.

One resident of Marfa has had as many experiences of the lights and involvement with theories about the cause of the lights as anyone. In 1943 he arrived in Marfa to train pilots at the air base. Long hours during night training exercises when he was positioned at the end of the runway of the nearby airfield gave him ample opportunity, between pilot landings, to observe the sky. "And the night sky at that time was even darker than it is today," he says. "It was wartime, there were few vehicles on the roads, and the ranches did not have electricity."

When the lights did appear, he described them this way: "We saw these small objects off in the distance. They moved laterally more than vertically. They moved towards us and away from us. They were soft in nature, not a harsh light, pale greens, pale blues, pale yellows, soft reds, but no harsh color. Often oblong, with no rough edges, they moved vertically but not much. At no time did we ever find the lights hostile or threatening. They didn't run at us, their movement was more slow than fast, very simple, very small, the size of a light bulb."

How do you look for the lights? According to him, "With a great deal of patience. Or, if you are young, with your girlfriend and a six-pack of beer".

How often are they out? "They are not out every night, in my opinion. They may be down in the grass, but I don't think they're there every night. Probably two nights out of three is a good guess."

The attitude of the locals towards the lights? "Oh, yeah, if you want to call them that. They're little old fellahs out there. They're here. It's just a different sort of thing. They live with it. The lights are like neighbors."

He has no definitive theory about the cause of the lights and strongly resents those who capitalize on the lights to make a name for themselves. Certainly Marfa can't be accused of that. Only in recent years has the Texas State Highway Department provided a parking space on U.S. 90 8 miles east of Marfa for cars to pull into. This is the viewing site.

Endless articles and a wide variety of theories exist about the cause of the lights. None have proved sound. For a well-researched little booklet on the subject, read Judith Brueske's *The Marfa Lights*. In fifty-one pages ($5.95), this book covers most of the major theories. Brueske is also the publisher of the local bimonthly *The Desert Candle*.

On a recent visit in May, the lights were visible on two nights out of two. They appeared only after dark, which was around 9:00 P.M. To see the lights, you have an easy guidepost. In the middle distance, looking south and slightly west from the roadside parking lot (the road runs east-west), there is a red light on the top of a pole. Look above and beyond this red light. Probably, you will see some pale lights, white, round, sometimes moving laterally and dipping perhaps, then for no good reason disappearing, then reappearing.

The show that night went on for forty minutes or so. A couple from Nevada were definitely unimpressed. A bus load of students from San Antonio were more interested in throwing frisbees around. The lights certainly weren't very dramatic, nor particularly colorful, and it required some imagination to make something out. The students were cold and faced an overnight train ride back to San Antonio, so they left. But the lights bobbed around, just above the ground, perhaps playing some game. The lights continue to appear most nights with no charge for watching. Each year at the Marfa Lights Festival, a committee meets to review the observations and findings of the previous year.

Golf Courses of the Big Bend Area

There are six area courses—in Alpine, Fort Stockton, Lajitas, Marfa, Pecos, and Van Horn.

Greens fees are reasonable but rise slightly on weekends. Electric and pull carts are available, with some variations on whether they may be taken on fairways. Refreshments can be obtained in the clubhouses, but it is advisable to take water with you as well. There is a practice range at all the courses except Alpine.

Morning watering takes place, so starting before 9 A.M. can be difficult, particularly in the summer. It is advisable to check ahead if considering playing on a Monday.

ALPINE COUNTRY CLUB

This a good beginner's course, not because it is easy, but because there are lots of hazards that make less experienced golfers nervous. For example, there are creeks to play over or alongside of, hidden sand traps, and overhanging trees that might have to be played from underneath.

This is a nine-green course with separate tee boxes to make a full round. The back nine are a longer a version of the front nine. There is no practice range. Electric carts must be kept on the cart paths. Pull carts may be taken on the fairways. Winter rules apply to balls in play.

On the par fives, tee shots can be put in the creek without too much trouble if anything over a three iron is used. Straight hitting is needed on several holes to stay out of trouble. The eighth green is interesting, since there is no such thing as an easy putt.

The clubhouse is located on Loop 223 (North Harrison Street), which intersects East Avenue E (U.S. 90) and Texas 118 (heading towards Fort Davis). The clubhouse and course are clearly visible from Loop 223, to the west.

PECOS COUNTY MUNICIPAL GOLF COURSE (FORT STOCKTON)

This is an excellent all-round course. While most fairways are wide enough to keep out of trouble, there are plenty of hazards in which to get entangled. The greens vary in style.

This is an eighteen-green course. The front nine holes have more elevation change and the larger proportion of challenges. However, the back nine are not short of merit, in particular the approach views for some greens. There is a practice range. Electric carts must be kept on the cart paths, and pull carts may be taken on the fairways.

There always seems to be a wind blowing here, which adds an interesting dimension to several holes. The back nine are often a relief after the difficulties of the front. The shot onto the eighth green is frequently a good challenge—a short iron or pitch shot with the wind over water onto a narrow green backed by rising ground.

The clubhouse is located off Hwy 285 North (heading towards Pecos), near the Pecos County Coliseum, down the same street as the airport. The course is visible from the elevated portion of I-10 as it crosses Hwy 285, to the north, and from Hwy 285, to the northeast.

LAJITAS ON THE RIO GRANDE GOLF CLUB

This is a putter's course. The greens are large and have unusual topography. Position is more important than distance on most holes. This is a nine-hole course with separate tee boxes to make a full round. The back nine are a longer version of the front nine. There is a practice range. Carts can be taken on the fairways to within fifty feet of the greens. Winter rules are in effect year-round on fairways, but balls in the rough must be played as they lie.

There is serious rough off many of the fairways, harboring members of unfriendly species, both botanical and zoological. The third hole, particularly when played for the second time, leaves no room for error. Placing the balls for all shots through the green is a problem for straight hitters and not-so-straight ones alike.

The clubhouse is located south of the main hotel building and is reached from FM 170 leading to the Lajitas Trading Post and RV Park. All three are posted on signs on FM 170. The course is not easily visible from the highway, but the trees and other green vegetation reveal its position.

MARFA MUNICIPAL GOLF COURSE

This is a good course for golfers who enjoy the short game. The greens are, on the whole, small, elevated, and angled towards the fairway, making them hard to hit in regulation and difficult to stay on when pitching, particularly from the sides and rear. Most greens are protected by a semicircle of trees. This is the highest golf course in Texas.

This is a nine-green course with separate tee boxes to make a full round. Tee boxes alternate, so on the second nine, some holes are shorter, while others are longer. There is a practice range. Electric carts must be kept on the cart paths. Pull carts may be taken on the fairways. The lie of balls in the fairway of the hole may be improved.

The views of the surrounding area make this course enjoyable. At the worst of golfing moments, looking out beyond the fairways is guaranteed to put things back in perspective. The sixth green, a par three hole, looks deceptively easy to hit and is hard to get into from practically every direction, if missed.

The clubhouse is located at the end of FM 1114, which leaves Texas 17 just north of the railroad tracks and U.S. 90 in Marfa, to the east. The road skirts the course.

PECOS' REEVES COUNTY MUNICIPAL GOLF COURSE

This course is for accurate hitters. Many of the longer holes are doglegs, and there are lots of fairway trees and other obstacles to avoid. Putting is a pleasure; the greens are excellent and putt true. Even on the smaller of the elevated greens a choice of chipping or pitching is possible.

This is an eleven-green course, seven of which are played a second time to make a full round. Lengths vary considerably between the first and second playing, and some holes are shorter the second time, while others are longer. There is a practice range. Electric carts may be taken on the fairway, with the ninety-degree rule usually in effect. The lie of the balls in the fairway of the hole may be improved.

The long par threes, long, straight par fours, doglegs, and the order in which the holes are played combine to make this a stretching course. The severity of the dogleg on the twelfth hole makes it the most interesting, and there is a severe temptation to cut the corner over a fenced out-of-bounds area.

The clubhouse is located on Starley, a street off Country Club Drive a block south of I-20. The course is visible from the I-20 overpass over Country Club Drive, to the south, and from Country Club Drive, to the north.

SUMMARY

	Men				Women			
	par	*hcap*	*slp*	*ydg*	*par*	*hcap*	*slp*	*ydg*
Alpine	70	66.4	111	5808	70	72.1	114	4868
Ft. Stockton	72	69.0	<2M>	6541	72	68.3	<2M>	4984
Lajitas	71	68.7	111	6212	73	<2M>	<2M>	5047
Marfa	72	70.0	115	6550	74	70.02	110	5786
Pecos	70	67.3	<2M>	6132	70	68.0	<2M>	5064
Van Horn	72	67.6	<2M>	5939	72	66.8	<2M>	4854

Abbreviations: hcap = handicap, slp = slope, ydg = yardage

VAN HORN MOUNTAIN VIEW GOLF COURSE

An aquaphobic's nightmare: water comes into play a surprising amount for a desert region course. The quality of the greens varies, but all require a light touch, and are well protected either by hazards or the nature of the ground surrounding them.

This is a nine-green course with separate tee boxes to make a full round. Most of the women's tee boxes are not maintained. The back nine are a longer version of the front nine. There is a practice range. Carts are allowed on the fairways, away from the tee boxes and greens. No relief for lie of balls. The course is closed on Monday.

The third green, a par three course, requires faith in one's ability to hit with an iron for a known distance; a huge tree blocks the view of the green and must be played over to hit it. A wide water hazard lies completely across the fairway, adding to the pressure. The green is raised, and not overly large, making a subsequent shot onto it, if necessary, also a challenge.

The clubhouse is located at the end of Golf Course Drive, which intersects I-10 and the I-10 Business Loop (the main street running through Van Horn). The course is visible from the I-10 overpass over Golf Course Drive, to the south.

Music in the Big Bend

Driving the roads of West Texas, travelers hopelessly scan the radio, searching frantically for some music but finding only stations of static with old Nashville hillbilly music or some powerful Mexican station blasting unfamiliar tunes. The thought comes to mind—what in the world do these folks do for musical entertainment? Rest easy, weary travelers, for there are as many kinds of music in the Big Bend and as many places to hear it as there are rocks and cacti and cattle on the range.

Mexican music, heard in the Big Bend for over four hundred years, is alive and well along the border. Mariachis, folkloricos, and Tejano bands continue to perform traditional Mexican ballads, corridas, and cumbias at concerts, public dances, and celebrations, such as the Marfa Lights Festival and Alpine's Cinco de Mayo Fiesta weekend.

Cowboy music—real cowboy music—is as old as the first open cattle range in the Big Bend. Since the early 1800s, cowboys of the area serenaded the moon and the cattle, either in music or poetry, accompanied only by the crackle of the campfire or the howling of coyotes. That same magic exists today in the Big Bend, and visitors flock by the thousands to hear cowboy music headliners, such as Craig Carter, Mike Stevens, and Clay Lindley.

Craig Carter's music is legendary in these parts. Craig performs across the globe, both as a premier country recording artist and as an upcoming actor. While Los Angeles claims him for short stays, Craig is more comfortable on his family ranch in the Big Bend. Between working cattle and mending fences, Craig entertains friends and fans throughout the area.

Craig can be seen in solo appearances in the patio or the Rio Grande Room at the Holland Hotel in Alpine, or at the Gage Hotel in Marathon. With his precision acoustic guitar and crystal-clear voice, Craig takes his listeners back to the days of campfires and tough trail rides. For larger crowds, Craig brings together his music cronies, the Spur of the Moment Band, giving audiences a blend of traditional cowboy music and modern country tunes that turn a tapping toe into a two-step faster than you can say "gimmeadraw." Joining Craig in the country and cowboy scene is Mike Stevens, who not only keeps horses and plays guitar, but is also a well-known guitar maker, crafting instruments for musical greats like Eric

Clapton. After leaving his job at Fender Guitars in California for the remote ranch land of the Big Bend, Mike established a workshop in Alpine and soon endeared himself to the inhabitants by performing old cowboy ballads. He is a regular at the Texas Cowboy Poetry Gathering in March and headlines at the Texas Mountain Western Heritage Weekend in September, both held in Alpine.

While not considered music, cowboy poetry is still sweet and easy to the ear. Locals and tourists alike flock to these gatherings to hear honest-to-goodness working cowboys spin tales of the range and poetry of the cowboy soul. One local favorite is Clay Lindley, billed as the "Cowboy Nerd." A border cowboy, Clay pokes fun at fellow trail hands and Mexican vaqueros alike. The Texas Cowboy Poetry Gathering, held the first weekend in March on the campus of Sul Ross State University in Alpine, is one of the most respected events of its kind. Over the three-day period, visitors are treated to sessions of poetry and music, both in auditoriums and around chuck wagon campfires. This is a very busy weekend in Alpine, so reserve hotel rooms early to see this unique event.

Okay, so you don't want the crowds and prefer hanging out with the locals. No problem, there's still plenty to do. Any weekend in the Big Bend, several nightspots offer a wide range of area talent and some good company as well. In Alpine, check the weekly *Alpine Avalanche* or at the Chamber of Commerce to see if there is any live music at the Cinnabar, the Civic Center, or Downtown Brown's. At the time of this writing, the future of Downtown Brown's is in some doubt. For some time now there has been excellent live music in Brown's garden on weekends and during spring and summer, featuring among others the Burners, a reggae and cumbia combo, and Spontaneous Combustion, known locally as Spon Com, a classic rock and blues group. Even if this site, and these groups, change, there will still be good live music to be heard in and around Alpine, since musicians live there and are just waiting for the chance to play.

Who are these musicians? Are they professionals, part-timers, or what? For some of them, they mix both full- and part-time careers. Some of the groups have made tape recordings for sale, and they also receive some money from the modest cover charge ($3 on average) for their appearances. All have other jobs, however; Charles Bell is an artist, Washtub Gerry works at McDonald Observatory, David Busey is director of the Chamber of Commerce, Robert Halpern is editor of the *Big Bend Sentinel*, Todd Jagger is a photographer.

Closer to the national park, in Terlingua, is the Starlight Theater. Once a movie house for the cinnabar miners of the area, the Starlight is now a classy restaurant and nightclub. The main attraction of the Starlight is the vintage show stage, which might feature comics or musical combos any night of the week.

Just down the road from the town is La Kiva, an extraordinary subterranean restaurant and club, featuring local musicians like Just Us Girls. These five talented women play a unique brand of border folk music, sung both in English and Spanish, and their lively stage show causes tourist stampedes to buy cassettes and CDs of the group.

The most remarkable thing about the area musicians is their diverse talent. Good examples are Dennis de Crenet and Steve Bennack. These music men can be heard with their respective anchor bands, the Burners, and Spon Com on Friday night. Saturday night they might be in Brown's Garden with their fusion blues band, the Blue Rain, only to top off the weekend at the Terlingua Cafe, also in the ghost town, for a Sunday jazz brunch. To find out who is playing when and where, consult the *Alpine Avalanche*, which appears on Thursday or the *Big Bend Sentinel*. Also look for posters, or ask at the Chamber of Commerce or your hotel, or call DTB's, the Starlight Theater, or La Kiva.

Another of Big Bend's musical example is Ron Steinman, perhaps the finest percussionist the Juilliard School of Music has ever sent to the wilds of West Texas. Ron directs the band at Sul Ross and plays with the Blue Rain band on weekends. You might catch Ron sitting in with any of the bands in the area, much to the delight of the crowds. Most musicians in the area prefer to play several different types of music, and it is not uncommon to find four or five members of different bands playing on the same stage—the "jam sessions" of old. With this kind of entertainment, locals and tourists alike are continually surprised at what a band in the Big Bend will produce. And the crowds who go to listen or dance at Downtown Brown's are likewise an easy mix of visitors and locals, of all ages, dancing with each other, dancing on their own, having a beer or two perhaps, but mainly and simply being a part of what has become an extraordinary social and musical feature of the Big Bend.

As you end your vacation and head out on these lonely roads, the old crackly AM stations no longer seem so lonely. They serve as a catalyst to your imagination—evoking those days of old on the range or those cumbias at the local Mexican dances. Pop in a cassette or CD of one of the local groups and put your mind back in one of the Big Bend's many watering holes, where the gentle mountain breezes mix with the music of the many entertainers in the area. Or turn off the radio, roll down the windows and listen to the coyotes crying a farewell. Your music tastes will never be the same.

The Old Man of the Desert

Living in a small house just off the Sul Ross State University campus is Hal Flanders and his wife Mary. How Hal came to Alpine and how he was named the Old Man of the Desert are connected; and anyone who has listened to the beautiful poetry spoken by Burgess Meredith on the video trilogy of the Chihuahuan Desert might be interested in knowing more about this dedicated conservationist and philosopher.

Although Hal lived and worked as an engineer in the northeast, as a naturalist he was familiar with the Big Bend area and had visited many times. Upon retirement, Mary and he spent five years traveling around the continent pulling a trailer and looking for a place to settle down. Alpine was their choice, and, after settling in, Hal found a group of young people, also "outlanders," as the newcomers to the area are known, working on desert research as volunteers. He identified with the aims and lifestyle of this group and soon became involved with them; this interest led to the start of the Chihuahuan Desert Research Institute and the making of the three-part video, *Land of Lost Borders*. Hal does not appear in the video, nor is his voice heard, but his are the thoughts and feelings which are expressed so movingly.

Hal spoke to me recently of how he arrived, and what the Big Bend country has done for him and can do for tourists if they give it time: "It was serendipity which brought us here, but I guess it is serendipity which holds a whole lot of people here once they visit here, more especially if they have the time to talk with some of the people around the area and get to know what makes this place up."

He continued, "I can't tell you the number of times I have been on a bus as a naturalist talking to people and have someone say: 'How can you live out here. It's just an impossible place to live, you can't even raise cattle!' Well, you live here very well, and if you wonder what all's going on here, this is a far more active natural area than, say, a big forest which is fairly sterile by comparison. But it happens at night.

"The Big Bend is a fascinating area visually, photographically. The animals, the organisms that live there, their coping mechanisms, who eats who, the whole place is absolutely fascinating. So if the tourist coming through here gets exposed to any of that he is quite likely to be captivated. But if he sees the Big Bend in four hours, which means he drove through it, then he's likely to miss a whole lot. You must invest a little something here, then the rewards will come.

"I've taken I don't know how many groups down the river, and watched the boisterous young people carrying on like banshees coming into the Santa Elena Canyon. But when they get in there and see all that fifteen hundred feet of limestone piled up over their heads, come down through that river and come out of there, they're speaking quietly and they are paying attention. They have just had an experience which changes their lives.

"Failing that, it is hard for me to see what is going to get us back in balance. Thoughtful people now, look at the culture and the way it is going, and can only decide that this is not a sustainable culture. We are going downhill, and we are ripping up the planet. We subsidize ripping up the planet. And no one pays any attention to putting it back. That's what the whole recycling effort is about: to put the raw materials which have been used and wasted back into the stockpile and let them be used again.

"So there is real therapy in being out there, and sleeping there. Don't go down the river through Santa Elena in one day. Take two or three days. This has to permeate you and, if it does, things come round right. Henry David Thoreau said, 'Learn wildness, and you are afraid of nothing.' Wildness is the preservation of the world and we must have places like these, especially the parks, because more and more people are going to get their head back straight in such areas. We are part of the planet; we are one of the many, many organisms which populate it, each with an equal right to be here.

"Life is the sacred thing on the planet, and you do not see that life very well exhibited except when you are out of doors."

In 1992 Hal was awarded Man of the Year by the Alpine Chamber of Commerce for introducing a recycling plan to the town.

Regional Artists

The Big Bend area, by virtue of its desert setting and low population, has attracted a multitude of talented artists and craftsman. Their talents are as varied as the landscape. Here is a sample of some of them:

Bob Bell of Alpine offers hand-colored prints of cowboys, Big Bend scenes, some watercolors, in the $100–$200 range.

Bob's brother, Charlie Bell, also of Alpine, makes handmade papers (stationery, art work, wall hangings). He uses many indigenous plants and fibers in his paper and teaches at Sul Ross State University. His price range is $10–$400.

John Blackman, West Murphy Avenue, Alpine, is a potter. His pottery features desert plants, animals and scenes. Prices are $50–$300.

Roger Cutforth from Terlingua produces primitive 12-inch-by-12-inch watercolors of desert images. Roger, who is English, has shown his artwork and photographs all over the world. *Houston Metropolitan* magazine noted his work as worth collecting and still reasonably priced, under $250.

John Davis is a clay constructionist and potter who makes beautiful, pastel-colored pots of flowers, desert images, and plants. He owns the J. Davis Studio at 510 West Holland in Alpine, (915) 837-3812. Prices are in the $100–$300 range.

James Evans from Marathon is a photographer who sells black-and-white images of Big Bend landscapes and people, priced under $200. Photographic lampshades, made completely by hand, feature desert plants and animals. The lamps are limited edition items since the material used to make the shades is no longer available from the manufacturer. Lamps and shades cost $450.

Todd Jagger from Fort Davis is a photographer and musician. Todd concentrates on dye transfer photographic prints of Big Bend National Park and the Fort Davis area. The dye transfer process is very labor intensive, and it can take as long as ten hours to make one print. His prices range from $150 to $300.

Maisie Lee from Marathon fashions beautiful wood sculptures, many of Indians, from pieces of mesquite found on the ranches of the Big Bend. Her prices range from $300 to $500.

Abby Levine from Fort Davis incorporates wood burning (pyrography) techniques into imaginative artwork, which include small boxes, yo-yos, mirrors, and dioramas featuring cowboys, cowgirls, and other western images. She masterfully includes objects such as cactus, barbed wire, rope, and leather in the framed pieces. Prices range from $50 to $250.

Lineaus Lorette from Fort Davis is a CPA who also makes handmade leather medicine balls and other athletic training equipment. Using the finest quality leather, he stuffs the balls with kapok. His equipment is used in the training programs of many professional and college football teams in the United States. Prices are $240 for the small balls to $300 for the large balls.

Tracy Lynch from Terlingua is a color photographer. Her beautiful cibachrome prints of the Big Bend area have been featured in many magazines, including *Texas Monthly* and *Texas Highways*. They sell for $250–$350.

Patty Manning from Fort Davis produces etchings and handmade masks. Patty is pursuing her master's degree in biology at Sul Ross State University. Her etchings are whimsical drawings of insects that sell for $180. The masks she makes are one-of-a-kind images, using many indigenous plants and animal horns and skins, all priced under $75.

Izzy Margoles, a long-time resident (forty years) of the region, paints landscapes in oil of the Big Bend and the Chihuahuan Desert for $400–$500.

Mahala Sibley is located at 114 North Sixth Street in Alpine, (915) 837-5029. Mahala uses her hand-painted tiles, some featuring desert images and ranch brands, in wrought-iron tables and trivets. She also does murals on commission. Trivets cost $45 and tables are $250.

Paul Wiggins from Terlingua makes belts and jewelry. Wiggins, a trained architect, makes colorful beaded-leather belts, hand-cast silver jewelry, and decorative concho belts that sell for $125–$275.

Also featured at Lovegene's Gallery in Marathon are recordings of some regional bands, including Craig Carter from Big Bend, the Terlingua Islanders, Todd Jagger and Jimmy Ray Harrell from Fort Davis, and Just Us Girls, an all-female band from Terlingua. Lovegene's is at 21 South 1st Street, opposite the Gage Hotel. (915) 386-4366.

River Trip Outfitters

GUIDED TRIPS AND RAFTS

Far Flung Adventures, P.O. Box 377, Terlingua, TX 79852, 1-800-359-4138 or (915) 371-2489. With their office in Terlingua Ghost Town, 13 miles from Lajitas, Far Flung Adventures has been an example of innovative river trips and effective promotion. They offer river vacations all over the Southwest and in Mexico.

On the Rio Grande, they offer day trips on Colorado Canyon (good for families) at $72 per person and, the most popular trip on the river, Santa Elena (20 miles) for $85 per person. There are two- and three-day trips on other sections of the river—Mariscal, where the bend actually hap-

Far Flung Adventures of Terlingua, Texas, was the outfitter for this trip through the Lower Canyons. Photo by Blair Pittman.

pens, and Boquillas, the longest and deepest canyon, but it's a mild trip and good for beginners ($300 for three days).

There are Music Trips featuring Peter Rowan, Steve Fromholz, and Butch Hancock, a slow three-day descent of Santa Elena Canyon from $410 per person, and Gourmet Rafting (Santa Elena, three-days, $550) with guest chef François Maeder from Crumpets Restaurant in San Antonio who serves haute cuisine on the riverbank. All overnight trips include tent accommodations and all meals; day trips include lunch. There are other trips with naturalist specialists accompanying the group.

This company has many years of experience and offers professional service with sound equipment and personnel. Call to make reservations.

The Whitewater Experience, 6005 Cypress Street, Houston, TX 7074-7609, (713) 774-1028. Long established on the river as a quality operator, this company specializes in group excursions. Don Greene, the owner, places the highest emphasis on the quality of the boat guides and the educational aspect of the experience. But this is also great fun, and former Texas Governor Ann Richards and her special guests, who were taken on the river by Whitewater Experience, seemed to agree. Call for rates and reservations.

Big Bend River Tours, P.O. Box 317, Lajitas, TX 79852, 1-800-545-4240 or (915) 424-3219. In business since 1971, this company is well equipped and staffed. Their office being located in Lajitas is an advantage to clients who are staying there. They offer trips through Santa Elena, Colorado, Mariscal, and Boquillas Canyons from a half-day float ($48) to Santa Elena (full-day $100). Two- and three-day trips ($205–$325), four- to seven-day trips ($415–$700), ten days ($985) and more, or a Buena Suerte Dinner Trip ($55). They offer discounts for children under twelve and for groups. "Fall is the best time to go, mid-October through Christmas. The river is magic; it helps people have fun and be children," says Beth García, the able general manager of Big Bend River Tours. Call for reservations.

Texas River Expeditions, 1-800-839-RAFT or (915) 371-2633. The newest arrival has actually been licensed for twenty years but has now turned to offering daily trips. The office is in the mall at Study Butte next to the Chevron station. The standard trips are offered and the rates are similar to the other companies: A half-day float is $48; a one-day trip to Santa Elena is $98; overnight to Santa Elena is $215; a three-day trip to Boquillas is $315. Call for reservations.

Outback Expeditions, P.O. Box 229, Terlingua, TX 79852, 1-800-343-1640 or (915) 371-2490. The office is located at the Y in Study Butte which means, for visitors who have not booked a trip in advance, Outback is the first float trip company they see. A useful description about each trip is given on their printed sheets—the length in miles and the features of each canyon. Trips range from half-day float ($39) to one-day Santa Elena ($90, but excludes lunch) to multi-day—from $170 for Colorado Canyon two-day, to ten days on the lower canyons for $1,100.

As with the other companies, for all overnight trips all you need to bring is your sleeping bag and personal gear. The park fee is added to all trips. Call for reservations.

Note: Most of the companies listed (especially Far Flung Adventures) also offer other trips: jeep tours, trips into Mexico, and horse trails.

GUIDED TRIPS

The Whitewater Experience. Canoe and kayak trips. See previous description.

Raft and Canoe Rentals

Desert Sports, P.O. Box 584, Terlingua, TX 79852, (915) 371-2602. Canoe rentals are available. A two-person canoe costs from $20 a day, including paddle, life jacket, and user fee (for being on the river). You provide your own food and have to pay the shuttle service for getting yourself and the canoe to the put-in point or from the take-out point. This can add a minimum of $55 for transportation (to the Colorado put-in point). Canoeing is a quite different experience from rafting. You have to work more carefully with your partner to avoid capsizing, but as a reward, you get more in tune with the river. Also, there are only two of you as opposed to perhaps five on a raft. Desert Sports plans to start up in a new location in Terlingua Ghost Town and to widen its services.

Bill Ivey's Rio Grande Outfitters Co., P.O. Box 211, Terlingua, TX 79852, (915) 371-2424. Bill Ivey offers raft rentals for $20 per person per day (minimum three persons). More than twelve years of experience in the self-guided raft rental business has given Bill Ivey a good feel for gauging the capabilities of clients against the current river conditions. As with the canoes, the cost of the shuttle can make a great difference in the price, depending on where the shuttle goes to or from. But there must be a nice satisfaction, for those who like doing the work, in navigating a canyon on one's own. Much depends on the level of the water.

SHUTTLE SERVICES

Big Bend Shuttle Service, P.O. Box 179, Terlingua, TX 79852, 1-800-729-2860 or (915) 371-2523. "We'll take you there and back, your vehicle or ours," is their motto. They can accompany you in your vehicle (with the canoe on the roof) to the river, bring the car back, and have it ready at the destination at the end of the river trip—at $10 an hour for driver's fee. If there is a chase vehicle involved (a second driver, and the company's vehicle), then the price is 50¢ a mile (total mileage, there and back), plus $10 an hour for personnel. If you need a put-in with a rented raft or canoe, then the price is 80¢ a mile both ways, plus $3 per person. Or, for those with their own vehicles who put-in themselves but require their vehicles to be delivered to the take-out point, it costs $85 to deliver the visitor's car to Santa Helena take-out, $30 for each subsequent vehicle. They also provide airport shuttle service from Alpine. See Chapter 1, "Big Bend National Park: How to Get There."

Scott Shuttle Service, P.O. Box 477, Marathon, TX 79842, 1-800-613-5041 or (915) 386-4574. They provide shuttles and canoe rentals ($35 per day, two-day minimum) from Marathon to any point. Rates are by the mile (80¢–$1), plus a per-person fee, depending on the type of road. This service is useful for those driving from the east who want shuttle service, with our without their own vehicle, to start at Marathon. It is also good for shuttles to the Lower Canyons. Bunkhouse accommodation is available in Marathon. See Chapter 3, "Marathon," for more information.

WHEN TO GO

Spring is a good time to go as temperatures are lower and there is usually the attraction of seasonal blooming. But water levels may not be too high, particularly if Mexico is diverting water from the Río Conchos, and the crowds during Spring Break can defeat the aim of the trip. This tributary of the Rio Grande comes from Mexico, joining the larger river at Ojinaga, and supplies most of the Rio Grande's water; when they drain it off for agriculture, there is less for the rafters.

Late summer rains usually help to increase the supply of water and lower temperatures. Otherwise, the fall is the best time if your schedule permits it.

HOW TO GO

On your own or with a guide will probably depend on your experience, motivation, who you are with, whether you want to do the work and take the risk, and on your budget.

Running the Rio Grande—or Pushing the Boat?

The Rio Grande is one of the three separate natural parts of the Big Bend; the Chihuahuan Desert and the Chisos (and other) Mountains are the other two. To get a feel for the river, it is necessary to get onto the river, by raft or canoe, with a trained guide or by yourself. This way you can get a sense of the motion of the current and the height of the canyon walls. You get a perspective from the level of the river itself. In the quiet of the shaded canyon, you may see a buzzard or a falcon circling high above, you may catch a glimpse of a catfish in the stream or see the flash of color from some wildflowers as you plunge into one of the rapids.

What part of the river to choose, how long to stay on the river, as well as which method (guided or do-it-yourself) and which type of boat (raft or canoe), will depend partly on the season. This, in turn, will affect the water level in the river. The cost of each option will be another factor, as will the number of people you are with. The options range from an easy half-day paddle downstream in a canoe, aided by a gentle current from Grassy Banks Campground, and traveling through pleasant but undramatic scenery, to a wild rush at high water with an experienced guide through the whitewater of the rockslide of Santa Elena Canyon, to a ten-day trip through the lower canyons, to a gourmet meal on the river, and so on. In money terms, you can pay between $39 and $48 for a half-day trip by canoe (no guide), to $650 for a seven-day Lower Canyons trip with Far Flung Adventures, one of the oldest companies on the river.

SANTA ELENA CANYON

This is the best-known and most dramatic stretch of the river. Depending on the height of the water, it offers a one- or two-day rafting experience, leaving the stark desert scenery and entering a new landscape of towering canyon walls that rise up to fifteen hundred feet.

When I took the river trip, the water was at its lowest point in eight years. Despite that fact, the trip had its exciting moments.

Our guide, a compact, blonde lady in her thirties, had been in the river-running business for several years, training in Utah and on the Zambezi in Africa. As tough as granite, she was capable of rowing non-stop for nine hours, (which was just about what she did) as well as loading, unloading, cooking meals, cleaning up, and seeing everything was shipshape on her raft and OK with her clients.

When our party of three had assembled in Lajitas with our guide, we were left with no doubt that she was not happy that we had been sold a Santa Elena trip. The water was so low, she said, the boat would have to be carefully handled through the rocks at the Rock Slide, perhaps even unloaded and lifted over the top. This would mean getting into the water, getting wet, maybe hurting an ankle or a back. Fortunately the clients' wishes prevailed, and we pushed off at 10:30 A.M. from Lajitas with a mound of luggage at one end which looked as if it would do for a seven-day trip.

After a short while it became clear that the water level was indeed really low. The oars, in constant use since the current was so weak, frequently caught the stones on the river bed. Sometimes, the boat would get stuck and we would bounce around trying to free it or step into the water (six inches deep) and give a push. Still—it was not unpleasant. There was bird life along the bank, cliffs loomed ahead, and we had a lunch stop; we heard dramatic stories of life on the Zambezi or colorful tales of personalities and lifestyles among the river-running community in Terlingua, where Far Flung Adventures, our river tour company, has its office.

We got out of the boat for lunch—a full and varied cold meat, cheese, bread, fruit, Gatorade affair—on the bank near some Indian cliff paintings. There was a cloth on the table and a practiced display of cleanliness in the food handling. We began to get some information about the geology, presented in exactly the right sort of way for the traveler who didn't want to be confused by too much technical detail at this point. Our guide pointed out, for example, "That cliff side looks exactly like a peanut butter sandwich."

We saw canyon wrens, ducks, hummingbirds, and buzzards. It was later the next day that we saw a peregrine falcon now returning to the area, although that is still a rarity. We smelled goats on the bank, saw burros grazing on the Mexican side, and once saw some Mexicans fishing. Otherwise there was no one there but ourselves. Our guide explained the rock formations and the plant life in more detail; we passed mesquite, tamarisk, and ocotillo bushes, and stopped at a candelilla camp, now defunct, where candelilla plants had been cooked to extract their wax. At this point, when we were up on the bank, somehow our raft broke free and started moving off slowly downstream. Our guide immediately hurled herself down the bank, cursing a blue streak and cutting her foot. The raft was caught. End of panic.

By five in the afternoon, our guide decided we should camp just before the mouth of the canyon, which lay directly ahead. There were tents and sleeping pads for our use, and we lay around in the sun or took a stroll while steaks, salad, and mashed potatoes were being cooked, with strawberry cheesecake to follow, coffee to drink, or beer for those who had brought it. A sound sleep of the pampered clients followed. The only requirement the next morning was to get up and eat tortillas with eggs and peppers, and sausage with salsa, before deciding how to take down the tent.

Back in the boat and going into the canyon it was easy to imagine, when the water level was twenty feet higher, how it might be very tricky maneuvering a raft by oneself, not to say foolish. But, in our situation, we had nothing to fear with only the tiniest amount of water spilling over the front of the raft when we dropped down through the rapids. We had plenty of time, and now thankfully some silence, to look at the towering cliffs rising vertically above us and casting the river into shadow as the canyon narrowed.

The fearsome Rockslide (usually Class IV in river terminology), the highlight of a usual run, came up. It was obvious, with all the boulders exposed above the water level, that we would have to squeeze our way through. And this is exactly what we did, in half an hour, by using the poles as levers against the rocks and by getting out and heaving and shoving it over the protruding stones. Our guide was delighted; we were pleased that she was pleased, and that the hazard had been easier than expected.

After another stop for lunch at Fern Canyon and a trip up the canyon to see the reason for its name, we continued to float down towards the exit of the canyon, still slowly, but not needing the oars so much. Life was discussed, and job and travel experiences shared. The beauty and power of the canyon had not been reduced by the lack of water; in fact we were going so slowly that we had more time to observe, at two miles an hour, what others going at five miles an hour might have missed.

Thoughts and reminiscences come easily in this sort of setting, when the trials of daily work and careers are forgotten. Our Far Flung van was at the right place at the right time (3:30 P.M.), which didn't come as a surprise since this organization has had seventeen years to get get it right. But it cheered our guide, since it meant an early start to cleaning up and getting ready to repeat the same thing the next day. No question but that the character and energy of our guide had changed what might have been a boring floating experience into something much wider in context and more memorable.

Some Itineraries from Alpine

Big Bend Circuit (Basic Route)
Miles: 220; minimum time: 5 hours; stops: 5 or 6
Travel east on U.S. 90 from Alpine, after having first purchased coffee and donuts to go from the Alpine Bakery. After 31 miles, you arrive in Marathon, the first stop. Allow ten minutes to walk through the lobby of the Gage Hotel, then cross over to the new wing, Los Portales. Check out the bedrooms in the old section and compare them to the new ones. Look at all the cowboy items hanging on the walls and also the Mexican and native American artifacts. If you would like to see a fine display of re-

gional art, cross the road to Lovegene's Gallery, which you can see from the front of the Gage.

The second stop, fifteen minutes later, is 12 miles south of Marathon on U.S. 385. Turn right onto U.S. 385 just as you leave Marathon on U.S. 90. This second stop is a historical marker which explains the name, Los Caballos, the rocky outcroppings along the side of the highway. It goes on to describe how the visitor is standing at a unique geological viewpoint and is seeing both the Rockies and the Appalachians (the end of the chain) from the same place.

Continue on U.S. 385 for 38 miles, at which time you will enter Big Bend National Park. Do not bother to stop at the Persimmon Gap Ranger Station just inside the park. Continue another 25 miles to Panther Junction, the park headquarters. Here you will need to buy a permit ($5) for your vehicle. You can look at the large topographical map of the park, browse the well-stocked bookstand, and pick up all sorts of free pamphlets. Outside you should not miss the short nature trail, which lists on a pamphlet (25¢) the twenty-eight species of desert plants that you will see growing on each side of the trail. Allow fifteen minutes here.

Turn left outside the park headquarters, travel 3 miles, then turn left again and begin your approach into the Basin. Seven miles later, you will have gone over the top of the rim and be inside the Basin itself. There you will find a ranger station, a post office, store, and the Chisos Mountains Lodge and Restaurant. Go into the lodge and browse in the lobby, then go outside to the verandah and look straight in front of you towards the Window, a cut in the mountain wall, through which you can see the desert.

No time for further sightseeing here, not on this schedule, so return to your car and drive out of the Basin. Back on the flat ground, turn left at the T-junction, and head for the west entrance of the park. After exiting the west entrance (20 miles) you will come to Study Butte. Here, if you arrive before 3:30 P.M., you will find the Road Runner Deli. This is the place to stop and eat or get something to go.

You may still have time, before heading north to Alpine, 78 miles from Study Butte, to make a short detour to Terlingua Ghost Town, four miles to the west on RR 170. There you can visit the general store, check out the river rafting trips at Far Flung Adventures, stop at the Terlingua Cafe, or throw the day's schedule out the window by deciding to spend the rest of the day south of the border, ending up with dinner at the Starlight Theater. But for those on the quickie itinerary, it is time to head home. If you have bought Chevron gas before leaving Alpine, you would have had the opportunity to pick up their free road log, which describes in detail all the points of interest on Texas 118 from Alpine to Study Butte and on into the Chisos Basin. You can also get this information-packed sheet at the Alpine Chamber of Commerce.

Big Bend One-Day Circuit (including Santa Elena Canyon)
Miles: 255; time: 7–8 hours; stops: 7 or 8

Follow the Big Bend Basic Circuit, and check at Park Headquarters about using the Santa Elena–Maverick Junction gravel road. Upon leaving the Basin and heading towards the west exit of the park, turn left 10 miles after the T-junction, where the Basin road joins the loop road, and drive 22 miles along the Robert Maxwell Scenic Drive to Castolon. Take time to stop at some of the roadside sights along the Scenic Drive. Stop in Castolon to buy a refreshment at the store. Get a pamphlet from the ranger station here or at the park headquarters that explains the history of Castolon. Check out, 1 mile further on, the Cottonwood Campground, in case you want to come back at a later date and camp here. Continue along the north bank of the Rio Grande until the road ceases at Santa Elena Canyon. Park your car, walk across Terlingua Creek, and enter the mouth of the canyon. Look up at the towering cliffs and watch for rafts coming downstream or birds soaring above you. You can go only a short distance into the canyon until the path dead-ends. Back at your car, and on the blacktop, look for a turn-off on the left, with a sign directing you to Maverick Junction. This is an easy, 12-mile gravel road which will take you directly to the west exit, saving 30 miles or so. Upon leaving the park, follow the same suggestions as in the Basic Circuit. You will probably be too late for the Road Runner Deli, so plan to have your daytime meal at the Terlingua Cafe in the ghost town. Return to Alpine.

Marfa-Presidio-River Road-Lajitas-Terlingua-Alpine
Miles: 232; time: 8 hours; stops: 5 or 6

After stocking up with coffee and donuts from the Alpine Bakery, head west on U.S. 90 to Marfa, 26 miles away. After 18 miles, stop for three minutes to read the historical marker on the left side of the road, which describes the Marfa Mystery Lights. This is the viewing point for the lights. In Marfa, observe the stately courthouse and drop by the lobby of the El Paisano Hotel on Highland Avenue to get an idea of the town's history.

If interest warrants it, detour upon leaving Marfa on U.S. 67 South via the Border Patrol headquarters to the old Fort Russell Army Air Base.

Peek inside the hangars and see the rows of aluminum cubes, which are a major part of the Donald Judd legacy. You are at the Chinati Foundation, and tours can be taken here Thursday through Saturday. Otherwise, simply observe the hangars and the concrete blocks in the desert from U.S. 67 as you pass.

Continue south along for 40 miles until you reach the ghost town of Shafter. Take fifteen minutes here to drive off the highway, through the village, across the creek, and past the cemetery, and you will arrive at some signboards which give a good idea of Shafter's history. Leaving Shafter, and before dropping down to the Rio Grande Valley, look for Lincoln's profile on the mountain ridge. Drive through Presidio, and head out on RR 170, stopping at Fort Leaton. Entrance fee is $2. Spend twenty minutes minimum in this museum, which will explain the history of the fort and the surrounding country. Ask about stopping at Closed Canyon, halfway down the River Road, in order to take a hike down the canyon. Passing through Redford, buy some provisions so you can snack while inside the canyon. Look for the Closed Canyon parking sign on the right side, and allow up to thirty minutes minimum for this shady walking tour. Continue to Lajitas on the Rio Grande, stopping at the Lajitas Trading Post to observe Clay Henry, the beer-drinking goat. At Lajitas Resort, enter the lobby of the Badlands Hotel, walk along the boardwalk, and have a refreshment in the restaurant or in the boardwalk drugstore. Continue 1 mile to the Barton Warnock Environmental Center and allow a minimum of thirty minutes here observing all the exhibits, including the outdoors nature trail. The entrance fee is $2.50. This museum closes at 4:30 P.M. Continue eleven miles to Terlingua Ghost Town where you will have to make a decision, depending on the time of day, whether to eat at the Terlingua Cafe or wait until the Starlight Theater opens. Read the "Study Butte and Terlingua" section to help you make up your mind.

Pinto Canyon Extension to the River Road Tour

At Marfa, continue west on Hwy 90 and, before exiting town, look for FM 2810 heading off left to the southwest. This road will take you across high empty rangeland before the asphalt runs out after 32 miles. At this point, the gravel road starts to descend steeply into Pinto Canyon, crossing one or two usually dry creeks, passing an abandoned mine, and you will see very little except some dramatic canyon scenery and perhaps some cattle. The road is passable to all vehicles of normal clearance, although a large RV might have problems. After 15 miles the road exits the

The Hoodoos, volcanic tuff formations. Part of Javelina Formation located on River Road between Lajitas and Presidio. Photo by Blair Pittman.

canyon; you will see the Rio Grande Valley ahead. Keep following the main track, bearing to your left when in doubt, and you will soon come to the small village of Ruidosa, where you could have a refreshment in the store. From here it is 34 miles to Presidio, where you can pick up the previously described route (Presidio-River Road-Lajitas-Terlingua). For an extra 30 miles or so, you will miss seeing Shafter, but you will see some wild and beautiful scenery.

Chihuahuan Desert Visitor Center, Fort Davis, Davis Mountains State Park, Prude Ranch, McDonald Observatory, the Davis Mountains Loop
Miles: 130; hours: 5–8; stops: 6–8

Head north on Texas 118 from Alpine, stopping at the Chihuahuan Desert Visitor Center after 22 miles. Open April 1–August 31, weekdays 1–5 P.M., weekends 9–6. Enter to the right of the highway and follow a gravel road until it ends. Read the section in Chapter 2 on this convenient and easy introduction to the desert and plan to spend at least half an hour. Continue to Fort Davis and visit the fort. One-half hour up to two hours, depending on how you feel about forts, should give you some idea of what life was like in a garrison fort in the last century. Plan to eat lunch in Fort Davis, at the Drug Store or at Cueva de Leon, or pick up some picnic items, barbecue from Raul's perhaps, to eat at a picnic site on the loop. Continue 4 miles north, enter the Davis Mountains State Park and drive up the Skyline Drive for a superb view over the prime rangeland to the south and southwest. Look in at Indian Lodge for its architecture, setting, and the lobby before exiting the park. Continue 1 mile to Prude Ranch for a quick view of a dude ranch, pick up some materials to help you to decide if you would like to go back and stay a while. A little farther on you will come to the McDonald Observatory where the Visitor Center is open until 6:00 P.M. Half an hour here should probably be enough. You may want to plan to come back for a daytime tour or for a nighttime Star Party.

Continue around the loop, after reading the description of sights and stopping places in the section on the Davis Mountains State Park. Upon your return to Fort Davis, turn to the right and drive south for 26 miles, returning to Alpine.

Texas 118 South from Alpine

Before leaving Alpine, pick up a copy of the Newell Chevron Road Log at the Chamber of Commerce or at the Chevron station. This free sheet, compiled in 1968, is still substantially correct and lists useful geologic information.

After leaving Alpine, the first point of practical interest is La Linda RV Park, on the left side at 4 miles. At 5,400 feet elevation, it is the highest

RV park around, and it offers hookups for $11. Set in a basin, surrounded by hills, it has a nice high-country feel to it; wildlife often encroach upon the campground.

Eighteen miles out of Alpine, on the right side of the road, is the Woodward Agate Ranch. One of the few ranches in the area to have turned to tourism to help supplement their income, the Woodward Ranch can do this partly because the cattle-grazing part of the ranch is on the other side of the highway, quite separate from the rock-gathering area open to tourists. On the right side, reached by an easy, winding dirt road after 1.7 miles, is the ranch house, rock shop and RV park. The latter (fifteen sites) is not well developed but is adequate for those preferring a rural setting. There are showers and a toilet. A hookup for the night is $11.50. There are separate showers and toilets for men and women. A further 2 miles along a bumpy road is the tent campground down by the creek. You pass through a gate (you are given the code), and you may have some cattle as neighbors (inquire at the ranch house before setting out). It is a nice setting all the same with Cathedral Peak in the background. The fee is $6.50 a night for primitive tent camping.

Rocks are what Woodward Ranch is known for, and their slogan is "Home of the Red Plume Agate." You can either buy in their shop or collect your own and pay by the pound (50¢). The latter is much more fun, especially for kids, and the people in the shop will direct you where to look (it is nearby) and what to look for. They will give you a bucket and a tool for scratching up the rocks. Before you go, it might be useful to look at some of the thirty different types of rocks identified outside the shop (geodes, petrified wood, red plume, etc.). When you get back, your collection will be identified and weighed. If you want to buy in the shop, there is a wide selection ranging from "polished biscuits" ($1), to opal pieces ($10), to cut and polished stones (up to $20), and then a selection of jewelry pieces going up to $250 for a pendant. Another option is the Opal Mining Tour for $15 per person. You will be taken to where the opal veins are and, since opal is fragile, shown how to mine. When you have excavated a piece of opal, you then have to negotiate with your guide on the price. There is no charge on this tour for non-mining children or other onlookers who just want to watch. A full-day tour of the whole ranch costs $25 per person. Call (915) 364-2271 for more information.

At 55 miles is the Last Frontier Cafe, serving breakfast all day (three-egg omelet, $3), snacks (ham sandwich, $2.75), and dinner (chicken-fried steak, fries, and salad, $4.95). Beer and wine are available. Occasional dances are held in the adjacent cement-built hall. The cafe is open 7:30 to 9:00 P.M. daily. Gasoline is also sold here. An RV hookup is $7.50. The telephone number is (915) 371-2376.

At 62 miles is the turn off, on the left, for remote Terlingua Ranch. A further 16 miles along an improved gravel road brings you to this two-hundred-thousand-acre ranch with around 4,700 individual property owners. The ranch is open to visitors, provides thirty cabins, and has RV and tent camping. This is a love-it-or-hate-it situation; probably with each passing mile, and with thoughts of no phone and no TV, your mood will change either for the better or worse.

This is a place for wandering, for enjoying the silence, for bird watching, and for using the pool and just chatting.

The cabins are wooden and comfortable; they have no kitchens, but there are barbecue pits. The price per cabin is $45 per night; for RV hookups it is $6 or $4; for tent camping, $3.

A restaurant serves complete meals every day 7:30 to 9:00 P.M. Choices include rancher or wrangler breakfasts ($4.25–$4.35), pork chops ($6.75), chicken breast ($6.25), catfish fillets ($8.95), or ten-ounce top sirloin ($10.95). Beer is available. Choose a cabin without a view of the earth-moving equipment; come only if you can entertain yourself or your companion; the scenery is stark and there is definitely a feeling of being off the highway. The telephone number is (915) 371-2416.

Big Bend Birding Expeditions has their office here, and Jim Hines conducts four-wheel-drive trips on the ranch and around the Big Bend area for a half-day or a full day, starting at $70 per person, with a minimum of two people. He also offers birding trips on the Rio Grande from two to seven days. Transportation can be the choice of the client: van, bike, horseback, or raft. What BBB Expeditions offers are expert guides, and the information on where best to see the most, also what bird species are in the area at a given time. Call (915) 371-2356 for reservations.

At 65 miles south of Alpine, standing on its own, is the Longhorn Ranch Motel and Matterhorn Restaurant, which includes twenty-four pleasant, modern rooms, grouped around a small swimming pool. The property, only six years old, has good views and conveys a feeling of desert isolation, but its biggest advantage is that it is only fifteen miles from the entrance to Big Bend National Park. Room rates are $40 for a single, and $50 for two, plus tax. This hotel is regularly used by Elderhostel groups. The telephone number is (915) 371-2541.

Included in the motel complex is El Matterhorn Restaurant, reflecting the country of origin of the owners. Open 7–11 A.M. and 5:00–8:30 P.M. (except for Monday), the restaurant offers lighter plates of chicken breast ($6.95), enchiladas ($5.75), and a small fillet steak ($7.95), as well as sturdier Texan fare.

Only 4 miles from Study Butte is an alternative type of accommodation with fine desert views. Wildhorse Station offers five different furnished cabins stuck on the side of a hill. Number One is a two-bedroom, with queen-size and double beds, a kitchen and bathroom, and includes linen and all dishes for $60 (two in one room) or $80 (four in two rooms) a night. Number Two is smaller, and includes one double bed, and one single bed for $40 for two, plus $10 per extra person. Number Three is larger, has three bedrooms, costs $60 for two persons, $100 for four. Two more cabins are being added. It is set back from the highway above the store with such beautiful views that the owners often sit outside in the front of the cabins, yet is highly accessible to the park. A tent camping site with showers and toilets is being added nearby. There is only a limited supply of food in the store, and a small, though well-priced selection of souvenirs. The telephone number is (915) 371-2526.

U.S. 385/FM 2627 to the Rio Grande

MARATHON — STILLWELL RANCH AND LA LINDA

Ten miles south of Marathon on U.S. 385, there is a pull-off and a sign referring to the nearby geology. "Los Caballos—Highly deformed rocks of the Ouachita fold belt, a northeasterly trending range, uplifted about 275 to 290 million years ago."

This sign indicates that this spot is very important geologically—in fact, unique in the country. Los Caballos (horses) is the name given to the clearly visible curved bands of white rock towards the tops of the hills on each side of the highway. Whatever the hills look like, they are important since they are the last visible evidence, the tail end, of the Ouachita range of mountains.

The Ouachita Range is actually a west-east range of mountains in Arkansas, but the name is extended to include ranges further afield but linked geologically and chronologically to this range. The age is very old: around 250 million years—the same age as the Appalachians. And this whole chain of mountains extends in a north and easterly direction and even appears thousands of miles further east in New England.

But nearby, towards the southwest on the horizon—and this makes for dramatic proximity—is a much newer chain of mountains, the Norte-Santiago Range (only sixty million years old), which stretches to the northwest and is the southernmost extension of the Rocky Mountains. So the "young" mountain range (volcanic) and the "old" mountain range (limestone) almost come together at this point. You can climb over the fence right next to the sign and for once are encouraged, by a ladder and a path, to step onto the land (which is private) to examine the "horses," which the rock outcrops resemble.

STILLWELL RANCH

Thirty-eight miles southeast of Marathon, bear left onto FM 2627 and 8 more miles will bring you to Stillwell Store and RV Park, (915) 376-2244. The RV park gets some extra business during spring break, when the Big Bend National Park campsites are full. But the majority of visitors to Stillwell Ranch have come to honor, get a glimpse of, or perhaps talk with Hallie Stillwell. If anyone epitomizes the steadfast values of pioneer life it must be Hallie Stillwell, who today, at age ninety-seven, is still alert, good-humored, and full of stories, thanks to an excellent memory.

Its Hall of Fame title gives little indication of a fascinating, custom designed three-room museum. Entry is through a stout wooden door—hand carved by David Busey, Hallie Stillwell's great-nephew, who also designed the building—which brings you into the entrance hall. Here, the walls are filled with citations, awards, keys, hats, and other items honoring the matriarch. Elsewhere, signed photographs from national and regional figures show the affection as much as the respect in which she is held.

First to catch the eye among the exhibits are, fittingly, guns, including the .38 Colt pistol Hallie carried when she went off to Presidio in 1916 to teach school—a time when Pancho Villa was raiding along the border.

The larger room, with wooden ceiling, overhead fans, and a fine, hand-carved Spanish chest, has, among other historical and cultural exhibits, a picture on the wall of Zapata's wedding. The two smaller rooms contain more memorabiliam such as copies of Hallie's marriage certificate (1918), her temporary teacher's training certificate (1916), the head of a bear roped by her husband Bill (who died in 1948), a picture of Hallie holding up a mountain lion she had just shot, a pie safe, a bedroll, and an ancient five-gallon Spanish demijohn, unearthed nearby, which was used for sacramental wine. Entrance is free but, like ten thousand people before you, sign the visitor's book. If you want to show appreciation and learn more about Hallie Stillwell, buy her book, *I'll Gather My Geese*, for $18.95.

RV park prices for pull-through RVs are $11.50 a night for two persons for full hookup and $2.00 per extra person. For tent campers, the price is $3.50 per tent. Showers and a laundromat are available. You will find groceries, ice, beer, and gasoline, and also some souvenirs. Hiking on the ranch is permitted, and camp fires may be lit (bring your own wood). There is a native plant trail to orient those who have just arrived in the region.

The Maravillas Canyon is on the Stillwell Ranch, and a jeep tour lasting five hours will take you into the canyon to see pictographs and Eagle Rock, the highlight. On the way there and back you will hear about the various flora and fauna of the northern Chihuahuan Desert. The cost is $30 per person, $15 for children.

There's a fascination in talking with any really old person, and when the memory is still so sharp, the sense of humor still very much alive, and the whole attitude totally down to earth, the fascination turns to great respect. Tucking into a bowl of strawberries, as we sat in the kitchen, Hallie Stillwell looked well and sounded lively. While we talked, her daughter Dadie sat next to us, and a granddaughter made a cake. She talked about the old days—they were hard, but then it was the only life they knew. The biggest change in rural life came with the arrival of electricity in the early fifties. A second profound change to ranchers was the elimination of the screwworm that was killing the cattle.

The Stillwell Ranch seems big—twenty-two-thousand acres—but it holds only three hundred head of cattle. Ten times that size is needed in West Texas to make cattle raising economically sound. Does she eat steak? She does, but forget about lamb. What about the increase in mountain lions? They are increasing in number, but they are not yet a critical problem. According to Hallie, what is not needed is for Yankees to come down telling folk how they should live their lives and how predators should be protected. Her memory ranged from farm management to lifestyles. She touched on one moving recollection of when her brother, being trained in the Army for World War I, contracted Spanish influenza. "He had just sent us a card saying he was better and going back on duty. Two days later, a letter came saying he had died. I don't think my mother ever recovered from it." He died over seventy years ago.

River Getaway
Heath Canyon Ranch is at the end of the road; FM 2627 stops here. The 622 acres and the adobe house that goes with it used to belong to the Du Pont Corporation. The company lodged VIPs or engineers here who

Hallie Stillwell on the Stillwell Ranch. Photo by Blair Pittman.

came to visit the fluorspar mine across the river at La Linda in Mexico. Fluorspar is used in making aerosol.

Until 1991 the mine, which is actually 23 miles away, was busy supplying the raw materials for the processing plant—which is directly across the river and still very visible—to deal with before shipping. Shortly before 1991, the Chinese started to mine fluorspar in great quantities, and the bottom fell out of the market. The population of La Linda fell from around three hundred to just one family of fifteen. But the closing down of the processing plant gave Andy Kurie, a geologist with the company for eighteen years, the chance to buy the house and land on the United States side of the river.

La Linda has the makings of a very useful river trip terminus. Boats coming down from upstream can take out at La Linda, where the passengers can clean up, have a good feed, and get back on the road. Similarly, those putting in at La Linda for the downstream trip through the Lower Canyons can enjoy an overnight stay and a trip across the bridge into Mexico before setting off.

The Open Sky Cafe must be one of the most remarkable border locations in the United States. Located on high ground in front of the bunkhouse, this efficient, one-room cafe turns out food made to order and cold drinks. You can eat inside or carry the food a few paces to a dining area beneath a thatch awning. Here below you is the Rio Grande, and to the left is Mexico. There's no noise, it is probably hot, maybe very hot. This is the end of the line; the paved road stops here. Only Mexican truck traffic continues, carrying, for example, U.S. frozen chickens. The cafe is open seven days a week or until supplies run out.

Accommodations include a bunkhouse arrangement with three rooms—two with two beds, one with a single bed—a shared kitchen, and a bathroom. The price per room, double or single occupancy, is $35. A cot in the room costs $10. There is also a trailer, which offers three bedrooms, one with a double bed, one with two twin beds, and one with a single bed. There is a shared kitchen and two bathrooms. It is the same price per room as for the bunkhouse. For the whole trailer, the price is $100. The accommodation is air-cooled, and linen is provided. There is also primitive camping down by the Rio Grande, with the use of showers at the house, for $3 per person per night. For reservations call (915) 376-2235 or (915) 386-4236.

WHAT TO DO

While you're in La Linda, visit Mexico. The views to one side are along the Rio Grande and up the mountain which is part of the Heath Canyon Ranch property (hunting in season is included in the accommodation price). The view directly to the front is over La Linda. The company housing is deserted and the plant is silent, a virtual ghost town except for the plant caretaker and a few members of his family. A trip across the bridge means first rousing, if it is early afternoon, a Mexican guard, who appears from the guard house with pistol stuck in his pants, for a cursory questioning. What there is to see is a small abandoned chapel; there are beer or soft drinks to buy from the only merchant, different types of rock can be examined at the place where the sorting was done in the old days, and horses can be rented for $4.50 per hour on a self-guided, unaccompanied basis.

Try wildlife watching and rock hunting. In addition to being on the river or taking a trip across the bridge into Mexico, there are trails to follow on the property. Since the ranch is situated between the Big Bend National Park and the Black Gap Wildlife Management Area, there are all sorts of possibilities for wildlife watching. And since there is a professional geologist in residence, Andy Kurie, who previously worked for the mining company, getting information on rock samples should be no problem either.

For adventurous spirits, it should be possible to arrange to travel with the manager of the mine when he travels once a week to Melchor Muzquiz, 85 miles south on a dirt road.

What is Cabrito?

Alpine recently celebrated its 4th Annual Cabrito and Menudo Cook-off, along with other Cinco de Mayo festivities, yet many people still call the Chamber of Commerce office to ask, "What is cabrito?" The following discussion should clarify the matter.

Cabrito literally means a young male goat, or "kid" in Spanish, usually less than one year old. In the recent history of the Big Bend area, cabrito was considered an occasional delicacy to some, and an important dietary staple to many.

The meat of the cabrito is high in protein, low in saturated fats and cholesterol, and high in B vitamins and other essential nutrients. While the husbandry of goats has been primarily for milk, the young males have traditionally served as an important, and in many cases, vital source of protein food.

In Mexico the goat is an essential part of life for the campesinos, or "rural people." It is cooked in many ways similar to other meats such as pork. One method is barbacoa: pit cooked over mesquite coals with a piquant sauce of the region. The cabrito cooked in such a manner is extremely tender and non-greasy; it is traditionally served with tortillas and a salsa fresca (fresh sauce) made from chiles, tomatoes or tomatillos, onions, cilantro, and sometimes avocados and cucumbers.

Cabrito is also roasted on a spit *(al pastor)*, butterflied and roasted at an angle to a wood fire *(asado)*, or stewed in a heavy pot with vegetables *(guisado)*. To a contemporary chef such as Grady Spears of Alpine's Reata Restaurant and a recent winner of the Alpine Cabrito Cook-off, cabrito offers a stimulating challenge to his culinary art. In the trail blazed in nouvelle Southwest cuisine by Santa Fe chef Mark Miller at his Coyote Cafe, cabrito has gained recent currency with the gourmet set.

To accompany your cabrito, I personally recommend a pile of fresh tortillas and a side dish of fresh lime slices, chopped red onion, and fresh chopped cilantro. To drink, a full-bodied beer such as Dos Equis, Pacifico, or Corona, or a medium-bodied red wine, such as St. Genevieve's Texas Red or a California zinfandel.

Regarding the menudo part of the cook-off, I hesitate to explain in detail what menudo exactly is, but there is nothing better than a good bowl of menudo when suffering from la cruda, or "hangover"—or just about any other infirmity for that matter.

My favorite menudo in this area is made by Lewis Gordon at the Ponderosa restaurant in Alpine. He knows the very important ingredient that most Tex-Mex cooks overlook: a pig's or calf's foot.

On the other hand, there is nothing in the world worse than a "bad" bowl of menudo, such as one entry in a previous contest prepared by the announcer of one of our local radio stations (the only one), sampled in spewing disgust by former Mayor Ernesto Gallego, City Manager Jerry Carvajal, and other judges at that past, but not forgotten, tasting.

Menudo is best served at about eleven Sunday morning—after a night at the El Apache Bar—accompanied by fresh cilantro, chopped onions, fresh lime slices, coarse oregano, a flour tortilla, and several cups of strong coffee.

Assess damage, retire early.